12/19 #2.00

D1559266

RENEWING THE SEARCH FOR A MONETARY CONSTITUTION

RENEWING THE SEARCH FOR A MONETARY CONSTITUTION

REFORMING GOVERNMENT'S ROLE IN THE MONETARY SYSTEM

EDITED BY
LAWRENCE H. WHITE, VIKTOR J. VANBERG,
AND EKKEHARD A. KÖHLER

CATO INSTITUTE
WASHINGTON, D.C.

Library of Congress Cataloging-in-Publication Data

Renewing the search for a monetary constitution/edited by Lawrence H. White, Viktor J. Vanberg, Ekkehard A. Kohler.
    pages cm
    Papers originally presented at an April 2012 symposium held in Freiburg-im-Breisgau, Germany.
    Includes bibliographical references and index.
    ISBN 978-1-939709-66-0 (hardback : alk. paper)
    1. Monetary policy—Congresses. 2. Money—Congresses. 3. Banks and banking, Central—Congresses. I. White, Lawrence H. (Lawrence Henry) II. Vanberg, Viktor. III. Kohler, Ekkehard A.

HG230.3.R46 2015
332.4'6—dc23
                               2014046061

ISBN: 978-1-939709-66-0
eBook ISBN: 978-1-939709-67-7

Cover design: Jon Meyers.
Printed in the United States of America.

CATO INSTITUTE
1000 Massachusetts Avenue, N.W.
Washington, D.C. 20001
www.cato.org

Contents

Introduction

Lawrence H. White

First drafts of the papers collected here were originally presented at an April 2012 symposium held in Freiburg-im-Breisgau, Germany, organized by the editors of this volume and conducted by the Liberty Fund, Inc.[1] The symposium was timed to mark the 50th anniversary of the 1962 publication of the important volume *In Search of a Monetary Constitution*, edited by Leland Yeager. Professor Yeager's volume was based on a fall 1960 lecture series he had organized at the University of Virginia. Our authors had a similar mandate to the one Yeager described giving to his lecturers, namely that they were "encouraged to take the broadest possible view, without worry about political practicality or about possible accusations of extremism," as if advising people "engaged in shaping the basic character of a monetary system, in shaping a 'monetary constitution'" (Yeager 1962, 1). Here we offer revised versions of the symposium papers with the aim of revitalizing public discussion of constitutional monetary reform.

The contributors to the Yeager volume (all but one) took the then unfashionable position that an explicit "monetary constitution"—a set of enforced constraints on the creation of money by government—would be useful. The position was unfashionable in the early 1960s because inflation was low and because most economists were optimistic that a discretionary central bank armed with the prevailing Keynesian wisdom would tame the business cycle. As Hugh Rockoff notes in his chapter of the present volume, the 1962 volume's warnings about central-bank discretion nonetheless "proved remarkably prescient because the Great Inflation was about to begin."

We are especially pleased to include contributions from James M. Buchanan and Leland Yeager, respectively, a leading participant in and the organizer-editor of the 1960 Virginia lecture series and the resulting 1962 volume. We dedicate the present volume jointly to the memory of Professor Buchanan, who passed away in January 2013, and to the prescient Professor Yeager.

Like the participants in Yeager's volume, ours ask: What is the case and what are the options for constitutional reform of the monetary system? In the past 50 years, central banks have delivered neither reliably sound money (but instead chronic inflation peaking in the Great Inflation of the late 1960s to early 1980s) nor smoother real growth (but instead a series of booms and busts leading to the Great Recession of 2007–2009, still lingering today in the United States and in Europe). As a result of this poor performance, many venerable ideas for monetary reform have been rediscovered and reenergized, including the cases for rules over time-inconsistent discretion, for a laissez faire or free-banking system, for a gold or commodity-basket monetary standard, and for targeting aggregate nominal spending. Noteworthy new reform ideas have been born, such as competing private irredeemable currencies, separation of the unit of account from the medium of exchange, and a prediction market to appropriately control the monetary base. Meanwhile new technologies for producing media of exchange and units of account have arrived in the marketplace, including redeemable community currencies, online-transferable "digital gold" accounts, and noncommodity cybercurrencies such as Bitcoin and its dozens of imitators. The time is ripe to rethink monetary regimes fundamentally rather than to continue confining ourselves to marginal tinkering with the instruction sets for status quo institutions.

The remainder of this introduction does not try to closely summarize the following chapters, which speak for themselves, but instead tries to introduce some of the fundamental issues they discuss.

Two sets of basic questions immediately arise when thinking of monetary institutions in constitutional terms. First, do we want constitutional provisions that *empower* government to act in the monetary sphere? Or do we instead want only provisions that *prohibit* government from interfering with money, much as the First Amendment to the U.S. Constitution bars Congress from abridging the free exercise of religion? Does anything special about money warrant a positive role for the state? For example, does money meet the technical criteria for a "public good"? Or do the general principles of property law (namely, following David Hume, the stability of possession, transfer by consent, and enforcement of contracts) already give us all we need in the way of rules for monetary institutions? Second, if government does undertake a positive role, how should constitutional-level rules be framed to specify its aims and its constraints? Which of many possible sets of instructions is best?

Our authors have differing views on both sets of questions. Some would affirm that a commodity money system needs only the Humean principles and not any positive government involvement on the grounds that markets have historically evolved robust contractual rules and institutional practices for coinage and commodity-redeemable money. Once government creates a central bank that issues a fiat money, however, some authors would agree that (second-best) constitutional rules are needed to limit money issue because there is no natural limit. Others (such as Leland Yeager) advance a positive role for government in specifying the unit of account. Still others would go further to empower government to conduct an ongoing monetary policy, controlling the economy's stock of money in pursuit of some objective. James Buchanan's chapter endorses a constitutional mandate for government to stabilize the purchasing power of the monetary unit (alternatively put, to stabilize some price index). Bill Woolsey proposes instead that a monetary authority should stabilize the path of total spending (nominal gross domestic product [GDP]), on the grounds that this would reduce "the disruption caused by efforts to stabilize the price level."

Yeager's chapter proposes excluding government from money production but having it play a role in establishing a new monetary standard, on the grounds that coordinating on the best standard is problematic if the market is left to its own devices. Yeager analogizes the unit of account to a unit of measure such as the meter or the yard. If government can help the economy coordinate on a standard unit of measure, can it not play a comparable role for the monetary standard? Robert Greenfield and Yeager's (1983) well-known "laissez faire approach to monetary stability" is inspired in part by Irving Fisher's (1925) proposal for a "compensated dollar." Fisher's proposal similarly emphasized the imperfection of the gold ounce as a measuring rod for value. Yeager proposes an alternative unit of account, a basket of commodities that would be less of an "elastic yardstick" than the fiat dollar or the gold ounce in the sense of having a more stable purchasing power.

Gold-standard advocates, whose favored system does not *directly* aim to stabilize the purchasing power of the monetary unit, would question the yardstick analogy. To them, because gold is a competitively produced commodity, a change in the purchasing power of gold is typically not like an arbitrary change in the length of a yardstick. For example, when productivity gains cheapen other commodities relative to gold, the rise in the purchasing power of gold is more like a rise in the price of the wood used in making yardsticks: it serves a signaling and allocative function.

Professor Buchanan believed that money is a special economic good that needs special constitutional rules. In various discussions in recent years, Buchanan granted that monetary arrangements can evolve spontaneously within a system of property rights, but he maintained that the evolved outcome wouldn't generally be efficient. Some type of money will emerge, but without an assurance that it will be the best money, because money has technical aspects of a public good. Other economists similarly point to the network property of money as an aspect that generates a relevant positive externality. The "commonly accepted" part of "commonly accepted medium of exchange," in this view, makes money inherently public. To say that money has aspects of a public good is to suggest that empowering the state is warranted if (and only if) it will remedy a market failure to capture all potential gains from trade. Because a role for the state *is* warranted here, but only a limited role, Buchanan believed, we need to specify an objective for the state to direct its activity in the monetary system.

The claim that money is a public good, or exhibits market failure, is controversial. Prima facie, money in its basic role as a medium of exchange lacks the technical characteristics of a public good. Money balances are a rival and excludable good—that is, a private good—and are efficiently provided by competing private mints (see Selgin 2011) and banks (see Lawrence White's chapter in this volume) under commodity standards. Although the use of money as a *unit of account* is nonrival and nonexcludable (one needn't own dollars to post prices or keep accounts in dollars), the market does not fail to converge on a common monetary unit, which is naturally tied to the commonly accepted medium of exchange on which it converges. One unit of account is enough, so there is no market underprovision (Vaubel 1984; White 1984).

However, the question remains of whether the market-chosen common monetary standard is the best standard available. If not, a case exists for affirming with Yeager that a switch to a *better* monetary standard can in principle be more efficiently made through government-coordinated collective action. This case is implicitly conceded by those who petition the government to act to put the economy back on a gold standard rather than only dismantle legal barriers to a parallel gold standard. Of course, in practice we need to take into account the costs of switching relative to the potential benefits, adjusted by the probability of actually getting a worse standard through collective action, before constitutionally deciding to empower government to make a switch.

As Viktor Vanberg and Ekkehard Köhler indicate in their chapter, constitutional governance and free-market competition are not mutually exclusive. A set of rules for government provision of money is only one kind of constitution. Instead one could have constitutional rules under which government provision is barred and private currencies freely compete. A monetary constitution of this sort could guarantee free choice among currencies while prohibiting government from meddling in contractual monetary arrangements (as when the U.S. Constitution proscribed the state governments from coining money or declaring anything but gold and silver a legal tender). As Gerald P. O'Driscoll, Jr., notes in his chapter, the economist Ludwig von Mises (1980, 454) argued along these lines that the concept of preserving sound money from a government's temptation to use inflationary finance "belongs in the same class with political constitutions and bills of rights." Vanberg and Köhler argue that better legal rules governing money—like better legal rules governing any human activity or institution—are a public good and so a legitimate matter for collective action. To say that all citizens nonrivally and nonexcludably enjoy the benefits of better legal rules regarding money is not necessarily to assume that all citizens must use the same money, but it would seem to require that all must be bound by the same legal system.

The Buchanan and Vanberg-Köhler papers raise the question of how a constitutional-level choice among monetary regimes can proceed in this day and age. The choice can be normatively modeled by placing decisionmakers behind a hypothetical "veil of ignorance" about their stations in life. But what do those behind such a veil know about how well a fiat-money system with (say) a price-level target will work in practice as compared to a system with a nominal income target or a gold standard with free banking? In the Vanberg-Köhler conception, the veil-of-ignorance norm does not in the least exclude knowledge of how real-world systems work in practice. Instead it simply requires, in the real world, that proponents of any monetary regime—for example, one that directs a central bank to target a price-level path—argue *at the constitutional level* for that regime's comparative benefits to the citizenry over alternative regimes, as if in preparation for a plebiscite.

Proposals to write new constitutional rules about money raise the question of how past written constitutional rules dealing with money, like those of the U.S. Constitution or the European Central Bank constitution, have fared in practice. A desirable characteristic of a monetary regime is that it be robustly self-enforcing, meaning that inevitably self-seeking participant behavior reinforces rather than undermines the regime. A cynic might say that a rule-bound central bank is like a married bachelor, a contradiction in terms, because central banks or their governments almost everywhere have proven themselves resourceful at loosening yesterday's constraints on the monetary authority. A regime without a central bank promises to be more robust in that respect (Salter 2013). The monetary rules of the U.S. Constitution (empowering Congress to produce coins but not to emit paper money, enjoining states from coining and from emitting paper money) are today honored in the breach, as Richard Timberlake (2013) has detailed in his recent book. The European Central Bank's constitution, which instructed the central bank to focus solely on price-level stability, has also been breached—triggering complaints and even official resignations in protest—by its participation in efforts to deal with sovereign debt crises. Politicians everywhere are prone to undermine rules that limit monetary discretion when such rules limit their fiscal discretion. Still, is not *some* explicit constitutional barrier better than none, even if only to serve as a focal point for protest?

Historical experiences with different monetary regimes, as broadly surveyed in the chapter by Peter Bernholz (and more specifically in the later chapters by Lawrence H. White and Gerald P. O'Driscoll, Jr.), indicate that gold and silver standards served as useful constraints on money issue by mints, private commercial banks, and later the central banks established under them. Since the scuttling of the classical gold standard in World War I, central banks have typically lacked tangible constitutional constraints. At most they have had temporary constraints such as pegged exchange rates, at least until the advent of inflation-targeting rules. Still, as Bernholz documents and seeks to explain, some central banks have been much better behaved than others. An understanding of how different behaviors have emerged from central bankers' different incentives under different institutional constraints is critically important to making an informed choice among constitutional constraints today.

The likelihood of returning to a commodity standard is surely lower today than in the past when, after a wartime suspension, a consensus was commonly in its favor. But low likelihood can be ascribed to *any* proposal other than retaining the status quo. Currently popular notions, when poorly informed and casually held outside constitutional deliberations, do not by their mere popularity determine what would, in fact, be the best monetary regime.

A concrete reform proposal much discussed in recent years, advanced most prominently by Scott Sumner, is to institute a system for stabilizing the level of nominal GDP along a smoothly rising target path.[2] A central bank could pursue such a target at its own discretion, as some suggest the Federal Reserve System did under Alan Greenspan in the 1990s when nominal GDP grew at close to 5 percent year after year, or it can be fastened on the central bank as a constitutional rule. Bill Woolsey's chapter critically discusses Sumner's most automatic version of a rule for a nominal GDP, in which the central bank creates a prediction market for nominal GDP and is bound to adjust the monetary base according to the market's forecasts.

Like any targeting rule, targeting the path of nominal income raises the question of where to put the initial target path. Do we start where we are, even if the economy appears to be underperforming? Some recent proponents of nominal income path targeting in the United States such as Christine and David Romer, formerly identified with Keynesian policymaking, propose to return to an extrapolation of the prerecession path, now well above the U.S. economy's current nominal income, which implies about a 10 percent one-time increase in the price level in the transition (assuming that the real income path does not shift up). Critics understandably object that nominal stickiness is unlikely still a problem five years after the 2009 recession, so the deliberate inflation would have net negative rather than net positive results. These critics see little sense in trying to return to the path along which the housing bubble formed.

The chapters by Bennett McCallum and Gunther Schnabl discuss other monetary policy reform proposals for a world of central banks. All such proposals raise the question of how to bind the central bank to the desired goals. We can write out rules, but how can we make them binding? Schnabl mentions the problem of the financial industry capturing central-bank policymaking in a world of revolving-door employment. The problem is exemplified by the Federal Reserve Bank of New York, where many officials were recent Wall Street bankers and members of the board of directors are *current* Wall Street (especially Goldman Sachs) executives. If the prospects for sticking to a particular rule depend on how central-bank officials are chosen, then either some other rule would be better or we need to add constraints on choosing central-bank officials.

Should provisions exist to suspend the monetary policy rule in emergencies? The answer would seem to depend on the type of rule. Proponents of a nominal income target rule argue that no suspension of such a rule would have been necessary to do the needful during the past financial crisis. On the contrary, the failure to maintain the nominal income path exacerbated the crisis. If a stable path of nominal income is assumed to be the best guide for a central bank, but the prevailing rule targets a money aggregate path, then a suspension of the rule is warranted in the event of a major shock to the velocity of money. Likewise, if a price-level path rule prevails, suspending it is warranted in the event of a major shock to the supply of real output. But even in such cases of an allowed suspension of the standard rule, the central bank's behavior can remain constrained by some other rule that then goes into effect. It shouldn't be that anything goes in a declared crisis. That would sacrifice the ex ante benefits of precommitment to rules, especially if the central bank has the discretion to decide when emergency conditions exist.

What about the periodic problem of a sudden government demand for money printing to finance a war effort? A constraint against financing an offensive war should be relatively uncontroversial behind the constitutional veil of ignorance. Should the monetary constitution also rule out money printing to finance a defensive war, on the grounds that less disruptive ways (borrowing and overt taxes) exist to divert the same material resources to the war effort?

The chapters by White, O'Driscoll, and Kevin Dowd consider possibilities for a monetary system regulated by competition and market institutions rather than by a central bank or government authority. A proposal to abolish the central bank obviously lies a step beyond giving the central bank a stricter mandate (O'Driscoll calls it "an extreme reform"). What constitutional rules best protect the viability of private payment systems? Are more than ordinary property law rules and their enforcement, including rules against fraud, needed?

Historical cases of free banking on a specie standard, as discussed by White, differ importantly from F. A. Hayek's 1976 proposal for open competition among private issuers of noncommodity or irredeemable monies (Hayek 1978). Evidence that free-banking systems have worked well on a foundation of contractual redeemability for commodity money does not show that competition among irredeemable private monies (as imagined by Hayek) would work well. Nor does it show that competitive banknote and deposit issue can overcome poor central-bank monetary policy in a regime in which the base money is fiat money issued by a discretionary central bank. It does seem favorable, however, to Milton Friedman's (1984) and George Selgin's (1985) proposals to reinstitute private competition in the issue of circulating currency under a strict rule regarding the stock of fiat bank reserves or under a strict target path for the price-level or nominal GDP. The relevance of historical free-banking cases to the Greenfield-Yeager proposal for a commodity-bundle standard is less clear, in light of the difference between a specie standard's direct redemption for the medium of account and Greenfield-Yeager's indirect redemption with separation of the media of account and redemption.

The track record of the Federal Reserve System's monetary policies over its hundred-year history, judged by inflation, price-level unpredictability, and real output variability, is "unenviable" at best, as O'Driscoll has noted elsewhere.[3] Central-bank histories around the world are equally or even more regrettable than the Fed's, with the exception of the Swiss National Bank's. Prompted by these poor records, O'Driscoll poses two alternatives for constitutional reformers: "Can central banks be constrained to a [beneficial] role, or must they be abolished? Can a 'bad system' be made better, or do we need wholesale replacement?" These are the central questions that our volume encourages monetary economists to examine.

One new possibility for superseding central-bank money does not involve *wholesale* replacement by legislation or constitutional amendment but *gradual* replacement by private alternatives that begin as parallel standards and win an increasingly larger market share. Dowd's chapter tells the fascinating stories of three such alternatives that have actually achieved loyal clienteles—the Liberty Dollar, e-gold, and Bitcoin—only to face legal obstacles thrown up by the U.S. federal government. The constitutional reforms necessary to unleash the potential of these new potential moneys are to remove all discriminatory legal restrictions that stack the deck in favor of status quo banks and funds transmitters. The Liberty Dollar and e-gold were innovative ideas for reintroducing precious-metal-based media in easily transferable forms. Bitcoin is something else again, a transferable private unit with a positive value, unbacked by redeemability. Unlike Hayek's proposed unbacked private currencies, Bitcoin is guaranteed (by clever programming) to expand in nominal quantity only gradually along a known path. It is produced by decentralized "mining" rather than by any central issuer who could issue more at will. Because its volume cannot be unexpectedly expanded, Bitcoin is free of the time-consistency problem that haunts Hayek's proposal—the temptation of a profit-maximizing issuer, when nominal expansion has no cost, to take the one-shot seigniorage profit from hyperinflationary overissue (White 1999, ch. 12). Bitcoin has no value guarantee, however, and its exchange rate against the dollar has in fact been quite volatile, which discourages its wider use as a medium of exchange. Still, starting from zero, the value of Bitcoins held by the public has risen in a few years to more than $10 billion (as of January 2013). It is a medium worth studying not only for its own sake but also for what we can learn about achieving credible monetary precommitment through transparent programming (Selgin 2013).

There is perhaps no more fitting way to conclude this introduction than to quote the final paragraph of the introduction that Leland Yeager wrote for the 1962 volume that has inspired the present volume. What he said about the state of monetary scholarship remains true, and his characterization of that volume applies equally to this one:

> A great deal of contemporary monetary scholarship … has concentrated on piecemeal and detailed study of our existing monetary structure and its performance. The reforms proposed have generally been correspondingly minor. Meritorious though this detailed work has been, it unfortunately tends to narrow the scope of the discussion, pushing aside and even subtly disparaging a concern with broader issues. The present volume is an attempt to redress the balance. In comparison with exclusive focus on detail, broad inquiries may bear upon different aspects of monetary theory and open new avenues of possible theoretical advance. In the long run, they may even have a wholesome influence on policy. If otherwise desirable and feasible, no reform must remain "politically unrealistic" except as thinking makes it so. (Yeager 1962, 25)[4]

Notes

1. The symposium's discussion leader was Hartmut Kliemt. The participating Liberty Fund fellow was Hans Eicholz. Also participating in the discussion were Roger Garrison, Jerry Jordan, and George Selgin. Their valuable contributions to the symposium are gratefully acknowledged.

2. See his blog, http://www.themoneyillusion.com. For more systematic expositions, see Sumner (2012, 2013).

3. See O'Driscoll (2013). For evidence, O'Driscoll cites Selgin, Lastrapes, and White (2012).

4. One reason for status quo bias in monetary policy research is that so much of the research is sponsored by central banks. See White (2005).

References

Fisher, Irving. 1925. *Stabilizing the Dollar*. New York: Macmillan.

Friedman, Milton. 1984. "Monetary Policy for the 1980s." In *To Promote Prosperity: U.S. Domestic Policy in the Mid-1980s*, edited by John H. Moore, pp. 23–60. Stanford: Hoover Institution Press.

Greenfield, Robert L., and Leland B. Yeager. 1983. "A Laissez Faire Approach to Monetary Stability." *Journal of Money, Credit and Banking* 15 (3): 302–15.

Hayek, F. A. 1978. *The Denationalisation of Money*, 2nd ed. London: Institute of Economic Affairs.

Mises, Ludwig von. 1980. *The Theory of Money and Credit*. Indianapolis: LibertyClassics.

O'Driscoll, Gerald P. 2013. "The Fed at 100." Cato Unbound website, December, http://www.cato-unbound.org/2013/11/04/gerald-p-odriscoll-jr/fed-100.

Salter, Alexander William. 2013. "Is There a Self-Enforcing Monetary Constitution?" Working paper, George Mason University, Fairfax, VA, October 9.

Selgin, George. 1985. "The Case for Free Banking: Then and Now," Cato Institute Policy Analysis no. 60, October 21.

———. 2011. Good Money: Birmingham Button Makers, the Royal Mint, and the Beginnings of Modern Coinage, 1775–1821. Ann Arbor: University of Michigan Press.

———. 2013. "Synthetic Commodity Money." Working paper, University of Georgia Department of Economics, Athens, GA, April 10.

Selgin, George, William D. Lastrapes, and Lawrence H. White. 2012. "Has the Fed Been a Failure?" Journal of Macroeconomics 34 (3): 569–96.

Sumner, Scott. 2012. "The Case for Nominal GDP Targeting." Mercatus Research, Mercatus Center at George Mason University, Arlington, VA, October 23.

———. 2013. "A Market-Driven Nominal GDP Targeting Regime." Mercatus Research, Mercatus Center at George Mason University, Arlington, VA, July 24.

Timberlake, Richard H. 2013. Constitutional Money: A Review of the Supreme Court's Monetary Decisions. New York: Cambridge University Press.

Vaubel, Roland. 1984. "The Government's Money Monopoly: Externalities or Natural Monopoly?" Kyklos 37 (1): 27–58.

White, Lawrence H. 1984. "Competitive Payments Systems and the Unit of Account." American Economic Review 74 (4): 699–712.

———. 1999. The Theory of Monetary Institutions. Oxford: Basil Blackwell.

———. 2005. "The Federal Reserve System's Influence on Research in Monetary Economics." Econ Journal Watch 2 (2): 325–54.

Yeager, Leland B. 1962. "Introduction." In In Search of a Monetary Constitution, edited by Leland B. Yeager, pp. 1–25. Cambridge, MA: Harvard University Press.

1. The Continuing Search for a Monetary Constitution

Leland B. Yeager

My assignment is to review the lectures of 1960 (published in Yeager [1962]). Detailed summaries are unnecessary here because they already appear in that book. Still, a brief review provides background for assessing newer proposals in the light of developments since 1960.

The Two Background Lectures

The first two lectures were meant not to advocate any specific reform but to provide background. Clarence Philbrook offered doctrinal history concerning the real-balance (cash-balance) effect (which belongs in any adequate exposition of the quantity theory of money) and concerning the curious persistence of the Keynesian concept of underemployment equilibrium. He dispelled a theoretical worry in Don Patinkin's book (1956, 1965) that general equilibrium might be unstable because of contagious intermarket effects.

Clark Warburton presented history, incidentally showing that theory is an essential tool but no substitute for examining business cycles episode by episode. In American experience, business downturns had typically followed exogenously caused slowdowns or reversals of money growth. (Warburton's extensive work on this and related topics was followed in 1963 by Friedman and Schwartz's detailed project.) Already a monetarist before Karl Brunner launched the term in 1968, Warburton was implicitly proposing steady money-supply growth. Later lecturers echoed that proposal explicitly.

Proposals

Among the later lecturers, only Murray Rothbard explicitly recommended stopping government's issue of money and leaving

1

that function to private enterprises. For him, money would consist only of private gold coins, as well as notes and deposits backed by 100 percent reserves of gold.

The 100 percent-reserve proposal is better known for a government-dominated system. Private-bank demand deposits (and banknotes, if any) would be fully backed by government-base money. George Tolley examined arguments for and against varieties of that proposal. Perhaps the main economic argument (as distinguished from a moral argument made by a few economists) is that 100 percent reserves would give the monetary authority tighter control over the money supply than it did have. Tolley mentioned the idea of having banks transfer their deposit liabilities to the Federal Reserve, so obliterating the distinction between demand-deposit money and base money.

Hundred-percent-reserve proposals got more attention in the 1930s than they get nowadays. My own view is that the fuzziness of just what now counts as money, together with the ongoing ingenuity of financial innovators, leaves such a requirement both impossible to specify in adequate detail and unenforceable against powerful incentives to evade it. Anyone who thinks otherwise is challenged to draft a law for accomplishing his purpose.

For Arthur Kemp, as for Rothbard, choice of a monetary system depends on concern for preserving personal freedom against state power. However, Kemp envisioned a restored governmental gold standard with fractional reserves against both government and bank money, one not much different from the gold standard before World War I.

James Buchanan considered predictability of money's value more important than stability as such. (In my view, though, consensus and expectations could better form around a target of zero price-level change than around some other number.) Buchanan's ideal monetary commodity would have a reasonably steady value against other goods and services because of high relative-price elasticities of supply and demand. Ordinary building bricks might be such a commodity.

Benjamin Graham envisaged government money based on (fractional) reserves of a composite of commodities, a formerly quite familiar proposal. He was less interested in monetary reform for its own sake than in associated benefits of stockpiling commodities and of stabilizing their prices and their producers' incomes.

Milton Friedman dismissed pure commodity money as costly in real resources and impossible anyway. He preferred fiat money managed by a central bank—not by an *independent* bank, however, but by one responsible to democratic authorities. (Since Friedman spoke, economists have by and large come to recognize more widely the virtues of central-bank independence.) He left presenting his famous rule to Richard Selden.

Jacob Viner rejected any definite monetary rule. The authorities should enjoy considerable discretion. Perhaps Congress should require the Federal Reserve to expand the money supply each year at whatever rate it judges would, if maintained during the preceding five years, have kept the price level stable over that period.

Willford I. King, while making an eloquent case for money of stable purchasing power, doubted the need for major institutional reform. The Federal Reserve, using primarily open-market operations, could achieve that result. (If necessary to resist inflation in exceptional cases, deposit growth might possibly be taxed.) Public confidence in a commitment to monetary stability would keep lags in the effect of monetary policy from being more than a minor problem.

Largely in view of lags, Selden advocated Friedman's rule for gradual and steady money-supply growth. The initially chosen growth rate could be subject to revision but not to frequent tinkering.

Developments since 1960

Developments both in the real world and in theory have improved our understanding of practical and theoretical issues and have expanded the range of possible reforms. We have experienced inflation, painful disinflation, the stagflation of the 1970s that discredited any simplistic version of the Phillips curve unemployment/inflation tradeoff, pegged exchange rates and their collapse, money first retaining some theoretical contact with gold and then giving way to fiat systems worldwide, changing proximate or instrumental targets in the conduct of monetary policy, and zigzags between accelerators' and brakes' giving way first to steadier policy and then to the current crisis and recession. Decades of experience have provided no unambiguous examples of inflation sustainably spurring growth of real output over the long run.

The past 50 years have brought major financial innovations. In the United States, these include interest paid on nonbusiness, demand deposits, money market funds, and other arrangements blurring just what policymakers should count as money. Derivatives have proliferated. Some of these innovations originated as wriggling around the interaction between price inflation and controls such as bank-reserve requirements and deposit interest ceilings, as well as around required capital ratios. The Federal Reserve experimented briefly (1979–82) with targeting on quantities of money or bank reserves only to resume targeting on the overnight interbank interest rate. Experience with policy failures and unintended consequences has supported public choice–theory skepticism about the benevolence and competence of government.

As for booms and recessions, each one has been a specific historical event, not to be diagnosed with a single theory to fit all episodes, whether an Austrian or monetarist or "real" theory. Two of the recessions since 1960 were triggered not obviously by tight money but rather by the oil embargo of 1973 and by collapse of the artificially inflated housing bubble in 2007. Yet even those episodes had a monetary aspect, as noted below.

In academia, events hastened the eclipse of Keynesianism. Monetarism temporarily displaced it as the dominant doctrine, then yielded to a variety of competitors: the exaggerations of new classicism, "real-business-cycle" theory, and—although I may exaggerate a bit—modeling the properties of imaginary worlds. Among policymakers, the current recession and sputtering recovery have brought a renaissance of crude Keynesianism even though it is questionable to try to remedy real discoordinating factors by "stimulating" aggregate spending, especially when bank-reserve money has already been made abundant (see "Annex on Recessions" in this chapter). Despite welcome deemphasis on a particularly dubious strand of it, Austrian business-cycle theory has not entered the academic mainstream.

Bennett McCallum ("McCallum Rule" 2013) and, more famously, John Taylor (Razzak 2001) have proposed rules for putting Federal Reserve policy on autopilot, resulting, they hoped, in less erratic macroeconomic performance. Another proposal receiving attention is for the Federal Reserve to target not on interest rates, not on some measure of the money supply, not on the price level or price trend, and certainly not on employment and real activity but rather on steady growth of nominal gross domestic product (GDP). Such targeting would avoid zigzags in policy, would achieve an approximately steady price level if the nominal growth rate equaled the growth rate of potential real GDP, and would permit appropriate and perhaps temporary rises or falls in the price level if productivity growth should deteriorate or improve. The question remains of just *how* the Federal Reserve would hit a nominal growth target.

Partly as a consequence of these real-world and academic developments, more radical reform proposals have gained attention. F. A. Hayek (1978) proposed competition in the use of national currencies and later launched his scheme for privatizing money. Other schemes to the same effect—"free banking" and the like—have gained attention.

Monetary Reform More Urgent Than Ever

More than 50 years of fiscal experience and financial innovation make the search for a new monetary constitution ever more relevant. The government's entitlement commitments, deficit spending, and debt keep soaring. The Federal Reserve's recent extreme base-money creation may arguably seem justified in the current economic slump. Yet these conditions presage extreme inflation unless somehow reversed in time. If the dollar should be destroyed, what might replace it?

On reflection, it must seem absurd that our unit for expressing prices, wages, debts, profit, and loss has a value no more objective and stable than the purchasing power of the scruffy fiat dollar bill. It is absurd that the U.S. government can borrow trillions of dollars payable in money that the Federal Reserve can simply create, if need be, in unlimited amounts.

Even if the dollar should somehow escape actual destruction, the question remains of how accurately the Federal Reserve could control the total quantity of ordinary money and close near-moneys. Central banks' leverage over money and nominal incomes through injecting or withdrawing bank-reserve base money grows ever weaker. How long will it be before the lever becomes so rubbery that the traditional system of monetary control becomes totally unworkable?

5

(Benjamin Friedman [1999] guessed about a quarter-century; also see Friedman [2000a, 2000b] and Brittan [2003: 151].)

Requirements of a Reformed—or Any—Monetary System

Determinacy

Any workable monetary system, old or new, presupposes "determinacy." At any time, the dollar must have a determinate (though not necessarily unchanging) value. The opposite would allow an unanchored and even self-reinforcing upward or downward drift of the price level. One such perverse system would be a phony gold standard defining the dollar and making dollar-denominated notes and deposits redeemable not in a fixed *quantity* of gold but in a dollar's *worth* of gold at gold's drifting price.

The dollar can be given a determinate value in either of two ways (or a hybrid of them): (a) controlling the total quantity of money or (b) keeping money on a commodity standard. Some *nominal anchor* is required, some nominal magnitude set otherwise than automatically by ordinary market processes. (Schumpeter [1970, 217–24, 258, and passim] called this anchor the "critical figure" of a monetary economy.) The anchor could be the dollar size of a total quantity of money centrally managed (directly or through interest-rate manipulation). Schumpeter suggested control over the *nominal* size of GDP, if only that could somehow be done. The second approach to determinacy sets the critical figure as the number of physical units per dollar of some commodity (or composite of commodities); in the United States until 1933, the dollar was defined as 23.22 grains (1.5046 grams) of pure gold. Because gold (or whatever the standard commodity may be) cannot be simply printed into existence but has its quantity and value naturally restrained by real factors, two-way convertibility between it and money defines the dollar's value by indirectly restraining the quantity of money.

Briefly, the reformed dollar could be made determinate either by central management of the total number of spendable dollars in existence or by interconvertibility with a definite amount of some commodity (or composite). Our current system is a hybrid: bank-account money is redeemable in centrally controlled and therefore artificially scarce base money. A reformed system should enjoy *transparency* about what it is and how it operates (something that the currently faddish Bitcoin system seems to lack).

Monetarism and the Quantity Theory of Money

Monetarism insists that for macroeconomic phenomena like inflation, deflation, boom, and recession, "money matters"— perhaps usually even "money matters most." (As Milton Friedman famously insisted, inflation is everywhere and always a monetary phenomenon.) Monetary order or disorder hinges on whether the actual quantities of whatever the public uses and holds as money equal, exceed, or fall short of the quantities demanded. Because transactions are accomplished in money or in credits denominated and to be settled in money, even apparently real-triggered recessions, such as those following the Organization of the Petroleum Exporting Countries' oil-price boost of the 1970s and the bursting of the housing bubble in about 2007, disrupted equilibrium between money supply and demand; attention to money's velocity can be illuminating.

The current neglect of monetarism calls for a clarification. That doctrine was never identical with a steady-money-growth policy, which would indeed work badly nowadays. Financial innovations have fuzzed up just what counts as money and so should be made to grow steadily.[1] But uncertainty about just how to count money cannot excuse inattention to it.

The quantity theory is the centerpiece of determinacy and of monetarism. With attention to the real-balance or cash-balance effect (discussed by Philbrook in 1960), the quantity theory explains how quantities of money (however exactly defined) affect nominal incomes and spending and so affect price levels in the long run and often real outputs in the short run. The theory holds true most straightforwardly, but not only, in a fiat-money system (Patinkin 1956, 1965). Without quite ignoring real disturbances, monetarism attributes price inflation, on the one hand, and deflation and depression, on the other hand, typically to an actual quantity of money exceeding or falling short of the total of cash holdings desired at thus-far-prevailing prices and incomes. Lags can explain the superficially puzzling case of stagflation.

Even more so than monetarism, the quantity theory is not a specific policy proposal. Nor is it the equation of exchange, $MV = PQ$. The equation is a tautology, valid by the definitions of its terms, that proves useful in expounding the theory and its applications. Propositions failing to square with it are wrong or incoherent. The tautological equation can be, but need not be, modified into an equilibrium condition for analyzing balance or imbalance between money's supply and demand.

The theory itself asserts a correspondence or parallelism between the quantity of money and the price level, which need not be tight except in the simplest of models. The theory is amply supported by historical and statistical evidence.

The theory—or my reasonably extended interpretation of it—does not insist that causation always runs *from* money *to* prices. The opposite is true for a small, freely trading economy under an international gold standard. There, the price level is aligned with prices in the entire gold-standard world, where supplies and demands, including supply of and demand for money, determine prices. The small economy's quantity of money adjusts through the balance of payments to the local demand for it at that price level. Essentially the same process works in a single city within a nationwide monetary system. Would we say that the quantity theory fails in such cases? Of course not. The *correspondence* between money and price level still holds.

The same is true in some proposed systems of free banking and private money issue considered below. Demands to hold money at the prevailing price level determine not only its total quantity but also its breakdown into quantities of the various kinds of money and near-moneys. The quantity theory illuminates decentralized as well as centralized monetary systems.

Doubts about the Quantity Theory and Monetarism

An argument against monetarism is that financial innovations have obscured what magnitudes aggregated together count as money. Yet respectable theory and models often deal in imprecisely specified aggregates and averages: goods, services, total output, labor, capital, the price level, assets, liabilities, equities, bonds, "the" interest rate, and so forth. Aggregating the various types of money into just "money" is no less legitimate in certain strands of theorizing. How narrowly or broadly to define "money" need not worry theorists as much as it should worry policymakers in today's systems.

A further requirement of reformed money is that to the extent possible it avoids booms and recessions characterized, as many have been, by an excess or particularly by a deficiency of money. At the same time, it should not try to cure or offset recession caused by mainly nonmonetary, "real," factors. The annex on recessions in this paper offers some further remarks.

Reformed Government Money

Proposals for reforming money under a system still operated by government predominated in the lectures of 1960. An old proposal, not described then, is Irving Fisher's compensated dollar (Patinkin 1993). The dollar would be given a supposedly steady purchasing power by occasional or even frequent adjustment of its gold content. That would not be a gold standard, however; gold enters the proposal mainly as a public-relations device.

The Federal Reserve's current approach of manipulating the interest rate on overnight loans between banks may be interpreted as an indirect way of trying to forestall and correct disequilibrium between actual and desired cash balances. Because the Federal Reserve can no longer measure, regulate, or even clearly conceptualize those quantities separately, it gives up trying to do so. Taking account of supposed symptoms, it merely tries to correct or forestall imbalances between money's supply and demand, currently by interest-rate manipulation. The foregoing is merely my perhaps overly sympathetic interpretation of what the Federal Reserve is or should be doing; it is not the official story.

Privatized Money

Despite political difficulties, proposals for privatization are worth hearing for four reasons. First, what is politically realistic can evolve.[2] Second, although horrible to contemplate, a collapse of the government dollar would call for drastic reform.

Third, keeping the government (or its agent, the Federal Reserve) from printing money will impose some discipline on its fiscal policies. Its special advantages as a borrower would diminish. Deprived of its power to issue money, the government could no longer inflate away its huge explicit debt and implicit obligations. Any default would then have to be straightforward. (Regrettably, though, nothing can absolutely prevent government subversion either of its own or a privatized monetary system, however excellent.)

Fourth, considering how private money might work provides opportunities for progress in monetary theory.

A privatized gold standard is simplest to describe. Each issuer of money, disciplined by competition and contract law, would provide dollar-denominated banknotes and deposits redeemable in a definite quantity of gold per dollar. A government gold standard, by contrast, is vulnerable to the government's abandoning it or reducing the dollar's gold content. Such full or partial repudiation of a private gold standard, violating the contracts made between private issuers and the holders of their notes and deposits, would be more difficult.

But gold is not the ideal monetary standard. Although sympathetic to privatization, some libertarians deplore the "constructivism" of devising and evaluating alternative systems; they insist on "letting the market decide." Our existing system, however, is far from the product of spontaneous evolution. It has been shaped over the centuries by numerous piecemeal government interventions. Shifting to a more market-oriented system, or even just clearing the way for spontaneous evolution, will require the government to dismantle its current domination over money. Just how it does so is bound to influence what new system emerges. Government's taxing, spending, regulating, and accounting are bound to influence how readily a new system catches on. The government cannot avoid, then, exerting at least a nudge on what new system evolves. Rather than just ignore that inevitable nudge, economists should analyze what sort of new system is most likely to work satisfactorily and be worthy of a nudge.

An Illustrative Proposal

My favorite reform proposal was developed with Robert Greenfield. I'll not go into great detail because my most recent attempt to refine it is readily available.[3] Better than gold as a monetary standard would be a basket of many goods and services like the basket used for calculating the consumer price index or some other broad price index. The dollar's stability against such a basket or index would bring near stability of a general price level. The question of how frequently the prices should be resampled or the index recalculated could be handled by interpolation of dates and by minor retroactive recalculation of redemptions.

Besides privately issued banknotes and checking accounts, checkable equity funds (not just money market funds) might come into use, and advantageously—if only capital gains taxes did not remain an obstacle. Redemption of dollar-denominated obligations would not be promised and accomplished in the many actual goods and services composing the standard basket because that would be too awkward for all concerned. Instead, redemption could be made indirectly, in quantities of one or more redemption media having actual market values equal to the number of standard baskets denominating the face values of the banknotes and deposits being redeemed.

The redemption medium or media might be gold or some one or more commodities or securities. Which one or ones is not a crucial issue, since redemption would take place in value amounts rather than in prespecified physical amounts of the redemption medium. The dollar-defining basket would remain the standard.[4] Advantageously, no specific base and reserve money would remain.

Most of the redemptions would probably not take place directly between note and deposit issuers and the general public. They would take place routinely at one or more clearinghouses maintained by the various issuing institutions. The clearinghouses might well sponsor a price index corresponding to the dollar's commodity definition, and they might operate a mutual fund as the redemption medium among members.

The ordinary person would no more need to understand the system's details than to understand the Federal Reserve nowadays. Profit-motivated arbitrage by professionals (explained in the works already cited) would almost automatically add money to or withdraw it from circulation to satisfy increased or decreased demands to hold it at the stable price level implied by the dollar's commodity definition. Money's supply and demand would be equilibrated without anyone's measuring or defining either of them or specifying just what instruments count as money. However it and near-moneys might be conceptualized, both their total quantity and also their breakdown into types and denominations would be demand-determined. Issuers would serve the preferences of users of their notes and deposits.

Prices would determine quantities, rather than causation running in the other direction; yet the quantity theory's correspondence between money and price level would hold.

Perhaps the most-discussed objection is that indirect rather than direct redemption is self-destructive (Schnadt and Whittaker 1993). I think that objection is just wrong (Woolsey and Yeager 1994; Greenfield, Woolsey, and Yeager 1995). A more substantial worry, already recognized in Greenfield and Yeager (1983), hinges on a contrast with direct redemption, as in a gold standard, whereby redemption (or its opposite, money issue) maintains equality of value between the dollar and its commodity content not only by affecting the quantity of money but also by directly affecting the supply of the standard commodity on its ordinary market. With indirect redemption, corrective pressures work only through the quantity of money and not directly on each of the markets for the commodities composing the standard basket.

This consideration recommends a highly inclusive standard basket so that the monetary pressures maintaining its one-dollar total value should not require any great part of the pressure (especially downward pressure) to operate prematurely on its sticky-priced components, hampering transactions in them. Other suggestions appear in the literature, such as taking account of an average over time of the price index implicit in the dollar's commodity definition or taking account of a core or "trimmed" index, whereby the relatively few commodities whose prices had risen or fallen the most over a specified period are left out of account, or implementing what would amount to stabilizing bets between money issuers and speculators so desiring. Expectations would work with the mechanics of the system to correct or forestall deviations of the dollar's purchasing power from its commodity definition.

I have described that reform not in detail and not as a definitive proposal. Here it serves as an example of one route to privatization. It is a proposal whose details reformers might well work out, along with alternatives.

A Stable Price Level?

Other reforms might also stabilize the general price level. But is that result desirable? The old issue is worth resurrecting. Most central bankers and politicians seem to have forgotten the old controversies and to have almost unthinkingly accepted a poorly articulated presumption in favor of chronic mild inflation. Even worse, they seem to pursue a year-by-year inflation-*rate* target, at best, rather than a price-*path* target; and if the rate should overshoot the target, well, "oops," no point in crying over spilt milk, no point in trying to reverse the deviation from a less inflationary path.

What arguments for steady mild inflation are available?[5]

- Chronic inflation and the consequently higher level of nominal interest rates supposedly allow expansionary monetary policy, when appropriate, to reduce real interest rates, even below zero. But interest-rate effects are hardly the essence of monetary policy. The quantity of money and the direct cash-balance effect remain important even if forgotten. And anyway, would a sound monetary reform retain a central authority practicing discretionary monetary policy?

- Charles Schultze (1959) argued that a background of rising prices eases market clearing relative to price and wage adjustments: necessary real cuts can be accomplished by merely lagging behind the upward nominal trend. But isn't this a matter of fooling people in a way that they eventually catch on to and allow for? Persistent money illusion is hard to rationalize. In a context of achieved and expected price-level stability, wage and price cuts would seem more normal than in a context of inflationary price uncertainty. In a dynamic economy, new sectors and occupations are always displacing old ones, and it seems reasonable that price and wage adjustments, not just quick plant closings and job losses, should ease the ongoing process. An uptrend in productivity and average wages already provides a cushion for some relative wage cuts to occur without nominal cuts. Price-level uncertainty impairs the formation and adjustment of relative prices; it worsens the signal-extraction problem. Monetary policy is no real remedy for labor-market frictions.

- Monetary expansion and the resulting price inflation, if at a sufficiently moderate rate, provide government revenue through seigniorage. This could be only a minor source of revenue for advanced countries.

- One argument of theoretical interest turns out to have little practical importance. Inflation could discourage accumulating wealth as real-money balances and close near-moneys and so divert saving toward productive capital goods instead, either directly or through purchase of securities floated to finance them. The capital stock thus increased would promote productivity and economic growth. This idea was set forth first and in greatest detail by Maurice Allais, so far as I know, and was later independently and more famously rediscovered by James Tobin and Robert Mundell (Yeager [(2003) 2011] cites and reviews these writings). Allais himself suggested that his capital-impairing effect of saving channeled toward accumulating money might be moderated by injecting any new money through loans to finance capital construction. Furthermore, dollar-denominated debts and claims are tools of the financial intermediation that helps channel saved resources into capital formation, so inflation that impedes using those instruments impairs capital formation. Also, as at least anecdotal evidence suggests, inflation, especially if severe, tends to divert saving from capital formation and securities to finance it into bidding up the prices of land and collectibles and into buying ostentatiously expensive residences, cars, watches, and the like, as well as foreign assets. Inflation complicates borrowing and lending and other contracting and planning for the long run. It distorts the tax system. It may divert resources into coping with it through financial, legal, and consulting activities and away from more straightforwardly useful production. (Yet such activities count as part of real GDP.) Leijonhufvud (1981) describes several such ways in which inflation can impair output and growth.

Another point against inflation is that real money balances are in effect a factor of production-providing services. Holding them economizes on costs of transactions, cash-balance management, and hedging against sales and other fluctuations. Loss of purchasing power through inflation is in effect a tax on holding cash balances, causing holders to economize on them and lose some of their services. For this reason, Milton Friedman (1969) advocated an actually declining price level so that the gain in the purchasing power of cash balances would offset an opportunity cost of holding them, namely, the loss of interest on alternative assets. Reducing the nominal interest rate to zero would remove both the opportunity cost of holding cash balances and the partial loss of their services. That result is appropriate, according to Friedman, because cash balances—of fiat money—are essentially costless to create.

A minority of economists recommends letting the price level sag mildly downward. Not trying to stabilize prices would avoid monetary manipulations and their "injection effects" that tend to distort relative prices, artificially depress interest rates, and have the consequences described by the Austrian theory of the business cycle. George Selgin (1997) argues persuasively, if not conclusively, for a sagging price level as gains in productivity reduce real costs of production (and letting prices rise temporarily when adverse shocks hit the economy). As Gerald O'Driscoll (2011) reminds us, "benign deflation" of that sort need not put a drag on real activity. In most of the second half of the 19th century, the United States experienced strong economic growth along with sagging prices. A monetary reformer should recognize that a price level behaving otherwise than in line with the value of a dollar-defining commodity or bundle presupposes central money management and rules out privatization.

Has inflation benefited or impeded real economic growth since recovery from World War II? David Rapach (2003 [statistics mostly from International Monetary Fund]) applied a vectoral-autoregression framework to time-series data from the 1950s to the mid-1990s for some 9 to 14 developed countries separately (rather than making explicit international comparisons). He found some evidence, if weak, that greater but still mild price inflation tended to depress real interest rates and so presumably promote capital formation and growth.

In short, the Allais-Tobin-Mundell effect described previously appeared to operate, if feebly. In contrast, Crosby and Otto (2000), applying a similar time-series approach to data for some 34 countries, found that moderate inflation rates seemed *not* to have significantly affected the capital stocks of most of those countries.

In any case, several developed countries have experienced milder price inflation than the United States. Table 1.1 shows a few comparisons of increases in per capita real GDP and the consumer price index between 1960 and 2006.

15

Table 1.1

ANNUAL PERCENTAGE INCREASES IN PER CAPITA REAL GDP
AND CONSUMER PRICE INDEX, SELECTED COUNTRIES,
1960–2006

Country	Per capita GDP	CPI
United States	2.24	4.26
Austria	2.72	3.65
Belgium	2.60	3.93
Germany	2.29	2.95
Luxembourg	n.a.	3.73
Netherlands	2.37	3.80
Singapore	5.62	n.a.
Switzerland	n.a.	3.07

NOTE: The percentages are calculated from beginning-of-year numbers at the FRED of the Federal Reserve Bank of St. Louis, http://research.stlouisfed.org /fred2/categories/32264. Most of the series begin with 1960. Taking 2006 as the final year avoids the distractions of the recent worldwide economic crisis. The figures for Germany refer to West Germany before 1990; then reunification diluted the country's per capita GDP. Although consumer price index numbers for the whole period are not available for Singapore, that country almost surely suffered less price inflation than the United States, since its dollar almost doubled in value against the U.S. dollar. n.a. = not available.

The precision and even meaning of such figures are open to question, of course, as well as the period chosen. Many factors besides monetary policy influenced output and prices. In a period of worldwide contagious inflation under fiat money, most countries, unsurprisingly, did suffer worse inflation than the United States.

Still, the conclusion seems plausible and significant that a few advanced countries, although indeed suffering appreciable inflation, restrained it better than the United States and without obvious impairment of output growth.

A flat price-level trend interrupted by only small and soon-reversed oscillations around it has intuitive appeal: something is special about *zero* change in money's purchasing power. The analogy between a stable money unit and fixed units of distance, weight, and so forth seems persuasive to me. Zero as the price-level trend is a kind of "Schelling point." (Thomas Schelling [1960, 56–59, 111ff] advanced the concept of a salient or focal point—a place, a number, or whatever—that people desiring to cooperate would spontaneously tend to converge upon in the absence of specific agreement.)

Money and Liberty

The Liberty Fund serves freedom in promoting discussion of monetary constitutions, including privatization. Indexes of economic freedom published by the Fraser and Heritage Institutes properly take account of how sound each country's money is. And economic freedom is a vital aspect of personal freedom.

Annex on Recessions

A monetary reform should recognize what business cycles are. It should avoid them to the extent that they result from monetary disorder (specifically, from money-supply tightness, which in turn may well follow too easy a monetary policy). Recession is a disruption of the intersectoral and intertemporal coordination explained in any good microeconomics course.[6] In a discoordinated economy, people are unemployed and businesses short of customers, even though people would gladly become better customers if they had jobs, and businesses would gladly hire more workers if they had more customers. That the price system can ordinarily accomplish tolerably good coordination is almost miraculous, given the many billions of domestic and international transactions to be accomplished—multilateral transactions, and not only between households and business firms but also between firms. Very many worker/employer and buyer/supplier contacts are established, maintained, broken, or restored; and many prices are gotten right or wrong. Sound business-cycle research should investigate the obstacles to transactions that worsen from time to time.

Clark Warburton, Milton Friedman, and others have focused on monetary obstacles. As they have shown, most recessions and depressions involve disorder of the money used in pricing and buying and selling, as well as of credits denominated in and ultimately to be settled in money. Does an economy-wide disruption of business trace instead to shocks to technology, tastes, or prices on particular markets, as supposed by the lately fashionable theory of "real" business cycles? Evidence for that idea is scarce. Even the (few) recessions of basically nonmonetary origin have a monetary aspect in that households and firms try to hold more money than usual in relation to their incomes and transactions. Diagnosis must take money into account; monetarism remains relevant.

But "real" factors sometimes do appear in economy-wide discoordination. It is counterproductive to try to remedy unsatisfactory realities by manipulating money—that is one of the teachings of monetarism itself. In the recession of 2007–2009, followed by only sluggish recovery, transactions were disrupted by the consequences of misguided policies, notably in housing and mortgage finance. Many financiers and real estate brokers took reckless and predatory advantage of the opportunities offered by perverse policies. Also belonging in the story is a background of excessive monetary ease promoting debt and causing a search for yield through exotic financial instruments.

Nowadays, furthermore, the media are full of accounts of how both existing policies and pervasive uncertainties cause households, firms, and banks to keep their options open by just holding on to their money. The uncertainties include not only the usual ones of recession but also uncertainties about looming and burdensome government policies regarding government deficits and debt, taxes, health insurance costs for businesses, and financial and environmental regulations. Often, however, we hear that the problem is not lack of confidence but lack of spending, of effective demand. But the issue is not one or the other. Lack of demand is a leading aspect of recession. Lack of confidence and lack of demand reinforce each other.

Even this situation might be alleviated, temporarily, by still more government deficit spending and by flooding the markets with so much additional money that consumers and firms and banks, despite obstacles and uncertainties, would venture some of their abundant funds on increased consumption, employment, and lending. But that would be only a short-run palliative, not a remedy.

Here we have another of the contrasts in economics between what is true or effective in the short run and what is true or effective in the long run. Extreme monetary/fiscal stimulus would leave—and already has left—an ominous and difficult-to-reverse overexpanded supply of bank reserves. Increased government deficits and debt, furthermore, would increase uncertainty about whether and when and which corrective measures would be taken.

Misdiagnosis of recession is evident in the current pervasive call for jobs, as if more jobs were the means to, rather than a happy result of, restored coordination. On C-SPAN's *Washington Journal* of July 27, 2010, Transportation Secretary Ray LaHood fielded a question about the (political) appropriateness of signs lauding highway projects as benefits of federal "stimulus" money. LaHood defended the signs in part as providing jobs for sign makers! Late 2011 TV ads to promote the exploitation of oil sands argued, "This resource has the ability [sic] to create hundreds of thousands of jobs." Calls for "green" energy (read subsidized or mandated energy) to provide jobs are pervasive.[7]

Such jobs-oriented argument puts tampering with resource allocation—trying to micromanage the economy—ahead of recognizing questions of economic coordination. An analogy would be to recommend jogging for a wheelchair-bound accident victim. Being able to go jogging would be the happy result of the patient's recovery, not a means to it.

It is preposterous to try to remedy economic discoordination without even understanding coordinating processes in the first place and without understanding what obstacles and inhibitions sometimes impede productive transactions. Evident ignorance of economics, even at the highest levels of government, must itself sap the business and consumer confidence necessary for business recovery.

Participants in the present volume presumably believe that well-considered monetary reform will help avoid repeating the causes of our current economic woes.

Notes

1. Arguably, a steady-growth rule might have worked well when first proposed. Failure to adopt it interacted with inflation and controls to spur wriggling around them by innovations that made the proposed rule no longer applicable.

2. Furthermore, as Philbrook (1953) argued, a tinge of immorality occurs when supposed experts contaminate their analyses with concern for being politically influential, especially without warning.

3. See Greenfield and Yeager (1983), Yeager (2010), and a considerable literature on the "BFH system" that Google turns up.

4. It should be obvious that such redeemability would not commit the fallacy of a phony gold standard under which the dollar would be redeemable in a dollar's *worth* of gold rather than in a specified physical amount.

5. Several of the arguments that follow are reviewed and criticized by Marty and Thornton (1995).

6. Gerald O'Driscoll aptly entitled his dissertation (1977) *Economics as a Coordination Problem*.

7. "Jobs" is not the only buzzword displacing facts and analysis. Many politicians and callers to C-SPAN unthinkingly recite words such as "growth," "education," "the children," "democracy," "pragmatism," "diversity," "fairness," "fair share," "the rich," "greed," "big oil companies," "corporate jets," "foreign aid," "illegal immigrants," "shipping jobs overseas," "China," "fair trade," "level playing field," "energy independence," "sustainability," and "carbon footprint." Word fads are not confined to politics and economics. Consider "incredible," "incredibly," "prior to," "subsequent to," and "advocate for."

References

Brittan, Samuel. 2003. "Currency Competition: The British Debate." *Cato Journal* 23 (1): 147–53.

Brunner, Karl. 1968. "The Role of Money and Monetary Policy." *Federal Reserve Bank of St. Louis Review*, July, pp. 9–24.

Crosby, Mark, and Glenn Otto. 2000. "Inflation and the Capital Stock." *Journal of Money, Credit and Banking* 32 (1): 236–53.

Friedman, Benjamin M. 1999. "Future of Monetary Policy: The Central Bank as an Army with Only a Signal Corps?" *International Finance* 2 (3): 321–38.

———. 2000a. "Decoupling at the Margin: The Threat to Monetary Policy from the Electronic Revolution in Banking." *International Finance* 3 (2): 26–72.

———. 2000b. "The Role of Interest Rates in Federal Reserve Policymaking." In *The Evolution of Monetary Policy and the Role of the Federal Reserve in the Last Third of the Twentieth Century*, edited by R. W. Kopcke and L. E. Browne, pp. 43–66. Boston: Federal Reserve Bank of Boston. http://scholar.harvard.edu/bfriedman/publications/role-interest-rates-federal-reserve-policymaking.

Friedman, Milton. 1969. "The Optimum Quantity of Money." In *The Optimum Quantity of Money and Other Essays*, pp. 1–50. Chicago: Aldine.

Friedman, Milton, and Anna J. Schwartz. 1963. *A Monetary History of the United States*. Princeton: Princeton University Press for NBER.

Greenfield, Robert L., W. William Woolsey, and Leland B. Yeager. 1995. "Is Indirect Convertibility Impossible? Comment." *Journal of Money, Credit and Banking* 27 (1): 293–97.

Greenfield, Robert L., and Leland B. Yeager. 1983. "A Laissez-Faire Approach to Monetary Stability." *Journal of Money, Credit and Banking* 15 (3): 302–15.

Hayek, Friedrich A. von. 1978. *Denationalisation of Money: The Argument Refined*. 2nd ed. London: Institute of Economic Affairs.

Leijonhufvud, Axel. 1981. "Costs and Consequences of Inflation." Chap. 9 in *Information and Coordination: Essays in Macroeconomic Theory*. New York: Oxford University Press.

Marty, Alvin L., and Daniel L. Thornton. 1995. "Is There a Case for 'Moderate' Inflation?" *Federal Reserve Bank of St. Louis Review*, July/August, pp. 27–37.

"McCallum Rule." 2013. *Wikipedia*, last updated October 18. http://en.wikipedia.org/wiki/McCallum_rule.

O'Driscoll, Gerald P., Jr. 1977. *Economics as a Coordination Problem: The Contributions of Friedrich A. Hayek*. Kansas City: Sheed Andrews and McMeel.

———. 2011. "Money, Prices, and Bubbles." *Cato Journal* 31 (3): 441–59.

Patinkin, Don. 1956. *Money, Interest, and Prices*. Evanston: Row, Peterson.

———. 1965. *Money, Interest, and Prices*. 2nd ed. New York: Harper & Row.

———. 1993. "Irving Fisher and His Compensated Dollar Plan." Federal Reserve Bank of Richmond *Economic Quarterly* 79 (3): 1–33.

Philbrook, Clarence. 1953. "'Realism' in Policy Espousal." *American Economic Review* 43 (5): 846–59.

Rapach, David E. 2003. "International Evidence on the Long-Run Impact of Inflation." *Journal of Money, Credit and Banking* 35 (1): 23–48.

Razzak, Weshah. 2001. "Is the Taylor Rule Really Different from the McCallum Rule?" Reserve Bank of New Zealand Discussion Paper Series DP2001/07, Wellington, October. http://www.rbnz.govt.nz/research_and_publications/discussion_papers/2001/dp01_07.pdf.

Schelling, Thomas C. 1960. *The Strategy of Conflict*. Cambridge, MA: Harvard University Press.

Schnadt, Norbert, and John Whittaker. 1993. "Inflation-Proof Currency? The Feasibility of Variable Commodity Standards." *Journal of Money, Credit and Banking* 25 (2): 214–21.

Schultze, Charles L. 1959. "Recent Inflation in the United States." Study Paper no. 1, Joint Economic Committee, 86th Cong., 1st sess. Washington, DC: Government Printing Office.

Schumpeter, Joseph A. 1970. *Das Wesen des Geldes*. Edited from manuscript (mostly drafted by about 1930) and with an introduction by Fritz Karl Mann. Göttingen: Vandenhoeck & Ruprecht.

Selgin, George A. 1997. *Less Than Zero: The Case for a Falling Price Level in a Growing Economy*. Hobart Paper No. 132. London: Institute of Economic Affairs.

Woolsey, W. William, and Leland B. Yeager. 1994. "Is There a Paradox of Indirect Convertibility?" *Southern Economic Journal* 61 (1): 85–95.

Yeager, Leland B., ed. 1962. *In Search of a Monetary Constitution*. Cambridge, MA: Harvard University Press.

———. 2010. "Privatizing Money." *Cato Journal* 30 (3): 417–38.

———. (2003) 2011. "Land, Money, and Capital Formation." In *Is the Market a Test of Truth and Beauty?*, pp. 209–24. Auburn, AL: Ludwig von Mises Institute. Reprinted from a 2003 Festschrift for Gerrit Meijer.

2. Still in Search of a Monetary Constitution

Hugh Rockoff

Remarkable Prescience

One would expect thoughtful discussions of monetary constitutions in the aftermath of financial crises—for example, in the wake of the crisis of 1907, or during the Great Depression, or today. And typically this has been the case. The U.S. National Monetary Commission, whose work led to the establishment of the Federal Reserve, was organized as a result of the panic of 1907. And 1936 witnessed the publication of two remarkable discussions of the Great Depression: Keynes's *The General Theory of Employment, Interest and Money* and Henry Simons's essay "Rules versus Authorities in Monetary Policy." The series of lectures that Leland Yeager organized at the University of Virginia in 1960 is something of an outlier. The U.S. economy then was doing fairly well, at least by today's standards, even if at the time some economists thought the economy could do much better. Indeed, Jacob Viner, the ideological outlier in the series, thought that discretionary Federal Reserve policy had worked well after the 1951 Treasury–Federal Reserve Accord (Yeager 1962, 254). According to Viner, things had gone better than they would have under a monetary rule, and "with the gains which one can reasonably expect time to bring in available statistical data, skills, and insights, the Federal Reserve will be able to perform even better in the future, if it is given adequate authority."

But things were about to change. Figure 2.1 shows the annual rate of inflation from 1955 to 1985. A vertical line shows when the lecture series was held. Inflation seemed to be under control, and it would remain so for the next few years. But in the mid-1960s, the "Great Inflation" would begin: three successive waves of inflation that would take the annual rate of inflation well into double digits.

Yeager had shown remarkable prescience in organizing a lecture series on monetary constitutions. Think how much economic trauma would have been avoided if some sort of monetary constitution had been adopted in the wake of the resulting volume of essays.

Figure 2.1
The Annual Rate of Inflation, 1955–85

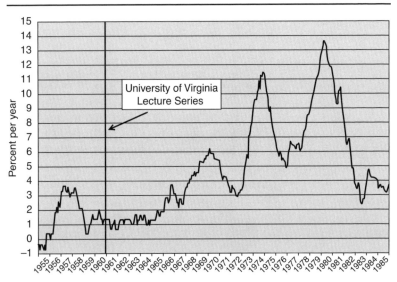

Source: U.S. Department of Labor, Bureau of Labor Statistics.

Note: I took the natural logarithm of the monthly consumer price index for all urban consumers, subtracted the natural logarithm of the same index 12 months earlier, and expressed the difference as a percentage.

All of the participants in the volume, with the exception of Viner, accepted the conservative political case for a monetary constitution: Governments often abuse the powers granted to them. Entrusting a government with an unchecked power to create money and thus to raise resources through an inflation tax is dangerous. Such a tax is largely hidden from the public because the public typically does not associate the losses imposed by inflation with the gains realized by the government. This was precisely the situation in the United States at the time of the Yeager volume: the Federal Reserve could, if it chose to do so, purchase large amounts of federal debt, thereby financing the federal government while creating inflation. Arthur Kemp (Yeager 1962, 152) quoted John Stuart Mill's *Principles of Political Economy* [(1848) 1909] on the dangers of governmental abuse of monetary powers:

> Profligate governments ... until a very modern period, seldom scrupled, for the sake of robbing their creditors, to confer on all debtors a license to rob theirs, by the shallow and impudent device of lowering the standard; that least covert of all modes of knavery, which consists in calling a shilling a pound that a debt of one hundred pounds may be canceled by the payment of a hundred shillings. It would have been as simple a plan, and would have answered the purpose as well, to have enacted that "a hundred" should always be interpreted to mean five, which would have effected the same reduction of all pecuniary contracts, and would not have been at all more shameless. Such strokes of policy have not wholly ceased to be recommended, but they have ceased to be practiced; except occasionally through the medium of paper money, in which case the character of the transaction, from the greater obscurity of the subject, is a little less barefaced.

But while the attendees, Viner excepted, agreed on the need for a monetary constitution, they differed on how a monetary constitution should be constructed. Murray Rothbard and Arthur Kemp favored a gold standard. Benjamin Graham and James Buchanan favored alternative commodity standards. Milton Friedman, George Tolley, Willford King, and Richard Selden considered the monetary system prevailing in the United States at the time of the Virginia lecture series—one in which the monetary base was produced by a central bank—and asked how it could be constrained to produce better long-term results. Clark Warburton's paper may be considered in this category as well, since he was an early and well-known advocate of a monetary rule, although his paper was an empirical one designed to show with a wealth of examples that "money mattered" for the business cycle.

A Gold Standard?

Rothbard advocated a "100 percent gold dollar." In Rothbard's world, fractional-reserve banking would be illegal. Banks could issue notes or deposits, but essentially they would be warehouse receipts for a fixed physical quantity of gold. Rothbard did not care for terms like "pound" or "dollar" with the understanding that they *meant* designated physical quantities of gold. A Rothbard banknote would simply say "Murray Rothbard promises to pay one gram of 24-karat gold to the bearer of this note on demand at our premises in Boston." And Rothbard's bank would have one gram of gold for every note outstanding. Anything else would be fraud.

One question that arises with respect to Rothbard's plan, and indeed with respect to all 100 percent monetary schemes, is whether near-moneys might be a problem. Rothbard believed that an asset was either money or not money. He saw no problem (Yeager 1962, 116, 116n22) with banks issuing "short-term debentures," even if these debentures were backed by long-term bank loans rather than 100 percent by gold. But if these debentures functioned, at least to some degree, as money—if they came to be used, for example, for making payments—then the same problems would arise under Rothbard's scheme as under more conventional gold standards. Fluctuations in the amount of debentures, and other near-moneys, could fuel business-cycle fluctuations. And the periphery of bank debentures would be subject to something akin to banking panics. Only if one were to go in the direction that Simons (1936) suggested and ban all short-term finance could the problem of a periphery of near-moneys be avoided. Friedman (Yeager 1962, 221) made a similar point in his contribution to the Yeager volume. Because real resources are required to produce a dollar under a gold standard (or other commodity standards), people will have a strong incentive to create substitutes. Friedman seems to have downplayed the risk that his own system of 100 percent money and money-growth rules could be undermined by the growth of money substitutes, but he recognized the risk with respect to the gold standard.

Kemp advocated the return to something like the pre-1914 gold standard, what Kemp called a "gold-coin standard." This is a good term for it. One of the distinguishing features of the pre-1914 gold standard was that legal-tender gold coins circulated from hand to hand as money. It was, however, a fractional-reserve system and therefore differed substantially from the 100 percent reserve system that Rothbard advocated. In Kemp's world, banks held reserves of gold but then issued banknotes and deposits that served as the basic components of the stock of money. Kemp accepted the basic libertarian argument for a gold standard: that it reined in, to an extent, the power of the government to raise resources through inflation. But he added an interesting supplemental reason for supporting a gold standard. By creating an easily transported and internationally accepted store of value, gold protected individual rights. As an example, he noted (Yeager 1962, 153) that the "father of Henry Bessemer, the inventor of the Bessemer steel process, caught in the disorder of the French Revolution, was able to re-establish himself as a die maker in England by virtue of a supply of gold coins. The vastly larger proportion of his wealth in French assignats turned out to be worthless."

Kemp's basic case for a return to the pre-1914 gold-coin standard, however, was the often-cited array of benefits of the historical gold standard. We can summarize them briefly as follows:

- Gold is in some ways the ideal material for making coins that circulate from hand to hand. It is beautiful, easily worked, and reacts with few other substances.

- The gold standard provided stable international exchange rates within the gold standard bloc, which encouraged international trade. The era of the classical gold standard, 1879 (when the United States rejoined the gold standard after the Civil War) to 1914 (World War I), is often looked to as a "golden age" of rising living standards, produced in part by international trade and specialization.

Because those exchange rates remained stable over long periods, the gold standard encouraged international capital flows as well as trade flows. Capital flowed from London (the world's center for international finance) in greatest volume to the English-speaking regions of new settlement: Canada, the United States, Australia, New Zealand, and South Africa. But it also flowed to many other areas of the world, including India, Latin America, the Far East, and Africa.

Maintaining exchange rates for long periods—the exchange rate between the dollar and the pound was basically unchanged between the end of the Napoleonic Wars and the beginning of World War I—required considerable discipline by governments. And that in turn meant that the public had to support maintenance of the gold standard at all hazards. It meant the development of what Buchanan (Yeager 1962, 191) referred to as a "mythology of money," a willingness of the average man or woman to "attribute the workings of the monetary system to the gods."

- The gold standard also provided some countercyclical employment adjustments. This occurred both directly because gold mining could be a countercyclical economic activity and indirectly through the Humean price-specie-flow mechanism. The direct mechanism, increased mining of gold during a slump based on the rise of the real price of gold (the fixed mint price relative to the price level), is usually ignored because it is not likely to have much practical significance and is not available to a country lacking gold mines. In a few circumstances, however, gold mining was an important economic activity. Between 1850 and 1860, the decade of the California gold rush, the male working-age population (15–75 years) in California increased by 144,955, from 82,272 to 227,227. At the same time, the free male labor force of the United States increased by 1,903,737, from 5,227,198 to 7,130,935. So gold-rush California (which included, to be sure, other activities besides gold mining) absorbed about 7.61 percent of the increase in the male labor force between 1850 and 1860.[1] This was enough to materially affect conditions in labor markets. But this was a rare event. One of the appeals of the more exotic commodity standards discussed in the next section is that they could provide more countercyclical benefits through this direct effect.

A prolonged slump of one country on the gold standard involving lower prices and income would produce a balance of payments surplus—as exports became more attractive and imports became less attractive—and a surplus in turn would produce an increase in the stock of money with a stimulative effect. A boom would tend to produce the opposite, a balance of payments deficit and a reduction in the stock of money. So automatic equilibrating forces were at work under the gold standard.

- Finally, and perhaps most important to advocates of the gold standard, as evidenced by the focus on it in the Yeager volume, the gold standard produced, relatively speaking, long-term price stability. True, prices could fall if the gold mines were not producing enough new gold to keep pace with the growth of economic activity or rise if abundant new mines were discovered. But the extreme inflations possible with paper money were simply not possible in a system anchored by gold. Although the discovery of the great goldfields of the Rand and smaller fields in Western Australia, the Klondike, and other areas produced an increase in world prices after 1896, the resulting inflation was moderate. Between 1896 and 1914 the gross domestic product (GDP) deflator, as shown in Table 2.1, increased only 1.96 percent per year in the United States and only 0.79 percent per year in the United Kingdom; the rate of increase of the consumer price index was 0.97 percent per year in the United States and 1.04 percent per year in the United Kingdom (the retail price index).

But a full description of the gold standard must look at the costs as well as the benefits. These were not inconsiderable. First, under the gold standard, real resources had to be used to produce the stock of money—resources that could be saved by relying on fiat money. In 1900, the U.S. monetary gold stock was equal to about 5.5 percent

Table 2.1

ANNUAL PERCENTAGE CHANGES OF KEY VARIABLES IN TWO
PHASES OF THE CLASSICAL GOLD STANDARD

Variable	1879–96	1896–1914
United States		
Consumer price index	−1.01	0.97
GDP deflator	−0.76	1.96
Real GDP per capita	1.57	0.98
United Kingdom		
Retail price index	−0.76	1.04
GDP deflator	−0.18	0.79
Real GDP per capita	1.24	0.92

SOURCE: http://www.measuringworth.com/.

of GDP. So a nice bonus was available, equal to about one year's growth in real GDP, if the United States were to convert from a gold-backed currency to a pure fiat standard.[2]

Second, although the price level could not rise to the astronomical heights possible under a paper-money standard, prices could both rise and fall under the gold standard. I have already noted the rise in prices from 1896 to 1914. The period before that, from 1879 (when the United States returned to the gold standard after the Civil War) to 1896, was characterized by a gradual deflation. Between 1879 and 1896, the GDP deflator fell 0.76 percent per year in the United States and 0.18 percent per year in the United Kingdom; the consumer price index fell 1.01 percent per year in the United States, and the similar retail price index for the United Kingdom fell 0.76 percent per year. To be sure, it was a mild deflation. Markets adjusted to some extent, and overall economic growth was strong. Real GDP per capita rose 1.57 percent per year in the United States and 1.24 percent per year in the United Kingdom (Table 2.1). These rates exceeded the rates of real GDP growth experienced in the following period of mild inflation. Friedman and Anna Schwartz (1963, 41–42) and more recently Bordo, Landon-Lane, and Redish (2010) have pointed to this period as one of "good" or at least relatively benign deflation compared with other deflations.

Although the deflation did not interfere with the strong surge of economic activity produced by the second industrial revolution, severe strains occurred, especially in the slump of the first half of the 1890s. It was an era of severe labor strikes. The reasons are complex, but several of the most famous strikes, such as the Pullman strike of 1894, were brought about in part by attempts to cut wages. Cuts in nominal wages might well have been avoided in a different monetary environment. And it was the era of farmer-debtor complaints about falling price levels. The western farmers who joined the populist movement may have conflated problems specific to their own industry, declines in the real price of agricultural prices, with the decline in the general price level. Nevertheless, populist hatred of the gold standard was intense. William Jennings Bryan won the Democratic nomination for president in 1896 by declaring at the Democratic Party convention that "you [Republicans] shall not crucify mankind upon a cross of gold." The gold standard survived the challenge, and opposition waned after the supply of gold began to rise more rapidly. But clearly political support for the gold standard in the

United States was circumscribed. The uncertainty produced by the populist challenge to the gold standard, moreover, undermined the economy, for example by producing outflows of gold when adherence to the gold standard was threatened. Price-level stability, if it had been possible to achieve, might have produced an even more robust economy than the mild deflation generated by the gold standard.

Third, what could not be done under the gold standard is what the Federal Reserve did in response to the recession of 2007–2009: deliberately increase the monetary base in hopes of rapidly restoring full employment. Under the gold standard the central bank (if one existed) was limited in its response to unemployment by "golden fetters," to use Barry Eichengreen's (1992) term, the need to protect the gold reserve of the central bank. In countries such as the United States and Canada, without central banks, discretionary monetary policy was obviously not possible.

An Alternative Commodity Standard?

Graham and Buchanan explored alternative commodity standards. Graham's plan, already well known by the time of the Yeager volume, would have backed the monetary unit with a set of "15 to 25" storable commodities. The idea behind Graham's plan was to improve on the gold standard in several ways while maintaining the advantages of a commodity-based currency. First, by broadening the range of commodities in the monetary basket, Graham hoped to improve long-run price stability. Under a commodity standard, the stability of the price level in the long run depends on the stability of the relative price of the monetary commodity or commodities. If that falls, as for example the relative price of gold fell in the 1890s with the discoveries in South Africa and elsewhere, inflation would follow. Having a broader market basket of commodities would reduce the likelihood of fluctuations in the real price of the monetary commodity. This was one of the ideas behind bimetallism—more long-run stability with two commodities than with one—but Graham's plan would take the idea even further.

Another advantage of a storable-commodity standard compared with a gold standard is that the former would spread the direct countercyclical employment advantages of a commodity standard more widely. As noted previously, the gold standard had produced

31

considerable employment during the era of the California gold rush, but that was obviously an atypical event. Making storable commodities part of the monetary market basket would increase the demand for them and moderate price fluctuations, a special concern of Graham's. Producers of cotton, historically impoverished southern sharecroppers (although that was changing), for example, would benefit if that commodity were included in the monetary basket.

A storable-commodity standard, of course, has many problems, not the least important of which would be the initial lack of the unquestioned public acceptance that is so valuable in establishing stable price expectations, the kind of support that developed for the gold standard in the 19th century. Graham's proposal, incidentally, had already been subjected to a searching and still valuable critique by Friedman (1951). In his paper, Graham responded to some of Friedman's criticisms.

Buchanan explored two exotic forms of commodity standards, a brick standard and a labor standard. Graham's plan had a better chance of being adopted because it would have been supported by the industries producing the commodities to be included in the monetary unit. But Buchanan's more exotic plans are worth discussing because they illustrate more clearly the potential costs and benefits of commodity standards.[3]

A brick standard, apparently first advocated by the economist C. O. Hardy, was just what it sounded like; the basic monetary unit would be a common brick rather than a specified quantity of gold. Obviously, replacing gold with bricks would mean giving up some of the benefits of the gold standard. Bricks could not be easily worked into coins that would circulate from hand to hand as money. They could not be used as a form of wealth by dissidents attempting to flee a tyrant. But a brick standard would have several potential advantages compared with the classical gold standard. Because bricks are made from widely available raw materials, the price level would likely be more stable than under a gold standard. Under the gold standard, as previously noted, you could have periods of inflation when new gold mines came on line and periods of deflation when existing mines were depleted. But under the brick standard, neither event was likely.

The stabilizing direct effect on employment, moreover, likely would be much greater under a brick standard than under a gold standard. Imagine a severe slump in which unemployment rose and wages and prices fell. Under a gold standard, demand for gold would still exist. The mint would stand ready to buy at a fixed price all the gold brought to it. People could still find work in the gold-producing industry. But the fixed costs of entering gold mining are so high that the effects on production and employment would be limited. During the Great Depression in the United States, some unemployed workers did return to the streams of California to pan for gold, but although an interesting phenomenon, it obviously could not do much to relieve unemployment. In contrast, one can imagine a much larger direct effect under a brick standard. Bricks, according to Buchanan (Yeager 1962, 176), can be produced in every locality in the United States. One can imagine hundreds of brick factories opening up and employing thousands of people, enough to make a substantial dent in the rate of unemployment.

A labor standard in which the dollar would be defined as a certain quality and quantity of labor would further strengthen the direct employment effect. Buchanan, citing an idea of Armin Alchian, described ATMs (automated teller machines) fitted with stationary bicycles. Someone who needed cash could go to the ATM, bicycle for a prescribed amount of time, and retrieve the appropriate amount of cash from the ATM. The bicycle might be hooked to the electrical grid so that the cycling would generate some useful power. The monetary system would become the "employer of last resort." As Buchanan points out, however, a problem exists with a labor standard that would need to be addressed. One of the basic functions of money is to serve as a store of value, a natural property of gold, bricks, and other storable commodities but not of labor. Buchanan suggested that the government could stand ready to go into the labor market and purchase labor if businesses and individuals wanted to cash in their labor notes.

Buchanan's plan for a labor standard bears a family resemblance (at least it shares a name) with the labor standard that the utopian socialist Robert Owen attempted. Owen's idea was that individual workers would offer their labor in exchange for "banknotes" that they could exchange for the labor of other workers. A butcher might offer 10 hours in exchange for notes. Later he might cash them in for 10 hours of labor by a carpenter. Although the experiment was tried, it was, as might have been expected, unsuccessful (Oliver 1958). It was hard to get enough people, with enough different skills, depositing their labor to make holding the notes worthwhile. An example of one of Owen's labor notes is shown in Figure 2.2.

Figure 2.2
AN EXAMPLE OF ROBERT OWEN'S LABOR-BACKED MONEY

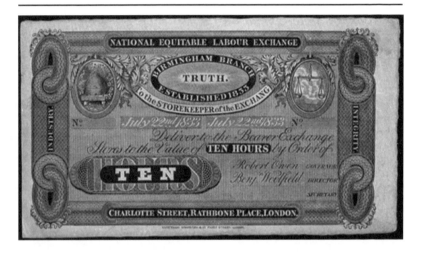

Friedman (1951), as I noted above in discussing Rothbard's and Graham's contributions, offered a trenchant criticism of commodity standards, whether gold standards or more exotic standards: although set up as pure standards by governments, entrepreneurs would soon introduce banking in some form, and so many of the problems inherent in modern systems would soon reemerge. Limiting the stock of money to the pure base money would be impossible. Here, to reiterate, Friedman seems to have missed the danger that his own policy proposal, stable growth of "the money supply," would falter because of the same problem, the growth of near-moneys or what has come to be called shadow banking.

Fiat Money Produced by a Central Bank?

The gold standard (or bimetallic standard) was abandoned by most of the industrialized nations in World War I, the most important

exception being the United States. The need for revenues over-whelmed all objections to printing money and generating inflation. This, of course, was nothing new. Britain had abandoned the gold standard during the Napoleonic Wars but returned to it afterward. The United States had abandoned its (de facto) gold standard during the Civil War but returned afterward. Restoration of the gold standard was widely expected after World War I. Indeed, this expectation probably helped sustain the values of the currencies of the warring nations. However, the gold standard never made a full comeback. Britain returned to the gold standard at a rate that overvalued the pound, a fact that Keynes blamed for some of the unemployment that plagued Britain in the 1920s. France returned at a rate that undervalued the franc. In principle, France should have allowed the resulting inflow of gold to expand its money supply, increase its price level, and gradually reduce its balance-of-payments surplus, but France preferred to "sterilize" the inflow. The United States also accumulated large amounts of gold during this period that it also sterilized. The result was considerable pressure on the rest of the world to follow contractionary monetary policies. The Great Depression, brought on in some measure by the policies of France and the United States, proved to be the deathbed of the gold standard. Country after country abandoned gold in the hope that devaluation and a more expansionary monetary policy would help alleviate unemployment. After World War II, the Bretton Woods system provided a role for gold, but the dollar was the true anchor of the system. Thus, the Federal Reserve replaced the gold mines of the Rand as the source of the world's monetary base. Although one could argue (following Viner) that the Federal Reserve had not done badly in that role during the 1950s, its performance in the 1960s and 1970s would not compare favorably with that of the gold mines of the Rand in the 1890s and 1900s.

Although the end of the gold standard was mainly the product of historical events—the two World Wars and the Great Depression—it also owed something to the revolution in economic thought. Keynes, who after World War I had referred to gold as a "barbarous relic" (1924, 172), helped establish the idea that governments needed to actively manage their macroeconomies. If unemployment was a major problem, then the monetary authority should try to lower interest rates. It might not be possible to lower rates very much if the economy was near a liquidity trap, and lower rates might not stimulate much investment spending. Monetary policy was weak; fiscal policy had to do the heavy lifting. But the monetary authority should not be prevented from doing whatever it could to alleviate unemployment by the artificial constraints of the gold standard. The gold standard, to sum up, had been sustained in the 19th century by widespread public support, by widespread support by economists and other financial experts, and perhaps by political systems that limited the influence of labor. By 1945 all of those pillars had been eliminated.

After the war, it was hoped that the new Bretton Woods system would provide the benefits of the fixed exchange rates of the gold standard while allowing governments to follow more aggressive countercyclical monetary policies. This hope, however, was not to be realized: rising inflation, especially in the United States, under-mined the system. Again, the driving forces were events in the real world: America's dwindling stock of gold and rising prices. But once again ideas were important. Had it not been for Friedman and other vigorous advocates of flexible exchange rates, including Yeager, fur-ther attempts might have been made in the early 1970s to reestablish a fixed-rate system. Instead, the modern system of flexible rates was tried and, despite many criticisms, has continued to survive.

Once one accepts the inevitability in the modern world of a mon-etary system based on a central bank that can create unlimited amounts of fiat money, the need for some form of monetary con-stitution is clear to anyone who fears unconstrained governmental power. But the basic libertarian political case for constraining central banks is not the only reason for doing so. Friedman's and Tolley's contributions to the volume identified several important additional reasons for reining in central banks with rules. Recounting these arguments here is worthwhile, as is seeing how they fared in the decades that followed.

One problem with an independent and unconstrained central bank, according to Freidman, is that monetary powers can also be exercised by the Treasury and in some cases by other federal agen-cies. Dispersal of power encourages shirking. Agencies may not act because other agencies are carrying the ball and likely to get the blame if things go badly. The central bank may not act because many other agencies exist with which to share the blame. The 2008 financial crisis in the United States revealed a closely related problem. Dispersal of power encourages everyone to get in the act. The Federal Reserve engaged in traditional monetary actions during the crisis. But we also had the Treasury's Capital Purchase Program, Term Asset-Backed Securities Loan Facility, and so on, and the Federal Deposit Insurance Corporation's Temporary Liquidity Guarantee Program. When things are happening, most bureaucrats want part of the action.

Second, the actual policies adopted by an unconstrained monetary authority would inevitably be, in Friedman's words, "highly dependent on personalities." Friedman cited two examples of very bad monetary policy that made his point. One was an episode that followed on the heels of World War I. The Federal Reserve followed a very expansionary monetary policy in 1919 that contributed to the high postwar inflation and then slammed on the breaks in 1920, producing a brief but severe contraction in 1920–21. Friedman blamed the governor of the Federal Reserve System, W. P. G. Harding, for both failures. A monetary rule of stable growth of the money supply, Friedman insisted, would have produced a better performance.

The most important example, of course, was the Great Contraction. Friedman pointed to the inaction of the Federal Reserve following the failure of the Bank of United States in December 1930 and argued that if the knowledgeable and dynamic Benjamin Strong, who had been the first president of the Federal Reserve Bank of New York and who died in 1928, had still been a major figure in the system, the Federal Reserve might have taken action and nipped the growing banking panic in the bud. Again, it is not hard to see that a monetary rule might have produced better results.

The failure of Federal Reserve policy in the 1930s was also addressed in Tolley's contribution. Tolley pointed to the contraction in the total money supply despite an expansion in high-powered money. A monetary rule would have forced the Federal Reserve to make even larger increases in the stock of high-powered money to maintain a fixed (or increasing at a fixed rate) stock of money. Tolley's main point, however, was that moving in the direction of 100 percent reserves would also have improved the stability of the banking system. Had the United States been on a 100 percent reserve system in the 1930s, the decline in the stock of money would not have been possible. Here, Tolley was endorsing the 100 percent reserve proposal of Henry Simons ([1934] 1948), which also has been endorsed by Friedman (1959). Tolley's (1957) main addition to the "Chicago plan" of 100 percent reserves, incidentally, was the proposal for the Federal Reserve to pay interest on reserves, a reform that was finally adopted in the wake of the 2008 crisis.

Subsequent experience strengthened Friedman's case for viewing the dependence of monetary policy on personalities as a matter of concern. Arthur Burns was chair of the Federal Reserve from February 1, 1970, to January 31, 1978, during the heart of the Great Inflation. Burns might have followed a tighter monetary policy and prevented or at least greatly moderated the inflation. But Burns saw inflation as a "cost-push" phenomenon rather than a monetary phenomenon that he could control. For Burns, monetary policy was better targeted toward maintaining an expanding economy. Again, a rule might well have done better.[4] Alan Greenspan was chair of the Board of Governors of the Federal Reserve from August 11, 1987, to January 31, 2006. For a time, Greenspan was widely hailed as a genius, as the Maestro, to use the title of an admiring biography by Bob Woodward (2000). Even Friedman became an enthusiast. Today, in the wake of the 2008 financial crisis, doubts have been raised about Greenspan's conduct of monetary policy. Perhaps after each recession, interest rates were kept too low for too long, thus fueling the real estate bubble that was the root of the crisis.

Third, Friedman identified excessive influence from bankers as a defect of an independent and unconstrained central bank. Central-bank actions have immediate effects on credit markets, so the players in financial markets are likely to exercise as much influence as they can on central banks to achieve the rates they desire. Commercial bankers, investment bankers, hedge-fund managers, and the like, moreover, constitute the experts that the media and the politicians turn to for an understanding of monetary policy. In that environment, a natural tendency exists to think of monetary policy primarily in terms of its effects on interest rates. Friedman objected strongly to the assumption that monetary policy works mainly through a small subset of interest rates—in particular, rates on short-term, government-issued securities. Both his theoretical and empirical work convinced him that direct connections linked changes in the stock of money and changes in spending on a wide range of goods, services, and assets. A prime example of the mistake of identifying monetary policy with interest rates, as Friedman saw it, was again the Great Depression.

Nominal interest rates fell during the early 1930s, a result that was widely interpreted as proving that monetary policy was "easy" and could do no more to ameliorate the slump. Friedman pointed to the decline in the stock of money as a signal that monetary policy was in fact "tight" and a major cause of the slump.

Although Friedman for a time had some success in convincing his fellow monetary economists to focus on the stock of money rather than on interest rates, in the long run the profession returned to the view that monetary policy was identical with short-term, low-risk interest rates. Macro models typically omitted an explicit equation including the stock of money. During the recent financial crisis, Keynesian economists such as Paul Krugman revived the Keynesian idea of the liquidity trap. They insisted that once short-term rates, especially the federal funds rate, were near zero, monetary policy ceased to have any effect on the economy. The realization that the Federal Reserve can still buy assets and affect interest rates even when the federal funds rate is near zero has undermined the identification of monetary policy with short-term interest rates, although not the broader idea that monetary policy works solely through asset prices.

In his discussion of rules, Friedman identified a fourth problem with discretionary monetary policy: some long-term cumulative effects of monetary policy are likely to be ignored when an unconstrained central bank moves from one short-term problem to another. Price-level stability, to be more specific, is clearly a desirable long-run goal of monetary policy. But the temptation for a monetary authority that is unconstrained by a price-level or monetary-growth rule is to meet the host of short-term problems that it encounters— an increase in unemployment; the bursting of a bubble in an asset market; an appreciation of the dollar, which hurts exporters; and so on—by expanding the money supply. A rule increases the visibility of long-term goals. Individuals often face the same problem and adopt rules for the same reason. We know that we should save for our retirement. So we adopt a rule of saving, say, 5 percent of our salary each week. Without the rule, we might forget our long-run goal as we deal each week with a more immediate set of problems and temptations. The absence of some sort of rule seems likely to have been part of the trouble with monetary policy during the Great Inflation. Some short-term problem, typically public concern about unemployment or a slowdown in the economy, always arose that could be addressed by increasing the money supply.

Together, to sum up, the Yeager volume's participants made a powerful case for adopting a monetary constitution. In some cases, they had done so by showing the potential merits of alternative systems, such as the gold standard or even the brick standard, and in some cases they had done so, as in Friedman's and Tolley's essays, by showing the dangers of leaving everything up to the discretion of the central bank. In the following years, most central banks did in fact come around to adopting some form of constitution, although not the form of explicit rule that most of the participants in the volume favored. In some cases, explicit price-level targets were adopted; in some cases, such as the Federal Reserve's "dual mandate," a "rule" was adopted that in fact permits a wide range of discretion. Although economists are not without influence, the main reason for the adoption of various forms of price-level rules by monetary authorities was simply the facts on the ground. By the time that Federal Reserve chairman Paul Volcker slammed on the brakes in October 1979, purely discretionary monetary policy had clearly failed. Central banks had to be constrained in some way to force them to take price-level stability into account.

What Kind of Rule?

Simons, in his famous paper "Rules versus Authorities in Monetary Policy" (1936)—a paper that was mentioned explicitly by many of the participants in the Yeager volume and that was clearly in the back of the minds of others—laid out what, for the volume participants, were the two main alternatives.[5]

A monetary rule of maintaining the constancy of some price index, preferably an index of prices of competitively produced commodities, appears to afford the only promising escape from present monetary chaos and uncertainties. A rule calling for outright fixing of the total quantity of money, however, definitely merits consideration as a perhaps preferable solution in the more distant future. At least, it may provide a point of departure for fruitful academic discussion (Simons 1936, 30).

Simons preferred a price-level rule to a monetary rule at the time because of the problem of fluctuations in the stock of moneys and near-moneys. The stock of money could not easily be fixed, of course, as long as fractional reserve banking existed. But Simons would not have been content simply with adopting 100 percent reserves. Simons believed that a wide range of assets possessed some degree of "moneyness." Short-term government debt was an obvious example. That degree of moneyness, moreover, was a matter of psychology. The same asset that was considered a safe and liquid store of value in 1929 might have been considered a dangerously illiquid asset in 1932. Hence, a monetary rule, such as fixing the stock of money, could not be adopted until financial reforms were completed that eliminated any risk that bank deposits and notes would not be redeemed and eliminated near-moneys. Indeed, Simons would go so far as to make most short-term lending illegal. Hence, fixing the stock of money was a reform for "the distant future."

Two of the participants in the Yeager volume, Milton Friedman and Clark Warburton, were famous for advocating the adoption of a monetary rule of stable money growth, even without the prior adoption of the far-reaching reforms of the financial system advocated by Simons. Their views are summarized, criticized, and ultimately defended in an excellent contribution by Richard T. Selden (1962). Friedman's case against a price-level rule was simply that with a price-level rule in place it was hard to hold the monetary authority to account. Many factors might conceivably affect the price level. The monetary authority could always invoke "other factors" if it failed to reach its price-level target.

The sort of monetary rule that Warburton and Friedman advocated, however, did not find much acceptance in the United States in the years after publication of the Yeager volume. During the time when Volcker was slamming on the brakes, an experiment, or at least so it was claimed, was made with controlling the money supply, and academics and journalists widely accepted that this experiment was a failure. The point is debatable. Even if we agree that a monetary rule was adopted, basing a conclusion about the efficacy of a policy on one trial under unusual circumstances hardly seems sound. However, no doubt exists that in the wake of the Volcker recession, the stock of money grew for a long while at a rate much exceeding the rates of growth that Friedman had earlier suggested were appropriate for long-run price stability, without producing a return to rapid inflation. Indeed, Friedman made

41

predictions (always dangerous for an economist) about inflation that did not come to pass. The result, for better or worse, is that monetary rules lost all traction with policymakers.

In Friedman's defense, one can say that he was always careful to note that his constant money growth rule was an interim suggestion, based on his reading of monetary history, and might well be replaced with something better as more experience and research accumulated. Indeed, Friedman went on to advocate other monetary rules. For many years, he advocated stabilizing the stock of high-powered money. And for a time he was content with Greenspan's management of monetary policy. With the exception of Allan Meltzer, who continues to advocate a monetary rule with adjustments for changes in velocity, however, few economists, as far as I am aware, now advocate a money-growth rule.

Economists, however, have been clever in thinking up a wide range of alternative rules. The "Taylor rule," which would have the central bank respond in a predetermined fashion to deviations of output and inflation from predetermined targets, is extremely influential. Some neo-Keynesian economists have suggested targeting fairly high rates of inflation because that would help "grease" labor markets. The idea is that nominal wages are relatively hard to reduce even when a reduction is called for by market forces. But with ongoing inflation real wages can be reduced simply by failing to increase nominal wages, a policy my university has discovered can be highly effective. Some neo-Keynesians, moreover, have advocated targeting high inflation rates to reduce debt burdens.

In contrast, a number of economists have advocated deflation. Deflation would naturally follow from Simons's rule (to be adopted after major reforms of the financial system) of fixing the money supply. Velocity would be stable once near-moneys—the source of most fluctuations in velocity, according to Simons—were eliminated. The price level would then fall at the rate of growth of real income. Nominal wages could remain fixed so that the benefits of income growth would be spread widely. Friedman's famous essay on the optimum quantity of money (1969) showed that the optimal policy in his model would be a continuous deflation, although Friedman did not subsequently advocate deflation as a practical policy. George Selgin (1997) made a detailed case for a "productivity norm," which would mean prices falling as productivity rose. Recently, considerable discussion has taken place in the United States of targeting the growth of nominal income, a variant of a proposal pushed by Scott Sumner. A major reason for the interest in this norm in the United States, I believe, is that it would encompass both of the Federal Reserve's mandates. A slump that produced a fall in real income while inflation remained constant would produce a fall in nominal income and give the Federal Reserve license to follow expansionary policies. An acceleration of inflation while real income growth remained constant would produce a rise in nominal income that would call for a contractionary monetary policy. There is not space here to analyze these proposals and the others that have been made in detail, even if I were up to the task. But the wide range of rules that have been advocated by economists shows that we are still far from agreement on the best monetary constitution.

Financial Crises

In retrospect, the main lacunae in the Yeager volume's papers, in my view, were discussions of how a monetary constitution should be structured so that a central bank could deal with financial crises without completely abandoning its constitutional constraints. Only Selden (1962, 355) addressed the problem directly. He reviewed the Warburton and Friedman proposals for monetary growth rules and suggested that monetary growth rules could be adopted "subject to one or more provisos which would release the central bank under certain contingencies.... One such proviso might be that the rule be abandoned whenever as much as 9 percent of the labor force becomes unemployed, or whenever a broad index of prices rises at a rate of 5 percent per year, for three months in a row."

Selden's suggestion is sensible, but it has two problems. One is timing. The financial crisis—the runs on financial institutions that Daniel Thornton and Walter Bagehot would have the central bank deal with—may well precede by some considerable time the rise in unemployment to the level that releases the central bank from the requirement to maintain a stable growth rate of the money supply. The damage, in other words, may already have been done before Selden's proviso allows the Federal Reserve to respond. The other problem is that Selden's suggestion does not specify any limits on what the central bank can do once it is in crisis mode. It would be better, it seems to me, if some explicit limits existed on what central banks could do even when responding to a financial crisis.

The problem here is similar to the constitutional problem of "war powers." We recognize that a state of war may require that the government be granted extraordinary powers. The U.S. Constitution, for example, provides that the right to a writ of habeas corpus can be suspended in time of war. And, in fact, the general assumption has been that the U.S. president has very broad powers during time of war that he would not have during peacetime. But cases exist when in retrospect it appears that maintaining peacetime constitutional constraints would have been better, rather than granting extraordinary powers to the president. The forced evacuation of Japanese Americans from the West Coast during World War II is a classic example. Similarly, we might want to allow the central bank a wider range of action during a financial crisis without abandoning all restraints.

Financial crises, I should add, do not need to occur with the frequency that they do in the United States. The United States has been especially crisis prone because legal restrictions on branch banking created a weak and segmented banking system and a savings-investment system that relied excessively on highly volatile capital markets for long-term finance. As Michael Bordo, Angela Redish, and I point out in a recent paper (2011), Canada, which has always permitted nationwide branch banking, has never had a banking crisis—not in 2008, not in 1930, not in 1907, not in all the years in the 19th century when the U.S. banking system was going up in flames. Still it would be prudent to assume that a financial crisis might strike and to grant the central bank the flexibility to deal with it when it does.

Two major issues concerning financial crises need to be resolved within the framework of the monetary constitution: (a) when should a central bank intervene, in other words, what set of events constitute a genuine financial crisis, and (b) how should it intervene, what tools and actions should it be permitted to use? The extreme positions on when intervention should take place were defined by Charles Kindleberger (1989) and Anna Schwartz (1986). For Kindleberger, almost any bad thing that happens in financial markets is a financial crisis justifying central-bank intervention: failures of financial institutions, declines in asset prices, adverse exchange rate movements, and so on. For Schwartz, in contrast, failures of financial institutions or declines in asset prices that do not affect the payments mechanism are mere pseudo-crises. Only when bank failures set off a panic that produces declines in the stock of money do we have a real crisis calling for central-bank intervention. The recent financial crisis, however, was centered in the so-called shadow banking system and did considerable damage without threatening the payments mechanism, or at least the payments mechanism as it was commonly perceived. Figure 2.3 shows the behavior of M2, Friedman's and Schwartz's preferred measure of the money stock, during the recent financial crisis. Evidently, a policy that looked to declines in traditional monetary aggregates to signal the need for action would not have triggered Federal Reserve interventions during the recent crisis. Some position between Kindleberger and Schwartz would seem to be prudent, but finding the right balance will not be easy.

Given the recognition that a financial crisis is in process, what form should intervention take? One school of thought holds that the central bank should not get involved with rescuing individual financial institutions from bankruptcy but rather should let the natural winnowing process of bankruptcy take place and should seek only to supply liquidity to the market as a whole. The opposed school holds that the central bank should do whatever is needed to prevent failures that might ignite a financial crisis. According to this view, the social costs of financial crises are too great to take any risk of allowing one to develop. Actions that the central bank might take include anything from organizing a private syndicate of backers—the Barings Brothers Crisis of 1890 is the classic case—to outright nationalization.

The term "nationalization" always produces passionate reactions. It warms the hearts of liberals (liberals in the American sense) and strikes fear into the hearts of conservatives. But all bankruptcies, at least in the United States, are and have been for many years in fact nationalizations. An official of the government, a judge, is placed in charge of winding up the affairs of the failed institution.[6] There is much to be said for subjecting failed financial institutions to traditional forms of bankruptcy administered by the judiciary. For one thing, judges are likely to be more experienced with bankruptcies than the bureaucrats put in charge when the bankruptcy is managed on an ad hoc basis by a central bank or some other agency of the executive branch during a crisis. And bankruptcy judges have a large set of legal and judicial precedents on which

Figure 2.3

THE M2 MONEY STOCK DURING THE 2008 FINANCIAL CRISIS, JANUARY 2006–NOVEMBER 2011

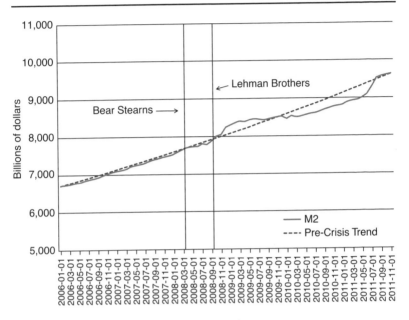

SOURCE: Board of Governors of the Federal Reserve System.

to base their decisions. Nevertheless, traditional bankruptcy may not give sufficient weight to effects of the failure of financial institutions on third parties and to the potential advantages of keeping a failed institution going through temporary injections of cash. The appropriate reform, it seems to me, would be to strengthen the monetary constitution by spelling out the role that the central bank could play in managing the bankruptcy of important financial institutions, and perhaps the penalties that it would be allowed or required to impose on various stakeholders—managers, directors, shareholders, and so on—to address the problem of moral hazard. This seems to be the aim of the Dodd-Frank bill, but it will be a long time before we know how the mechanism provided in the bill for dealing with the failure of a "systemically important" institution will work in practice.

Some of the authors in the Yeager volume assumed that financial crises could not arise if the proposals they advocated were adopted. Perhaps in Rothbard's world of a pure 100 percent gold-backed money or in Tolley's world of 100 percent central-bank reserves, banking crises, at least, would be impossible. Others may have assumed that the rules that they advocated could be used both in normal times and during financial crises, so that no special provisions of the type that Selden advocated would be necessary. Implicitly, the Warburton and Friedman monetary rules would provide a policy response to a banking panic, although not necessarily to stock market crashes, real-estate market crashes, and similar events. During a banking panic, the "money multiplier" would decline because the public would attempt to withdraw cash from banks, reducing the currency-deposit ratio, and banks would attempt to raise their reserve ratios by refusing to make new loans, allowing old loans to run off, and so on. If the monetary authority did nothing, the stock of money would fall. But if the monetary authority followed a rule of stable money growth, the authority would have to offset the fall in the money multiplier by expanding the monetary base by buying assets, providing loans to banks, lowering required reserve ratios, or other means. Thus, a monetary rule of keeping the money supply growing at a constant rate would automatically generate a response in the right direction to a banking panic. Friedman and Schwartz pointed this out in *A Monetary History of the United States* (1963). After recounting the gyrations of the stock of money during the Great Depression, Friedman and Schwartz (1963, 545) concluded as follows:

> How different the history of that fateful dozen years [1929–41] might have been if the money stock had grown steadily at its average rate of 2½ per cent per year, let alone at the higher long-term historical rate, instead of first falling by one-third from 1929 to 1933 and then doubling from 1933 to 1941.

A price rule might generate a similar response to a banking panic. But given the likely long lag between a banking panic and the price effects, the response generated by a price rule might be less timely than the response generated by a monetary rule.

How did the Federal Reserve do in the most recent crisis? We can refer, again, to Figure 2.3. Overall, by chance or design, the Federal

Reserve kept relatively close to the idea of maintaining normal growth of the key monetary aggregate in the face of the crisis, although in spring 2009, the growth of M2 slowed, eventually falling below the precrisis trend level. And some critics of the Fed during this period complained that the Fed was not doing enough. But although price rules and monetary rules provide some guidance in financial crises, it would seem that some special provisions need to be made to guide the handling of monetary policy during financial crises.

Conclusion

Leland Yeager's decision 50 years ago to organize a lecture series and the resulting volume on monetary constitutions proved remarkably prescient. Although at the time, discretionary monetary policy seemed to be doing well, the Great Inflation, which eventually engulfed the United States and much of the rest of the world during the second half of the 1960s and the 1970s, was about to begin. In the wake of that inflation, many countries adopted some form of price rule to rein in their monetary authorities. Think how much damage might have been avoided if the world had listened to the message of the Yeager volume and subjected its central banks to the restrictions of a monetary constitution in the 1960s.

The volume's participants, however, did not speak with a common voice and did not leave a clear blueprint for a monetary constitution. They debated the merits of commodity standards such as gold compared with fiat standards. They debated whether some form of monetary growth rule or some form of price rule would work better when the goal was to constrain a central bank that could issue fiat money. And they gave little thought to how a monetary constitution could be constructed to provide the central bank with the appropriate flexibility to deal with financial crises. In short, despite their valiant efforts, and those of many economists in the years that followed, we are still in search of a monetary constitution.

Notes

1. The data are from the *Historical Statistics of the United States*, millennial edition (Carter et al. 2006, series Aa2553–2577, Ba341). Data for the female labor force are not available for 1850.

2. The data are from Carter et al. (2006, series Cj1, Ca9, and Ca13).

3. Buchanan's essay, I believe, was intended for this purpose, rather than as a practical proposal for reform.

4. Although they differed sharply on the causes of inflation, Burns and Friedman had a long, and I understand it, mostly friendly relationship. Burns had been Friedman's professor when Friedman was an undergraduate at Rutgers.

5. I discuss Simons's views in detail in Rockoff (2000).

6. In the United States, financial institutions can do "chapter 11 bankruptcies," in which the court may allow the firm to continue in operation while providing protection from creditors in the hopes that the firm will later be able to emerge from bankruptcy. Lehman Brothers filed as a chapter 11 bankruptcy.

References

Bordo, Michael D., John Landon-Lane, and Angela Redish. 2010. "Deflation, Productivity Shocks and Gold: Evidence from the 1880–1914 Period." *Open Economies Review* 21 (4): 515–46.

Bordo, Michael D., Angela Redish, and Hugh Rockoff. 2011. "Why Didn't Canada Have a Banking Crisis in 2008 (or in 1930, or 1907, or …)?" NBER Working Paper no. 17312, National Bureau of Economic Research, Cambridge, MA. http://www.nber.org/papers/w17312.

Carter, Susan B., Scott Sigmund Gartner, Michael R. Haines, Alan L. Olmstead, Richard Sutch, and Gavin Wright. 2006. *Historical Statistics of the United States: Earliest Times to the Present.* Millennial ed. New York: Cambridge University Press.

Eichengreen, Barry. 1992. *Golden Fetters: The Gold Standard and the Great Depression, 1919–1939.* NBER Series on Long-Term Factors in Economic Development. New York and Oxford: Oxford University Press.

Friedman, Milton. 1951. "Commodity-Reserve Currency." *Journal of Political Economy* 59 (3): 203–32.

———. 1959. *A Program for Monetary Stability.* The Millar Lectures no. 3. New York: Fordham University Press.

———. 1969. "The Optimum Quantity of Money." In *The Optimum Quantity of Money and Other Essays*, pp. 1–50. Chicago: Aldine.

Friedman, Milton, and Anna Schwartz. 1963. *A Monetary History of the United States, 1867–1960.* National Bureau of Economic Research Studies in Business Cycles, vol. 12. Princeton: Princeton University Press.

Keynes, John Maynard. 1924. *A Tract on Monetary Reform.* London: Macmillan.

———. (1936) 1964. *The General Theory of Employment, Interest and Money.* New York: Harcourt, Brace & World.

Kindleberger, Charles Poor. 1989. *Manias, Panics, and Crashes: A History of Financial Crises.* Rev. ed. New York: Basic Books.

Oliver, W. H. 1958. "The Labour Exchange Phase of the Co-operative Movement." *Oxford Economic Papers* 10 (3): 355–67.

Rockoff, Hugh. 2000. "Henry Calvert Simons and the Quantity Theory of Money." Departmental Working Paper, Department of Economics, Rutgers University, NJ. http://search.ebscohost.com/login.aspx?direct=true&db=ecn&AN=0843013&site=ehost-live.

Schwartz, Anna J. 1986. "Real and Pseudo-financial Crises." In *Financial Crises and the World Banking System*, edited by Forrest Capie and Geoffrey E. Wood, pp. 11–40. New York: St. Martin's Press.

Selden, Richard T. 1962. "Stable Monetary Growth." In *In Search of a Monetary Constitution*, edited by Leland B. Yeager, pp. 322–55. Cambridge, MA: Harvard University Press.

Selgin, George A. 1997. *Less Than Zero: The Case for a Falling Price Level in a Growing Economy*. Hobart Paper 132. London: Institute of Economic Affairs.

Simons, Henry C. (1934) 1948. "A Positive Program for Laissez Faire: Some Proposals for a Liberal Economic Policy." In *Economic Policy for a Free Society*, pp. 40–77. Chicago: University of Chicago Press.

———. 1936. "Rules versus Authorities in Monetary Policy." *Journal of Political Economy* 44 (1): 1–30.

Tolley, George S. 1957. "Providing for Growth of the Money Supply." *Journal of Political Economy* 65 (6): 465–85.

Woodward, Bob. 2000. *Maestro: Greenspan's Fed and the American Boom*. New York: Simon and Schuster.

Yeager, Leland B. 1962. *In Search of a Monetary Constitution*. Cambridge, MA: Harvard University Press.

3. The Value of Money as a Constitutionalized Parameter

James M. Buchanan

The half-century that we mark with this conference has not witnessed progress toward the constitutionalization of money with agreed-on improvements in economic performance. If anything, professional economic discourse has experienced retrogression. Before the early 1960s, and before the Keynesian capture of the politicians—capture that allowed them to exploit economists' arguments to their own advantage—some tempered hope may have existed that a meaningful monetary constitution might somehow come into being.

Such hope was dashed, however, as the Kennedy era of Keynesian enthusiasm came to dominate economists' attention. Henry Simons's (1936) earlier admonitions concerning discretionary authority were almost totally ignored as establishment economists imagined themselves in positions to manipulate macroeconomic magnitudes as dictated by well-defined end objectives. The simple and most elementary principle of public choice had not yet come into focus as political entrepreneurs seized the elements of the Keynesian logic that favored their own retention in elected office.

The alleged tradeoff between inflation and unemployment was both analytically and empirically smothered by the stagflation of the early 1970s, as backed up in earlier explanatory "natural rate" models, which were themselves precursory to formal models that embodied expectations more explicitly. As might perhaps have been predicted, the models that embodied expectations were overextended as their logical implications came to inform policy thrusts that reflected both academic and public attitudes. The earlier exuberance of economists playing with Keynesian models vanished only to be replaced by almost comparable exuberance concerning the ability of markets to internalize all deviance from preferred end states, and especially as compared with governmental intrusions. The "market works" attitude, as applied to institutions, incorporated the false premise that all valued "goods" are partitionable and hence amenable to entrepreneurial arbitrage.

In 2011, I presented a paper titled "Ideology or Error" (Buchanan 2011) in which I argued that the failure of economists to predict or even understand the Great Recession was attributable to scientific error rather than a market-fundamentalist ideology, as claimed by Anatole Kaletsky (2010) and others. The basic error was the failure to incorporate those elements of midcentury welfare economics that represented genuine contributions to economists' understanding. In particular, economists generally did not recognize the value, and hence the relevance, of Paul Samuelson's taxonomy of goods, along with the underlying logical implications (Samuelson 1954). For goods that descriptively fit into the polar case of "publicness," exhibiting both nonrivalry and prohibitively costly exclusion, Samuelson argued that markets could not be expected to work toward efficiency. Rent-seeking entrepreneurs could not, in such cases, be predicted to act so as to shift the economy toward the Pareto frontier. Some goods might be produced that might be classified as substitutes (e.g., Coasian lighthouses; Coase 1974), but the potential gains from trade would not be exhausted. The market-generated equilibrium would remain a commons tragedy in the absence of explicit collective action.

The fundamental error here was inherent in the economists' generalized neglect of attention to the parameters that define the market game as such, that is, to the constraints within which voluntary exchange processes may be expected to generate outcomes that warrant positive evaluation. More explicitly and more generally, the error is located in the implicit presumption that markets can create their own rules. Conventions and practices will, of course, characterize all exchanges, from the simple to the complex. But there can be no legitimate claim to the effect that the results become "efficient" merely by the fact of observed existence.

Constitutionalization

It is relatively straightforward to argue that the monetary structure of a market economy should be constitutionalized rather than allowed to emerge anarchistically or to be subjected to arbitrary political manipulation. In a paper that I presented in Stockholm in 2009 (Buchanan 2010), I argued in some detail that neither anarchy nor ordinary politics offers effective monetary predictability and stability. Participants in a smoothly working market economy, in either of these settings, are subjected to major cost burdens if, in any transaction, they must make predictions about the expected value of the monetary unit quite apart from predictions about the expected value of the goods and services that are traded.

In my 2009 paper I did not, however, discuss particular features that may be required in an effective monetary constitution—features that make this constitution different from more familiar constraints. In the latter, constitutional provisions are applied primarily to the processes through which political action may be undertaken. The constitutional focus is on the means through which outcomes are to be generated rather than on the outcomes themselves. Such outcomes are open, so to speak, in the sense that they are allowed to emerge so long as the processes of their emergence are constitutionally permissible. By implication, multiple outcomes are possible among which the allowable process of selection produces the chosen alternative.

The monetary constitution differs in that here the outcome itself is the direct objective. That which is to be accomplished, to the extent that is possible, is stability in the value of the monetary unit itself, with less relative attention or emphasis on the means or processes through which the result is to be achieved. Because money, as such, is not a "good" that has final end-use, nonmoney value, there is no meaningful preference ranking over varying quantities of issue. Here the classical neutrality theorem applies. Stability in the value of the unit is the aim—stability that may be attained through small, medium, or large quantities of the units in being. This value, in itself, is not one among alternatives, any of which may be selected.

The unit of money (the dollar in the American context) may be usefully compared with ordinary units of measure. Intrinsically, no ranking is meaningful, say, between metric and nonmetric systems. What is required is consistency in application. The problem reduces to one of pure coordination. To refer to another familiar example, no intrinsic difference exists between right-side and left-side road transit. The objective to be sought is uniformity. To vary the rule or convention from one day or one week to the next would unduly impose major adjustment costs on all users of road facilities.

To fulfill its parametric role in the inclusive exchange nexus, money must be of invariant value and must be perceived to be so in public attitudes. The placing of reform emphases on processes, such as a Friedman-like rule for monetary growth, may require a multistage translation between the instruments and the desired end state. My argument here is that the effective monetary constitution must begin from the preferred end state—namely, the value of the unit of money—and then proceed backward, so to speak, to the processes or instruments through which the objective might be attained.

Admittedly, the index-number issue looms large in the approach suggested. What, precisely, is the value of the unit of money, the dollar, that should be understood to remain invariant? Experts may analyze and discuss the alternatives, but the point to be emphasized is that *any* general and inclusive index, so long as it is clearly defined, suffices. What is required is clarity and understanding of the index that is embodied in the constitutionalized structure. Participants in the economy, regardless of roles, should not be burdened with the unnecessary task of predicting what index of money value is to be the "parameter of the week."

The instruments and processes that may be used by the constitutionally designated monetary authority need not be narrowly defined. So long as these instruments and processes do not violate general constitutional limits, the monetary authority may be granted considerable flexibility beyond the obvious power of money issue itself.

Getting There from Here

As empirical evidence has shown, the effectiveness of central banks varies directly with the degree of independence from political control. Broadly interpreted, the achievement of such independence may be treated as a first step toward constitutionalization. However, the location of monetary sovereignty cannot be properly lodged in the monetary structure itself, as by the banking institutions or some agency as representative of a banking cartel. Ultimate control must remain with the collectivity while being outside the machinations of ordinary or postconstitutional politics.

To a degree, this result may be achieved if the monetary authority is explicitly recognized as a constitutional unit, as opposed to one that operates within a legislative mandate alone. In the American context, a formal amendment to the U.S. Constitution would be required, one that would establish and legitimize an independent body charged with the task of securing the single objective, that of maintaining the value, as defined, of the monetary unit, the dollar.

Because the objective is defined as an end state—namely, stability in the value of the monetary unit—there is no concern with problems presented in alternative reform proposals. The definition of what is and what is not money, a major problem for Friedman-like rules for monetary growth, need not arise. Growth in the quantity of money, under any definition, becomes an emergent result of actions taken in pursuit of the specified target.

Similarly, the package of instruments that the monetary authority may use in its furtherance of the objective need not be defined beyond some insurance that these instruments fall within broad constitutional regulatory powers. The choice of instruments here may, of course, depend on the banking and credit institutions in being, because these institutions might be themselves changed with the constitutionalization of money. The monetary authority should not be constitutionally charged with objectives that extend beyond stability in the value of the numeraire. To add other objectives may create situations in which conflicts arise, out of which the benefits of the central single objective may be sacrificed.

Suppose that a constitutionally recognized monetary authority is established with the defined end state in place. What is to ensure that this objective is achieved? Officers of the authority somehow must be made personally accountable as monitored by attainment or failure to attain the designated target. Constitutional authorization must make provision for removal of responsible officers when failure occurs.

As this generalized discussion indicates, it becomes relatively easy to imagine and to propose the establishment of an institutional structure that would work more or less as desired. Such an exercise remains ideal theory, however, and fails to address the problems of transition. We do not, and cannot, commence from an empty organizational chart. We necessarily start from an institutional status quo that is unlikely to be reformed without major conflict. Almost universally, putative reformers are remiss in their failure to attend to problems that arise in any efforts to "get there from here"—failure to recognize the power of the status quo, whatever this may be.

With the constitutionalization of money, however, such reform need not require institutional revolution to the same extent as might be relevant for other reforms. Relatively less overt conflict with forces that defend the institutional status quo may describe a possible transition. Central banks are in existence, and these institutions can be readily reauthorized as constitutional units with properly redefined powers. In the American context, the Federal Reserve Board can quite simply be renamed as an authority with recognized constitutional standing, with both officers and current employees grandfathered into the newly defined entity. The redundancy that might be present in an initial change can be eliminated by attrition. The means of making the transition suggested here reduces a major share of the pecuniary interest in maintaining the status quo, leaving only the Fed watchers as primary losers, those who secure rents from discretion in current monetary policy.

The institutional and organizational changes required are surely within the set of practicable possibilities. Perhaps a more difficult barrier to effective parameterization of money may be the necessary accompanying shift in public attitudes, that is, in the psychology on money. Persons who use money in all roles must somehow come to treat the value of the monetary unit as invariant, simply as a measuring rod. To an extent, of course, persons carry on their ordinary affairs without conscious awareness of variability in this value. This variability is, however, imbedded in the terms of trade and amounts to a burden on all transactions.

I shall not discuss the particular tools and instruments that a monetary authority, once established as a constitutional agency with a narrowly defined single objective, might use in ensuring that the desired stability results. Nor am I competent to examine possible changes in the complexities of the institutions of the financial sector that might be made necessary by the basic monetary reform proposed. For a central example, the degree and extent to which banking regulation must itself be brought within the control of the constitutional authority will remain beyond the limits of my discourse in this paper.

Emphasis must be placed, first and foremost, on the primary purpose of any monetary reform—namely, that of removing the institutional sources of instability, the anarchy that best describes the setting with multiple near-moneys in the Great Recession, along with the overt politicization of money as an omnipresent threat. "Between Anarchy and Leviathan": I used this as a subtitle to my book *The Limits of Liberty* (Buchanan 1975). And it applies with especial descriptive relevance to the monetary foundations of the inclusive political economy.

References

Buchanan, James M. 1975. *The Limits of Liberty: Between Anarchy and Leviathan.* Chicago: University of Chicago Press

———. 2010. "The Constitutionalization of Money." *Cato Journal* 30 (2): 251–58.

———. 2011. "Ideology or Error: Economists and the Great Recession." Paper presented at the Summer Institute for the History of Economic Thought, University of Richmond, June.

Coase, Ronald H. 1974. "The Lighthouse in Economics." *Journal of Law and Economics* 17 (2): 357–76.

Kaletsky, Anatole. 2010. *Capitalism, 4.0: The Birth of a New Economy.* New York: Public Affairs Press.

Samuelson, Paul A. 1954. "The Pure Theory of Public Expenditure." *Review of Economics and Statistics* 36 (4): 387–89.

Simons, Henry C. 1936. "Rules versus Authorities in Monetary Policy." *Journal of Political Economy* 44 (1): 1–30.

4. The Constitutionalization of Money: A Constitutional Economics Perspective

Ekkehard A. Köhler and Viktor J. Vanberg

The title we have chosen for this chapter may sound redundant because in some sense any economic approach that deals with constitutional matters, including monetary constitutions, must of course adopt a "constitutional" perspective. By "constitutional economics perspective" we mean, however, not just a perspective that focuses on constitutional issues. Instead, we refer thereby to the distinct theoretical paradigm that has its principal roots in James M. Buchanan's work. And, as we seek to show, this paradigm approaches the problem of monetary constitutions in a quite specific manner that differs from—without being necessarily incompatible with—other theoretical perspectives that have been applied to the issue of how monetary regimes are or should be organized. Introductory remarks with which Leland Yeager has prefaced the 1962 book that the present volume revisits provide a suitable starting point for characterizing the specific features of the constitutional economics perspective, which we summarize in more detail below (Yeager 1962a). About the contributions collected in his *In Search of a Monetary Constitution*, he notes: "Each of the lecturers was invited … to approach his task as if he were an advisor not merely to administrators of existing monetary arrangements, nor even to legislators considering limited changes, but rather to men engaged in shaping the basic character of a monetary system, in shaping a 'monetary constitution'" (Yeager 1962b, 1). And he adds that though the contributors shared "a roughly similar conception of the 'good society'" regarding "the decentralized organization of economic life by means of markets, money, and prices as indispensable to human freedom," their recommendations showed a "perplexing diversity" with their disagreements hinging on both "matters of facts" and "on personal values" (Yeager 1962b, 1–2).

Our aim in this chapter is to show how the perspective of constitutional economics can help sort out some of the "perplexing diversity" by explicitly distinguishing between matters of *legitimacy* and matters of *prudence* in constitutional choice or, put differently, between, on the one hand, the question to whom, exactly, economic advisers mean to address their constitutional proposals (a question whose answer depends on where one locates the source of constitutional legitimacy), and, on the other hand, the question of what kind of prudential arguments can motivate the addressees to accept the advisers' recommendations. The central tenet of constitutional economics is that constitutional regimes, monetary or otherwise, can ultimately derive their legitimacy from no other source than the voluntary agreement among the members of the group that are subject to the respective regimes.[1] Accordingly, advisers must ultimately address their proposals to these members, such as the citizens of a polity that is to choose among alternative rules or regulations. This implies, with regard to the second question, if advisers want their recommendations to find acceptance, the arguments they offer in their support must appeal to the common interest of the ultimate addressees, convincing them that they can benefit from heeding the advice. In other words, advisers must seek to convince their addressees that prudent pursuit of their own interest requires them to choose what is recommended.

Our purpose with this chapter is not to add another proposal to the numerous suggestions to be found in the literature for how monetary constitutions ought to be devised, nor is it to judge the theoretical or empirical validity of the conjectural content of such suggestions. Our project is essentially an exercise in conceptual clarification, namely to examine a representative subset of existing proposals in light of the two preceding questions. We first ask whom the respective authors appear to have in mind as the addressees of their recommendations, in particular if their proposals may be interpreted, or reconstructed, as advice to the "ultimate addressees" about how they can advance their common interest. And second, we ask if the kind of arguments that authors provide in support of their respective proposals appear, in principle, to be capable of securing agreement among the addressees.

The chapter is organized as follows. The next section explains in more detail the distinction, central to the perspective of constitutional economics, between the two questions noted: (a) the question of *legitimacy* in constitutional choice, that is, the issue of who is the proper addressee of constitutional recommendations, and (b) the question of *prudence* in constitutional choice, that is, the issue of what arguments the addressees should, in their own interest, prudently consider in choosing among alternative constitutional provisions. Next, we seek to identify in general terms the principal types of monetary regimes that have been proposed and that seem to exhaust the spectrum of potential alternatives. In light of the suggested classification, the following section provides a review of the debate on monetary regimes. The next two sections analyze the principal regime proposals, asking to whom they are supposedly addressed and, in particular, if they are portrayed by their advocates in terms that might appeal to citizens' common interests. The final section concludes the paper.

To Whom Do Economists Address Their Advice?

Constitutional economics studies how the rules of the game that govern human interaction and cooperation affect the nature of the social processes that unfold within these rules. As a *theoretical science* it seeks to explain how rules evolve or are established, how they are enforced, and what effects they exert on the behavior of the individuals to whom they apply. As an *applied science* it provides, based on its theoretical and empirical insights, advice for how rules should be devised if certain effects on the patterns of actions that unfold within them are desired. As in any applied science, the advice constitutional economics provides comes in the form of hypothetical imperatives—or conditional ought statements—that tell their intended addressees what they should do *if* they wish to achieve certain effects or results. In contrast to categorical imperatives that call for unconditional compliance, the validity of hypothetical imperatives can be critically examined. They are irrelevant if their addressees have no desire to achieve the result the recommended measure is predicted to produce. They are false if the recommended measure is in fact not capable of producing the predicted result. And they are inefficient if other measures, from the addressees' perspective, are more suitable for achieving the desired outcome.[2]

Public choice theory, from which the Buchanan-inspired research program of constitutional economics emerged, originated with a critique of traditional welfare economics as the principal applied counterpart to theoretical economics, censuring that it provides policy advice in terms of what in essence are irrelevant hypothetical imperatives. Welfare economists, so public choice theorists argue, remain typically ambiguous about whom they mean to address their policy advice to. Ostensibly their recommendations for how to improve or maximize "social welfare" are addressed to politicians who are endowed with authority to decide policy measures on behalf of the citizenry. However, in phrasing their advice as if politicians were benevolent dictators who pursue no other aim than to maximize the common good, welfare economists overlook that real-world politicians seek their own interest within their own particular constraints and that what serves their interest and garners them votes may well differ from what the general welfare calls for. To the extent that this is the case, politicians will find the welfare economist's advice for how to maximize social welfare of little help for dealing with the problems they seek to solve.

Constitutional economics adds to the public choice critique the charge that if, alternatively, welfare economists were to address their advice not to politicians but to the citizens as the ultimate sovereigns in a democratic polity, their hypothetical imperatives would still be irrelevant because citizens would hardly be interested in being told how the welfare economist's factitious measure of aggregate welfare can be maximized. They would surely be more interested in learning about how their own well-being would be affected and are unlikely to approve policy measures that fare well in terms of the economic adviser's welfare function but come at the citizens' expense.

The upshot of this reasoning is that if economists want their advice—be it addressed to politicians as agents or to citizens as principals of democratic polities—to find an audience, they must appeal to interests that the respective addressee can be assumed to pursue. Constitutional economists do not negate the pragmatic role of advice to politicians who are interested in instructions for how they can be more successful in the competitive environment to which they are exposed. But they insist that only the citizens can be the proper ultimate recipient of the kind of advice that welfare economics is presumably meant to provide, namely, advice on how the community as a whole can be made better off.

In their interpretation of what making the community as a whole better off entails, welfare economics and constitutional economics are both *individualistic* in the sense that they define *community benefit* in terms of what benefits the community's individual members. They differ fundamentally, though, in terms of how individual preferences figure in their respective assessment of community benefit or social welfare, a difference that one of us has described elsewhere as the contrast between the *utility-individualism* of welfare economics and the *choice-individualism* of constitutional economics (Vanberg 2008, 28ff.; 2009, 3ff.). The utility-individualism of welfare economics treats individuals as mere metering stations from which the utility values that enter into the theorist's calculation of aggregate welfare would have to be read. In contrast, the choice-individualism of constitutional economics treats individuals as the sovereigns who must be respected as the only ultimate judges of their own interest and whose agreement is the only conclusive indicator of what serves their common interest. In other words, the constitutional economist insists that, if individuals are respected as the ultimate sovereigns, only that which benefits all members can qualify as "community benefit," and the ultimate test of what benefits all members can only be agreement among all.

Respecting individuals as the sovereigns to whom policy advice is to be ultimately addressed and whose consent is the only ultimate test for what counts as common benefit means that economists, in providing such advice, submit their reasoning to the requirement of stating their arguments in terms that appeal to the presumptive interests of the individual constituents. Economists must ultimately convince those individuals that what is recommended serves their common interest. Policy advice that meets this requirement consists of two kinds of claims: namely, conjectures about the factual consequences that the proposed policy measure can be expected to produce and conjectures about the desirability of these consequences for the addressees to whom the advice is directed. Applied to policy advice on monetary regimes that concerns us in the present context, this means that from a constitutional economics perspective such advice has to be critically examined in light of the following questions:

1. Is the advice explicitly or implicitly addressed to the individual constituents of the jurisdiction that is to adopt the proposed regime, or can it be reconstructed as such?

2. What are the consequences that the proposed regime is predicted to produce?

3. Can these consequences be assumed to serve the common interests of the constituents, such that the regime from which they are predicted to result might be expected to command general agreement?

4. Is the proposed regime in fact capable of producing the consequences it is claimed to produce?[3]

Questions 2 and 4 concern purely factual matters; they fall squarely in the domain for which the advising economist can properly claim authority. Questions 1 and 3 concern matters of evaluation on which only the addressees are ultimately entitled to judge. Or, stated in terms of the previously mentioned distinction between matters of prudence and matters of legitimacy, questions 2 and 4 concern the issue of what regime should be prudently chosen if certain outcomes are desired; questions 1 and 3 concern the issue of what legitimizes the choice of regimes.

The literature on monetary regimes focuses mostly, if not exclusively, on questions 2 and 4, whereas questions 1 and 3 are rarely explicitly addressed. Typically, authors seem to presuppose that the consequences they predict their favored regime to produce are "desirable" without seeing any need to explicitly argue for whom and for what reasons they can be said to be desirable. By contrast, our interest in this chapter is the exact opposite. In reviewing examples of what we regard as the principal alternative proposals for monetary regimes to be found in the literature, we leave aside the issue of the adequacy of the factual claims about causes and effects that the proposals entail and focus exclusively on the proposals' evaluative dimension, examining them in light of questions 1 and 3.

Before we embark upon this task, however, we first specify what we intend to include as "principal alternative proposals" in our analysis.

Monetary Regimes: Between Unhampered Market and Unhampered Politics

James M. Buchanan, who was among the contributors to Yeager's 1962 collection, has recently renewed his call for constitutionalizing money as a necessary reform for escaping the polar evils of "monetary anarchy" and "politicization," which both are inimical to effectively working markets (Buchanan 2010). Responding to Buchanan's paper, Steven Horwitz (2011, 332) has charged that the term "monetary anarchy," if it is meant to denote a regime of "competitive money production" and "free banking," disregards that such "laissez-faire in money" is not anarchic in the Hobbesian sense but presupposes that "the right *general* constitutional protections for private property, contracts, and the rule of law are in place" (emphasis in original). Beyond these general constitutional protections that any effectively working market requires, so Horwitz argues, no further special constitutional provisions are necessary for money to serve the function that Buchanan seeks to secure.[4]

Of interest at this point is not the substance of the issue that Horwitz raises, to which we return later, but the fact that it indicates the need to be more specific about what we mean by "monetary constitution." Any monetary regime, be it in the private or the public sphere, that operates within a framework of rules can in the most general sense be said to be "constitutionalized," but the term "monetary constitution" is typically used in a more specific sense, implying that specific rules pertain to the production and use of money that go beyond the general system of rules that otherwise govern the operations in markets and in politics. Horwitz's "unconstrained" or "unhampered market" (2011, 332, 334) for money on the one side, and "an *unrestrained* government monopoly" (334, emphasis in original) on the other, fall, at opposite ends, outside the range of monetary constitutions in the more specific sense of the term. Advocates of "unhampered markets" would not want to see the private production of money subjected to stricter rules than those that apply "to most of the other goods that markets produce" (332), while advocates of an "unrestrained government monopoly" do not want to subject the public production of money to rules more rigorous than those that apply to ordinary day-to-day politics. Not many authors seem to explicitly advocate either of these polar cases. Most of the proposals for monetary regimes that can be found in the literature explicitly or implicitly start from the presumption that the production of money ought to be subject to specific rules. They differ in how they specify the particular requirements that they wish to inscribe in a monetary constitution as well as in terms of their preferences for private over public production of money or the reverse. Figure 4.1 shows the spectrum of the principal alternatives.

In the remainder of this chapter, we look at proposals for monetary regimes that exemplify the foregoing principal alternatives, examining them in light of the questions previously noted:

Figure 4.1
The Principal Alternative Proposals

Principal Alternative Proposals

| Unhampered market | Regulated market regime | Competitive regime combining private and public money | Restrained political regime | Unconstrained political regime |

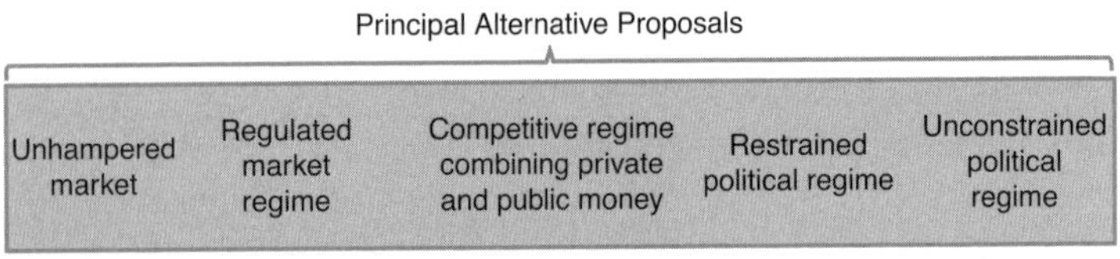

- Do their advocates address their advice implicitly or explicitly to the citizens-constituents of the polity that is to decide on the organization of its monetary affairs, or can their arguments be reconstructed as such?

- Do the arguments that they advance in support of their favored monetary regime appeal to presumed common interests of the citizenry?

In examining proposals for monetary constitutions in light of these questions, one must keep in mind that such proposals must be supported by arguments that are of relevance at the *constitutional level of choice*, that is, by arguments that inform their addressees about the relative merits of alternative rule regimes. This reminder is not as superfluous as it may appear, because, in particular, advocates of "free-market regimes" do not always pay due attention to the critical difference between the subconstitutional and the constitutional level of choice. Murray Rothbard's (1956, 250) comment on "exchanges on a free market" may serve as an illustration:

> Such an exchange is voluntarily undertaken by both parties…. The fact that both parties chose the exchange demonstrates that they both benefit. The free market is the name for the array of all the voluntary exchanges that take place in the world. Since every exchange demonstrates a unanimity of benefit for both parties concerned, we must conclude that *the free market benefits all its participants*. (emphasis in original)

Rothbard's argument is in agreement with the perspective of constitutional economics in insisting that voluntary agreement among the parties concerned is the ultimate source from which legitimacy in social affairs is to be derived. Its shortcoming lies in the fact that it blurs the difference between the constitutional and the subconstitutional level of choice to which constitutional economics seeks to draw attention. It blurs the difference between the issue of what legitimizes transactions *within a market order*, that is, at the subconstitutional level, and the issue of what legitimizes the *market order itself* as a constitutional regime. As much as we may be convinced that "the free market benefits all its participants," we must distinguish between the voluntary agreement, by which the parties legitimize the exchange transaction they voluntarily conclude within the market order, and their agreement to the "rules of the game," from which the market order itself derives its legitimacy. Contrary to what Rothbard's argument suggests, the voluntary agreements that legitimize market exchanges cannot per se legitimize the market as a constitutional order. The latter can derive its legitimacy only from agreement expressed at the constitutional level, at which the choice among alternative constitutional regimes is at stake. And such agreement is not tested by the agreement to transactions within the rules of the market but by individuals' preference for the market order compared to potential alternative arrangements.

The same caveat applies where the choice among monetary constitutions is concerned. With the formula "Financial Power to the People!," Friedrich Hayek (1975) expresses a well-founded preference for a monetary regime in which individuals are free to choose among competing moneys according to whatever they consider preferable for the kind of uses they have in mind. Yet, here again, we need to distinguish between the subconstitutional and the constitutional level of choice. Through the voluntary choices they exercise within such a regime, individuals do not per se express their agreement to the regime itself. To be sure, the freedom of choice they can enjoy in a competitive regime may well be an attractive feature that makes them inclined to opt for it. But the important point is that proposals for such a regime must be argued for in constitutional terms, that is, with arguments that tell the addressees why such a monetary constitution promises to serve their common interests better than relevant alternatives. The fact that it gives "financial power to the people" on the subconstitutional level cannot by itself prove that this is the case.

The History of the Debate

Because our objective is to discuss distinct monetary proposals that exemplify the previously mentioned principal alternatives with regard to questions 1 and 3, we need to specify a representative subset from the vast number of proposals that have been discussed among economists. This can be achieved by a systematic classification of the proposals with respect to their legal-institutional characteristics and the working properties that the institutional arrangement is expected to exhibit. With regard to the explicitly or implicitly defined legal-institutional framework (the monetary constitution), the focus of our analysis is on proposals that require a distinct set of monetary rules in addition to the general requirements for a functioning market, "enforcing property rights and contracts among private parties" (in analogy with Brennan and Buchanan [1981, 59]). In the case of the working properties, we adopt the analytical framework of the theory of monetary institutions (White 1999) and classify proposals first as competitive or monopolistic monetary orders (Figure 4.2). For example, a central bank that is subject to commodity-reserve-currency rules to emit legal tender will be classified as a monopolistic monetary order, while a gold-anchored free-banking system is classified as a competitive monetary order, even if both proposals include constitutional rules that define what money is or prescribe technical modalities for its creation. They differ in terms of whether or not they are open for "access" (North, Wallis, and Weingast 2006): the latter illustrates an open-access monetary order and exhibits competitive working properties, whereas the former illustrates a closed-access monetary order and exhibits monopolistic working properties.

The different categories among which we distinguish (Figure 4.1) resemble those defined by Brennan and Buchanan (1981). The category "unhampered market" is analogous to their regime "free market in money with no governmental role" (Brennan and Buchanan 1981, 59). The second category, "regulated market regime," includes proposals that require at least one specific rule in addition to the legal-institutional framework in which markets in general operate, thus qualifying in a proper sense as "monetary constitution." The gold-anchored free-banking proposal is a prominent example of this second category, as is Brennan and Buchanan's "pure commodity money, with governmental definition of value" regime. Our category "regulated market

Figure 4.2
The Range of a Monetary Constitution and Monetary Orders

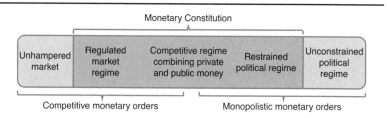

regime" is, however, meant in a more general sense to include proposals that are based on informal rules without any government involvement or on such archaic minting rules as the one on weights and measurements implied in the Bible in chapter 25, verses 13–16, of the book of Deuteronomy (the Deuteronomic code) and chapter 19, verses 35–36, of the book of Leviticus. The third category, "competitive regime combining private and public money," includes proposals that account for at least one parallel currency besides legal tender. The government may be empowered to issue domestic money, but competitive entry is permitted. This category corresponds to what Brennan and Buchanan (1981, 60) define as "governmental money issue, but competitive entry." Finally, what we describe in our classification as "constitutionally restrained political regimes" is equivalent to what they define as "fiat money issue constrained by constitutional rules." In addition to proposals in which central banks are constrained by a distinct monetary constitution, our classification includes, as the polar opposite to an "unhampered market" in money, regimes in which political forces are in effect unconstrained in how they manage money. A pure example for this latter category would be an omnipotent dictatorship with a centrally administered economy. It should be noted, though, that even if a monetary constitution exists de jure, it may have no constraining force. The German Reichsbank from 1938 on is a paradigm example of such a drained monetary constitution that allows for an unconstrained political regime.

In view of the abundance of proposals that have been submitted in the long-standing debate on monetary issues, we must limit the scope of our analysis. In the first instance, we look at proposals from the late 1920s on only, for the following reasons: first, discussions in the sense of a debate on alternative monetary rules did not start before the 1920s, when financial turmoil spread in numerous nations that had entered World War I. Second, this discussion was marked by a new trend in monetary economic thinking, as Hayek showed in identifying stabilization policy as a new paradigm in monetary politics (Hayek [1932] 1965; see also Hayek 1994, 88–89; Keynes and Henderson 1929). Third, the Great Depression refueled the debate on alternative monetary rules, especially with regard to bank regulations, minimum reserves, and most notably unprecedented monetary proposals[5] (Köhler and Kolev 2011). Fourth, the debate on how to organize the monetary arena "was practically closed by 1875" (Smith [1936] 1990, 6). Discussions in monetary economics between 1875 and World War I had been devoted to technical issues of how to adopt a prudent central-banking system rather than to the issue of choice among monetary regimes.[6] Fifth, in contrast to the latter, the post-1929 debate eventually inspired a renewal of the mid-19th-century debate on free banking (Meulen 1934; Smith [1936] 1990).[7]

For the noted reasons it is not only justifiable to limit our analysis to proposals from the late 1920s on but also advisable to subdivide the sample we plan to look at into three periods (see Figure 4.3). The first group includes proposals that were advanced until the end of the 1960s, when the first inflationary tendencies in the United States and the ensuing economic turmoil heralded the end of the Bretton Woods system (Yeager [1971] 1997, 307–20). The second group includes proposals that were submitted since the 1970s. The partition between these two periods is reasonable because, first, the collapse of the Bretton Woods system restarted the debate on alternative rules for the monetary constitution, as exemplified not only by the revival of the free-banking debate in the mid-1970s (Klein 1974; Sechrest [1993] 2008), but also, and most notably, by the Lucas critique that challenged Keynesian monetary politics (Lucas 1976) and by the debate on the time inconsistency problem in public choice and monetary policy (Buchanan 1962; Friedman 1968, 1971; Kydland and Prescott 1977).

Second, the shortcomings of the neoclassic synthesis, exemplified by increasing inflation and decreasing economic growth rates,

Figure 4.3
THE THREE DEBATES IN MONETARY ECONOMICS

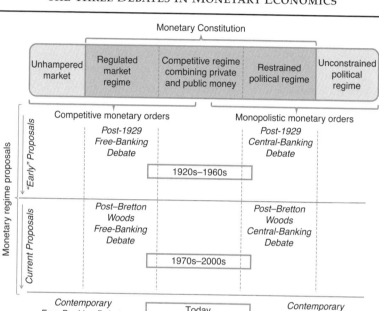

led economists to discuss the working properties and institutional arrangements of a flexible exchange-rate regime, especially with regard to central-bank independence and optimal monetary policy targets, reviving the rules-versus-discretion debate of the 1930s (Kydland and Prescott 1977 and Simons [1936] 1948, respectively). Hence, a full-blown search for an optimal monetary constitution and its subconstitutional properties took off. Third, a paradigmatic shift in discussions on monetary policy from (neo-)Keynesianism to a monetarist paradigm occurred that eventually motivated major European central banks to adopt a monetary policy like the Bundesbank (Janssen 2006), which switched from the neoclassic synthesis to a monetarist approach. Again, a new trend in monetary economics and policy emerged. Fourth, the collapse of the fixed-exchange-rate regime supported the European monetary integration,[8] which eventually motivated a number of scholars to rediscuss the previously mentioned free-banking idea but, most notably, to include new and unprecedented proposals for a free-banking system (Tullock 1975; Hayek [1978] 1999, [1979] 1999; Klein 1974). Receiving a renewed interest among economists, a diversified free-banking debate developed again and saw its peak in the late 1980s and the new free-banking school debate of the early 1990s.

The third group of proposals in our sample is selected from the contemporary debate on alternative monetary rules and monetary policy that started as the housing bubble rose and culminated in today's financial and sovereign debt crisis. This "contemporary debate" is partly reminiscent of the preceding two debates: several of the presently advanced monetary proposals, the principal arguments as well as the envisaged institutional arrangements, are adapted or simply repeated from earlier debates. If we discuss, nevertheless, proposals advanced in the contemporary debate as a separate group, it is because—when exhibiting the common threads that run through the entire debate—we can identify more clearly those aspects that are of particular interest for our specific purpose, namely, to focus attention on the categorical difference between arguments that concern matters of legitimacy and arguments that concern matters of prudence in the choice of a monetary constitution.

In the sections that follow we take a closer look at the three specified debates. Each started as a reaction to large-scale events: the first, in response to the Great Depression; the second, after the collapse of the Bretton Woods system; and the third, during the financial crisis.

"Early" Proposals of the Post-1929 Debate

We summarize the monetary regime proposals in the order in which they appear in the first debate, beginning with the 1920s idea to reintroduce a gold standard with open access to private issuers (Mises [1912] 1924, 1928).[9] Ludwig von Mises's student Hayek also embraced this distinct free-banking proposal in "Monetary Nationalism" ([1937] 2011). Proposals in favor of a free-banking system were also contributed by Henry Meulen and Hayek's doctoral student Vera Smith (Meulen 1934; Smith [1936] 1990).[10] It is very common among economists either to defend the gold standard against criticism (e.g., Machlup 1925) or to support the new stabilization policy paradigm, especially after 1929 (Hayek [1932] 1965). Hayek contributed a monopolistic proposal as an alternative pari passu to Mises's (1928) free-banking proposal (Hayek [1937] 2011, 105). Although he knew that it might be "impracticable," he argued for an international central bank, 100 percent reserves, and a monetary policy that follows either a productivity norm or a constant-money stock goal (Hayek [1937] 2011, 101–16).[11] With this combination of several institutional arrangements, Hayek took account of the seminal works in monetary theory of the time (Hicks 1935; Lutz [1936] 1962; Simons [1936] 1948; Smith [1936] 1990). As promoted by the old Chicago School, 100 percent reserves became a widely accepted institutional arrangement in continental and Anglo-Saxon debates for more than 20 years. The focus on the rules-versus-discretion issue prepared the ground for the future rise of monetarism in the Chicago School (Friedman 1948; Simons 1948).

By the end of the 1930s, the commodity-reserve currency proposal was submitted to the Anglo-Saxon debate by Frank Graham (1936, 1942) and Benjamin Graham (1937, 1944). By the 1940s, the proposal was adopted by many economists (Hayek [1943] 1948; Eucken 1949) and held its ground until the monetarist revolution in the beginning of the 1960s.[12] As a matter of fact, Friedman, who still embraced this idea in the 1950s, critical of the working properties of the Graham plan, later favored a constant money-growth target for monetary policy and, based on his seminal work with Anna Schwartz (Friedman and Schwartz 1963), eventually argued for an optimal money-growth target by the end of the 1960s (Friedman 1968). Advocating free-fluctuating fiat moneys, Leland Yeager, who describes himself as a supporter of Friedman's ideas, made the case for flexible exchange rates in his dissertation (Yeager 1952). The commodity-reserve scheme, however, persisted throughout the 1950s. It has been restated by Benjamin Graham in 1962 and underlies the proposal for the brick standard (Buchanan 1962).[13]

Of particular relevance for our chapter, however, is that Buchanan—broadly in line with Hayek (1960)—already called for a "genuinely constitutional attitude" in the discussion of an appropriate monetary regime that ensures "monetary predictability" (Buchanan 1962, 183). With this aim, Buchanan went beyond the purely technical debate on monetary regime proposals, directing attention to the constitutional dimension.

At the same time, Murray Rothbard published his proposal in favor of a 100 percent gold dollar. In line with Mises, Rothbard denies that "money" can "originate as a new fiat name, either by government or by some form of social compact" (Rothbard 1962, 103). In contrast to Mises, Rothbard wants to roll back fractional-reserve banking and combines his proposal for a gold standard with 100 percent reserves.[14] Rothbard's amalgam of ideas is referred to in this chapter simply as the Rothbard proposal.

Most visible in the post-1929 debate have been, however, adherents of the Keynesian proposal. The Keynesian paradigm dominates the discussion in monetary economics and policy since the end of World War II with its pro-stabilization-oriented monetary policy recommendation (Keynes and Henderson 1929; Keynes 1936).[15] Keynes rejected any return to a rule-based monetary regime after the collapse of the gold standard (1936). He called for "the enlargement of the function of government, involved in the task of adjusting to one another the propensity to consume and the inducement to invest"— that is, to use monetary policy as a tool—"as the only practicable means of avoiding the destruction of existing economic forms in their entirety and as the condition of the successful function of individual initiative" (Keynes 1936, 380).

Proposals of the Post–Bretton Woods Debate

The collapse of the Bretton Woods system also marked the peak of Keynesian monetary economics and the breakthrough of the monetarist trend in economic thinking. The concept of rational expectations and the attention drawn to the time-inconsistency problem supported the latter camp and paved the way for the counterrevolution. The blueprint of the upcoming monetarism had been laid down earlier by Friedman (1960, 23) in these terms:

> It means that the central problem is not to construct a highly sensitive instrument that can continuously offset instability introduced by other factors, but rather to prevent monetary arrangements from themselves becoming a primary source of instability. What we need is not a skilled monetary driver of the economic vehicle continuously turning the steering wheel to adjust the unexpected irregularities of the route, but some means of keeping the monetary passenger who is in the back

seat as ballast from occasionally leaning over and given the
steer wheel a jerk that threatens to send the car off the road.[16]

This argument in favor of a depoliticized, rule-based, monopolistic monetary constitution clearly reflects the spirit of the Knightian
Chicago School, especially with respect to uncertainty.

Giving up the commodity-reserve currency (Friedman 1953, 1968;
Friedman and Schwartz 1963) and the 100 percent idea (Friedman
1967),[17] monetarism turned into a pure central-banking school that
quickly gained support in the economics profession. Monetarism
gained the status of a paradigm in monetary discussions. The central-
banking debate took off and was from then on devoted to either
the issue of a monetary policy target or to the problem of how to
prudentially design the central bank and other regulative institutions. Numerous empirical investigations have proven that flexible
exchange rates and an independent central bank that is committed to
price stability contribute to low inflation (e.g., Alesina and Summers
1993). Transparency and accountability are of major concern in this
research because they encourage "good" decisionmaking and shield
the independence of the central bank from attacks on its democratic
accountability (Goodhart 2003, 109). However, the renunciation of
the constant-money-growth concept in the 1990s led to a paradigm
shift toward a neo-Keynesian approach, the most prominent adherents of which have dominated monetary policy discussions ever
since (Woodford 2003). The current neoclassic/neo-Keynesian consensus on monetary policy emphasizes a targeted interest rate and
pays "curiously" little explicit attention to the quantity of money
(Yeager 2010, 420n). In the pre–financial crisis discussion in monetary economics, Olivier Blanchard, Lars E. Svensson, and others
have further questioned a strict inflation target, arguing instead for
a flexible inflation target to account for supply shocks.

The preceding summary of the discussion around the idea of a
depoliticized central-bank constitution may suffice for the purpose
of the present chapter. However, we still need to take a closer look at
the debate on proposals in favor of a competitive monetary regime
between the 1970s and the 2000s.

The post–Bretton Woods debate on competitive monetary regimes
started with Benjamin Klein's article on competing currency
schemes (1974). Hayek credits the article in his proposal for the

"Denationalization of Money," which was motivated by the upcoming European monetary integration process during the mid-1970s (Hayek [1978] 1999). Hayek's idea was to deregulate the monopoly of the central bank by allowing commercial banks to emit money. Private notes should compete against legal tender and eventually set off a discovery procedure for the most successful currency. The money user, the citizen, becomes the sovereign of the monetary arena. This proposal motivated several other scholars to endorse similar competitive proposals. The most prominent are Greenfield and Yeager[18] (1983) with their proposal for what they call a BFH-system (named after Black [1970], Fama [1980], and Hall [1982]); the George Selgin and Lawrence White proposals for free banking; and Buchanan's proposal for the European Monetary Union (EMU).[19] These proposals, as well as the Rothbard proposal, are discussed below as representative examples of the younger debate on a competitive monetary constitution.

The Greenfield-Yeager proposal belongs to the group of BFH proposals that were discussed in the new monetary economics (Cowen and Kroszner 1994). Like Hayek's *Denationalization* proposal, the Greenfield-Yeager BFH proposal "would almost completely depoliticize money and banking" (Yeager [1983] 1997, 358–59). Linking financial deregulation with the "government announcement and promotion of a new ... unit of account," BFH adherents call for a separation between the functions of money as a unit of account and as a medium of exchange (Cowen and Kroszner 1994, 80).[20] This is how Yeager ([1983] 1997, 359) describes the scheme:

> The government would define the new unit [of account], just as it defines units of weights and measures. The definition would run in terms of a bundle of commodities so comprehensive that the unit's value would remain nearly stable against goods and services in general. The government would conduct its own accounting and transaction in the new unit.

As he argues, separating the unit of account of "defined purchasing power from the medium of exchange would ... avoid macroeconomic disorders" ([1983] 1997, 359). Exchange media, though, are not defined in a BFH system—they are basically "lacking"—which is seen as an advantage because, as Yeager points out ([1983] 1997, 359), it prevents any fractional reserve pyramids. He supposes that people would rather pay with checks if there were no base money. In this sense the BFH proposal is a scheme to eliminate outside money. It favors a "cashless" economy, in which money is an artifact of banking.[21] Selgin and White (1994), O'Driscoll (1986), and Cowen and Kroszner (1994) have criticized the BFH proposals. Lawrence White (1984a) doubts the capacity of a BFH system to sort out inferior money producers. In addition, he doubts that economic agents in an unregulated world without a central auctioneer would be likely to converge on a unit of account that is not a unit of outside currency (White 1984a, 703). In his view, a unit of account emerges "wedded to a medium of exchange" (711).

The Selgin[22] (1988) and Lawrence White (1983, 1984a, 1984b) free-banking proposals operate as follows: private banks emit redeemable money. The emitted volume depends on the costs of carrying (for the emission bank) and the preferences of the money users for the extent to which their money should be covered by securities or gold. The method to prevent overissue of bank notes is the ability to return notes to the issuing institution for redemption. This disciplining function is feasible only as long as a monopoly in note issue and inconvertibility are prohibited. In addition, a lender of last resort as well as a central bank hinders the realization of such a proposal. A necessary requirement is an interbank clearing institution that settles claims among issuing banks. To restrict money supply, Selgin and White embrace gold.

As he notes, Buchanan's 1990 proposal for a monetary constitution for an effective European Union "closely resembles" Hayek's earlier proposal (Buchanan 1990, 13), except that Buchanan allows for competition among the European currencies but does not envisage private money emission. His proposal of a fiat-currency competition for the European Union rests upon a "constitutional provision" that impacts "directly on the legal relationships among persons and indirectly on the operation of the monetary authorities (13): "Citizens of Europe, of each and all of the separate nation-states of the federal union, must be legally-constitutionally allowed to transact affairs, to make contracts enforceable in their own courts, in the monetary unit issued by the central bank of *any* of the nation-states of the union, including the discharge of all monetary obligations, and specifically the payment of taxes to any and all political authorities" (13). Buchanan's unique contribution is that his proposal—in contrast to the previously mentioned competitive proposals—focuses not on technical issues but on the problem of public choice among constitutional rules. This is why Buchanan applauds Peter Bernholz (2003) for examining "the characteristics of political regimes and the identification of circumstances that might bring constitutional reform more closely to the realm of the politically possible" (Buchanan 1990, 1).[23]

The Contemporary Debate

Under the influence of the financial and sovereign debt crisis, the most recent debate on central banking has partly refocused on post-1929 issues such as the liquidity trap, vagabonding liquidity bubbles, or money as a source of economic instability. The tension between the lender-of-last-resort function and fiscal stimuli has redirected the discussion to issues of public choice, regulation, and bank supervision, including the too-big-to-fail problem. Monetary economics is currently experiencing a Keynesian revival. Apart from these crises-centered issues, the core debate on the future of monetary policy is currently devoted to alternative targets for monetary policy. Claudio Borio (2008) and William White (2006) call for a broader perspective on monetary aggregates to account for asset price inflation; Axel Weber (2008) calls on central banks to prevent long negative real interest rate periods. Paul de Grauwe opts for a modification of the reserves for the same reason. Selgin recommends nominal gross domestic product (GDP) targeting as an alternative to the predominant Fed monetary policy targets (Selgin 2010, 471). He also reaffirms Scott Sumner's nominal GDP future targeting to account for speculation in the open market (Sumner 1989, 1995), supposing that these targets "significantly reduce the discretionary element in monetary base adjustment" (Selgin 2010, 472). Such a targeting would, in Selgin's view, come "close to making the monetary supply adjustment process an entirely automatic one" (472).

The free-banking debate, too, has received renewed attention since the outbreak of the financial crisis. Two lines of arguments can be identified and traced back to the time when the gold standard collapsed: one is an American-Austrian development that advocates the "return" to a free-banking system with a 100 percent minimum reserve backed by gold (Rothbard 1962; Huerta de Soto [2006] 2011; Bagus 2009), whereas the other is a more heterogeneous

Anglo-Saxon development that offers many proposals for a distinct free-banking system, including the participation of the central bank. The Rothbard adherents and the Selgin-White group divide with regard to where they locate the source of legitimacy as well as with regard to the institutional specifics of their respective monetary schemes. Surprisingly, neither Hayek's nor Yeager's proposals have received attention in the most recent debate, even though the latter has reaffirmed his arguments (Yeager 2009, 2010). Buchanan's approach has also found little attention among monetary economists, including his most recent plea for the constitutionalization of money (Buchanan 2010), to which we return in the next section.

Figure 4.4 summarizes the preceding overview of the three debates.

The Addressees of the Principal Proposals

Having summarized the post-1929 debate on monetary regimes, we examine in this section major constitutional proposals in light of the question of where their advocates locate the source of legitimacy and, accordingly, to whom they mean to address their advice. More specifically, applying the constitutional-contractarian "internal standard of evaluation" (Vanberg [1986] 1994, 209) as the measuring rod, we ask whether they consider—explicitly or implicitly—the individuals who are to live with the suggested monetary regime as their ultimate addressees and whether they support their proposal with arguments that—again, explicitly or implicitly—aim at convincing these individuals that heeding the advice offered is in their common interest.

When applying the contractarian-constitutionalist standard of legitimacy, we must distinguish, of course, between the *ultimate* and the *proximate* addressees of the arguments that authors offer in support of their respective proposals. The point of applying the contractarian-constitutionalist standard of legitimacy can obviously not be to classify proposals for monetary regimes according to whether or not their advocates directly address their arguments to the citizens. We should surely expect them to argue in terms that are meant to impress their academic peers. The relevant question that we need to ask is, first, if in so arguing they explicitly or implicitly acknowledge that the citizens are the sovereigns to whom their proposal must be ultimately justified and, second, whether what they portray as the

Figure 4.4
SIMPLIFIED OVERVIEW OF MONETARY REGIME PROPOSALS
DURING THE THREE DEBATES IN MONETARY ECONOMICS

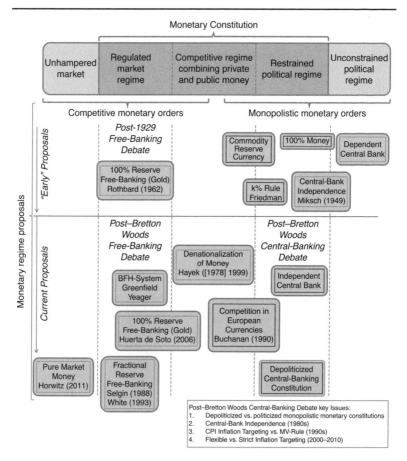

virtues of their proposals may potentially appeal to citizens' common interests. In light of this twofold question, we classify proposals into the following categories: (a) proposals that explicitly apply the contractarian-constitutionalist internal standard of legitimacy; (b) proposals that can be interpreted to implicitly apply this standard; (c) proposals that neither explicitly nor implicitly consider the citizens' common interests as the ultimate source of legitimacy in constitutional matters but are argued for in terms that can be reconstructed as appealing to such interests; (d) proposals that implicitly refer to external standards of legitimacy, that is, to criteria that are supposed to allow for judging the appropriateness of monetary regimes independently of what the citizens themselves consider a desirable constitution; and (e) proposals that explicitly refer to external standards of legitimacy.

Not surprisingly, Buchanan is the author who most explicitly appeals to the citizens as the sovereigns from whose consent monetary regimes—no less than other institutional arrangements—ultimately derive their legitimacy, and his proposal is the only entry in our category (a). Although the constitutional-contractarian thrust of his arguments on monetary issues can be traced back to his contribution to the Yeager volume (Buchanan 1962), it has been more explicitly stated in Buchanan's joint contribution with Nicolaus Tideman (Buchanan and Tideman [1975] 2001, 411)[24] and systematically developed in *Monopoly in Money and Inflation*, coauthored with Geoffrey Brennan (Brennan and Buchanan 1981). Approaching the issue of what may qualify as "legally justifiable" in monetary matters in light of the question of "what are the ultimate criteria in evaluating the basic institutions of a desirable social order" (53), Brennan and Buchanan propose a contractarian answer.[25] As noted before, they argue that if one rejects "the existence of (or at least general agreement on) external ethical norms … the criteria for evaluation of institutions must in some way be *derived from individuals themselves*" (53, emphasis in original). And this implies, as they suppose, that the "test of 'legitimacy'" must be whether or not an institution "could have been, or could possibly be, agreed on by all persons" (54).[26] More recently Buchanan (2010, 254) has advocated the inclusion of money in a "conjectural Hobbesian" contract as a remedy for its instability under the status quo. As he puts it, such a constitutional contract ought to "also embody the requirement that the monetary authority itself be bound by the rules of the basic contract. Beyond narrow limits, discretion on the part of the authority goes outside the dictates of constitutional criteria" (257).

In proposing an unhampered market regime, Horwitz (2011) does not explicitly refer to the citizens as the ultimate sovereigns in constitutional choice. Invoking a Mengerian explanation of the emergence of money, he "assume(s)" that "gold is the choice emerging out of this process." Yet, arguing that the emergence of gold as money can be explained along the lines of Menger's methodologically individualistic account (Vanberg [1992] 1994, 150) is not the same as answering the question of the gold standard's legitimacy as a constitutional regime. Horwitz's reasoning rests implicitly on Mises's regression theorem, which is commonly cited by today's Austrians in support of the claim that gold should be the one and only commodity used as money.[27] In this sense, Horwitz's argument for a gold-based monetary regime, constrained only by the general provisions of the private law, can be said to appeal tacitly to an "external" criterion of legitimacy, as opposed to the "internal" standard of normative individualism.[28] No reasons are provided for why the constituents should have an interest in agreeing to his plan for monetary anarchy, which we accordingly classify into our category (d).

With regard to the fractional-reserve free-banking proposal advocated by White and Selgin, we come to a mixed conclusion: Lawrence White does not explicitly address the citizens but the "public" in general (e.g., White 1983). Because the citizenry would be "vulnerable to the errors of monetary policy," he concludes that it was "vital that some means of real protection be available" (281). In discussing arguments against the nationalization of money, he implicitly recognizes the citizens' role as the sovereigns in the monetary arena when he criticizes central-banking proposals for overlooking the "possibility that consumers prefer commodity money to fiat money strongly enough to consider the resource costs worth bearing" (294). He even appears to refer to consent as the ultimate source of legitimacy: "Consumers would conceivably consent to the replacement of a commodity currency by a fiat currency only if they themselves enjoyed the resource savings" (295). And although he seems to be critical of hypothetical contractarian arguments, he de facto affirms the citizens' status as the ultimate judges when he argues, "Economists are not in a position to divine consumers' true preferences in a hypothetical constitution-like choice and thereby to design optimal social institutions for them" (294). In support of his claim that commodity money "could most plausibly be silver or gold," White (299) argues, "The point here is not to re-establish a link between government-issued money and a precious metal; it is to phase out government-issued money," because a "conversion to a precious-metal based monetary system seems our best hope for a competitive supply of outside money." Gold is favored as a means to achieve the proximate aim of a consumer-sovereign monetary constitution, that is, in terms that may be meant to appeal to citizens' interests.

Where Selgin finds the source of legitimacy in constitutional matters is not so clear in his early writings. Similar to Horwitz, he seems to rest his proposal implicitly upon an external criterion, arguing as if the evolutionary emergence of gold as money would provide normative legitimacy to gold as the single commodity to be used as money (Selgin 1988, 16–21, 47; see also Sechrest [1993] 2008, 11). Later Selgin avoided such ambiguity in his proposal by providing prudential arguments in favor of a "naturally scarce reserve medium (such as gold or a 'frozen' stock of central bank money)" (Selgin 2000, 97–98) that might play a role in recommending such a regime to the citizens. Although such arguments and, in particular, White's above-quoted arguments would seem to allow for an interpretation that places their proposal into either category (b) or (c), this is in conflict with their explicitly stated intention "to base the legitimacy arguments on Rothbardian normative analysis" (Selgin and White 1996, 86), a statement that would put their proposal squarely into category (e).[29]

Yeager's (2010) reaffirmation of his and Greenfield's inside money standard proposal (Greenfield and Yeager 1983) neither addresses a potential constituency nor appeals to natural rights or any other external criterion. Yeager motivates his reappraisal in Milton Friedman's and Anna Schwartz's words; they who assert that "widening of the range of options [in monetary constitutional choice] and keeping them alive—is … the major contribution of the burst of scholarly interest in monetary reform" (Yeager 2010, 417). He explicitly endorses the proposal as one of many possible proposals, without any claim to universality. Prudential arguments are the main reason for preferring a commodity standard (Yeager, 2010, 422–42): gold would be too volatile since its value would be determined by more factors than by industrial demand.[30] As is presented in the next section, Yeager's arguments can be interpreted in ways that place his proposal in category (c).

The Rothbard proposal has been restated in the recent debates by such authors as Jesús Huerta de Soto ([2006] 2011), Jörg Hülsmann (2008), and Philipp Bagus (2009), who explicitly refer to natural rights as an "external" criterion of legitimacy that can, supposedly,

be identified without regard to what the individuals involved consider as constitutionally desirable.[31] Their respective versions of the
Rothbard proposal clearly belong in category (e).

Huerta de Soto's book *Money, Bank Credit, and Economic Cycles*
([2006] 2011) has been described as "the final and decisive proof
that fractional reserves are incompatible with a) a proper defense
of private property rights, b) morality, and c) a stable economy"
(Sechrest [1993] 2008, 1). By using the term "sin" when reviewing
various episodes in banking history, Huerta de Soto ([2006] 2011,
88, 92, 97) indicates his claim to know what is morally "right."
Deriving his principal arguments from a historical-evolutionary
theoretical and ethical perspective, he advocates the 100 percent
reserves requirement as a tradition-honored positive norm that, in
line with gold, requires unconditional institutional application to
prevent a collapse of the monetary system (Huerta de Soto 1988;
[2006] 2011, 518).[32] Even his followers describe his approach as a
"formal ethical theory" (Bagus 2009) that derives distinct monetary
rules from externally set criteria to legitimize the Rothbard proposal for a nonfractional-reserve free-banking system (Huerta de
Soto [2006] 2011, ch. 29).

Arguing in a similar spirit, Hülsmann (2008, 238, 10–11) states in
support of his Rothbardian monetary regime proposal:

> There is no ... legal, moral, or spiritual rationale that could
> be adduced in justification of paper money and fractional-
> reserve banking.
>
> Mises integrated the theory of money and banking within
> the overall theory of subjective value[33] .... In Rothbard's
> work, then, the Austrian theory of money found its present
> apex. Rothbard not only developed and refined the doctrine
> of his teacher Mises; he also brought ethical concerns back
> into the picture, stressing natural-law categories to criticize
> fractional-reserve banking and paper money. Our work is
> squarely built on the work of these two writers. Important
> living authors in this tradition are Pascal Salin, George
> Reisman, and Jesús Huerta de Soto.[34]

A similar line of argument can be found again in Bagus's (2009)
monetary reform plan. Referring to Rothbard (1962, 1995) and
Hülsmann (1998, 115), Bagus wants the central bank assets to be
raffled off and, in line with Walter Block (2004, 2006), calls for a

"libertarian punishment of statists," suggesting that "a libertarian Nuremberg Trial" be held against the persons responsible and "collaborateurs" (Bagus 2009, 115). While such a "monetary reform" is portrayed as "necessarily just"—and, in line with Rothbard (1995, 11), as inevitable because "the banking system is headed for a mighty crash in any case" (Bagus 2009, 122–24)—"most plans for monetary reform" are dismissed as "unethical" (Bagus 2009, 126). Such ethical verdicts notwithstanding, Bagus describes his own proposal as "value-free economic analysis."

Even if it has not played a role in the most recent debate, a closer look at Hayek's proposal for the denationalization of money may be useful because it provides an opportunity to reemphasize the importance—in the case of monetary regimes as well as in other institutional matters—of distinguishing between the constitutional and the subconstitutional level of choice when the issue of constitutional *legitimacy* is at stake. Hayek ([1976] 1999, 121) explicitly refers to the individuals as the sovereigns when he argues:

> But why should we not let people choose freely what money they want to use? By "people" I mean the individuals who ought to have the right do decide whether they want to buy or sell for francs, pounds, dollars, D-marks, or ounces of gold. I have no objection to governments issuing money, but I believe their claim to a *monopoly*, or their power to *limit* the kinds of money in which contracts may be concluded within their territory, or to determine the *rates* at which monies can be exchanged, to be wholly harmful.[35]

Yet such reference to individuals as sovereign choosers should not be confused with a contractarian-constitutional argument for the monetary regime that Hayek wants to advocate. That people, if allowed to choose at the subconstitutional level, would opt for the currency they prefer as money users does not mean that, if faced with a constitutional choice among alternative regimes, they would necessarily opt for the regime that Hayek favors. At the constitutional level, they would need to be given reasons for why they can expect this regime to serve their common interests better than feasible alternatives. And, in fact, the prudential reasons, such as the "utilization of knowledge" argument that Hayek provides in support of a competitive monetary regime may well be restated as appeals to citizens' common constitutional interests. Furthermore, even if Hayek has been explicitly critical of social contract theory, in his writings one can find sufficient evidence for the claim that he implicitly accepts the contractarian standard of legitimacy (Vanberg [1983] 1994, 207). In this sense his proposal could, in a broad interpretation, be classified in category (b) but belongs surely in category (c).

At the end of this section, we must conclude that the majority of the participants in the monetary debate, including the advocates of a depoliticized central-banking system (e.g., McCallum 2010), make no explicit reference to the citizens-constituents as the ultimate sovereigns in constitutional matters and that Buchanan's constitutional economics perspective on money has been of little influence in drawing attention to the issue of legitimacy in the choice of monetary regimes. In particular, the Austrian and free-banking groups have remained entirely immune to the contractarian-constitutional insistence on the citizens-constituents as the ultimate addressees to whom constitutional proposals—including monetary regime proposals—have to be justified. It is noteworthy that the advocates of a competitive monetary constitution are divided into two camps—on the one side a group that fights for the preservation of the Rothbard proposal condemning fractional-reserve free banking, on the other side a number of authors who have neither completely decoupled their reasoning from external (natural rights) standards nor explicitly developed an alternative normative foundation. In general, how little explicit attention has been paid to the whole debate on the issue of legitimacy in choosing among alternative monetary regimes is surprising.

Regime Proposals and Citizens' Interests

The fact that most of the proposals for monetary regimes that we have examined here neither explicitly nor implicitly refer to the citizens as the ultimate sovereigns in constitutional choice does not, of course, mean that the arguments offered in their support might not be of relevance within a contractarian-constitutionalist framework in the sense that they may help inform citizens as to which among alternative regimes promises to serve their common interests best. In other words, whatever the respective authors' own views in matters of legitimacy may be, they may well provide arguments on the working properties of monetary regimes that citizens should prudently consider in choosing their monetary constitution. With this in mind, we use the remainder of the chapter to take a second look at some of the proposals discussed above, specifically proposals classified in categories (b) and (c) of Figure 4.5, to see if their advocates support them with arguments that citizens would have reasons to consider in evaluating alternative proposals, even if they are not so framed by their respective authors.

All proposals that we look at[36] have in common that they argue for monetary regimes to be constrained by rules that are meant to avoid anarchy as well as political arbitrariness in the monetary arena; that is, they all propose a *monetary constitution* in the proper sense of the term. Yet, although they all require a special legal framework for the money sphere, they differ in the kind of institutional arrangements that they favor. On the one hand is the group of free-banking advocates (Yeager, Hayek, and White), who want to constrain money issuers by the disciplining force of competition, and on the other hand are the central-banking advocates (Goodhart, McCallum), who opt for a rule-based, depoliticized central-bank regime. Of interest in the present context is whether the arguments that the advocates on either side provide may serve to convince citizens that their common interests are better served by one regime than the other.

What, according to Hayek, speaks against monopoly in money from the perspective of the citizen is that "governments in history have used their exclusive power to issue money in order to defraud and plunder the people" (Hayek [1976] 1999, 120). Referring to the explorative potential of evolutionary competition, Hayek points out that "all monopolistic government limits the possibilities of evolution …, because it would preclude the possibility of trying alternative methods" (Hayek 1994, 152). Competition in currency and market entry, so he argues, allows for the discovery of yet unknown institutions and business practices for how to organize money and will work toward stable currencies to the benefit of citizens (Hayek 1990, 52). Money issuers, including the central bank, would be subject to the disciplining power of the market because they are "depending on success in keeping the value of the currency constant" (52).[37] Hayek has in mind working properties such as these when he claims, "At this moment it seems that the best thing we could wish governments to

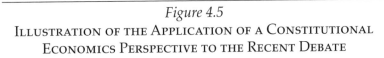

Figure 4.5
ILLUSTRATION OF THE APPLICATION OF A CONSTITUTIONAL
ECONOMICS PERSPECTIVE TO THE RECENT DEBATE

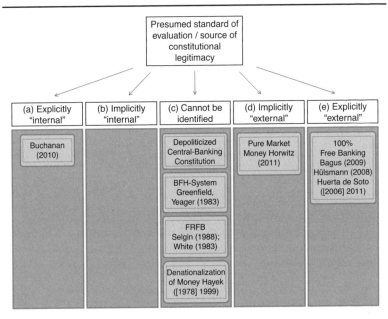

do is for, say, all members of the European Community, or, better still, all the governments of the Atlantic Community, to bind themselves mutually not to place any restriction on the free use within their territories of one another's—or any other—currencies, including their purchase and sale at any price the parties decide upon, or on their use as accounting units in which to keep books" (Hayek [1976] 1999, 121).

To sum up, Hayek's prudential arguments for a competitive monetary constitution can be understood as being directed at "the people" as their ultimate addressees, giving reasons why it is in their common interest to agree upon the denationalization of money. As he notes, "One cannot help wondering why people should have put up for so long with governments exercising an exclusive power over 2000 years that was regularly used to exploit and defraud them" (Hayek [1978] 1999, 141). Similarly, White and Yeager base their proposals on arguments appealing to citizens' common interests, claiming that under a competitive regime, the value of money will be more predictable and stable because the supply of money will be automatically brought in line with the preferences of the money users.

Yeager (2010, 425) argues that the expected patterns of a demand-determined money will ensure that note issuers supply "the quantity of money that the public desires to hold at the price level predetermined by the dollar's basket definition" because competition requires money issuers to "serve the preferences of their note- and deposit-holders."[38] Under such a regime, he argues, money users will be able to control the money supply process instead of being at the mercy of a central bank that is mandated to control the value of money on their behalf. This is surely an argument that an adviser may use who wants citizens to put an end to monopoly in money.

White disagrees not only with the specific institutional features of Hayek's denationalization but also with Yeager's composite index. Nevertheless he also stresses as its desirable property that competitively issued money would tend to "erode the monopoly profit government currently enjoys in the production of outside money" (White 1983, 298). A competitive monetary regime, he argues, would allow for "discovering" which money may serve the "consumer's preferences best" (292), adding: "Even if the market process will eventually converge on a single type of money ... the time spent is not a wasteful aspect of competition that may be efficiently supplanted by government edict. Government would not be in a position to know what the market process would have selected as most suitable" (293).

Advocates of central banking have criticized the competitive supply of money, arguing that money is a public good that evolved "naturally" over time and should, therefore, be subject to public or "higher" law.[39] They also provide prudential arguments for the necessity of a monopoly in money. On the grounds that inflation is "always and everywhere a monetary phenomenon" (Friedman 2003, 85) in that "it is and can be produced only by a more rapid increase in the quantity of money than in output" (Wood 2003, 29), they argue that money should be controlled by a central institution.

McCallum (2010), one of the very few central-bank advocates who has commented on the recent free-banking debate, rejects all three of the preceding proposals for a competitive supply of money. His arguments against a gold-based standard—as suggested in White's free-banking proposal—resemble Friedman's earlier arguments. Friedman (1960, 5–7) claimed that such a regime would have a strong tendency to evolve into one with "fiduciary elements" so that, as McCallum appends, it finally culminates in "commodity currency in which the commodity is paper or, today, digital storage capacity" (McCallum 2010, 442). This argument mirrors the central-banking school's long-standing view that "inter-bank control via clearing mechanism" is an "illusion" (Smith [1936] 1990, 158). Accordingly, the monetary constitution is assumed to work properly if, and only if, the power of controlling money supply, regulation, and banking supervision is monopolized. Hayek's proposal is rejected on the ground that it would create a multiplicity of banknotes (McCallum 2010), an outcome that is regarded as inferior compared to a regime in which the medium of transaction coincides with the medium of account. According to McCallum, a separation of the two functions would burden money users with increasing transaction costs as they face a multiplicity of currencies.[40] In addition, McCallum argues, Hayek's denationalization would suffer from "dynamic inconsistency" and "could only be sustainable if the issuer were to provide potential users with a contractual commitment to redeemability in some acceptable medium—and this would require, that the legal system will enforce such contracts" (McCallum 2010, 443). McCallum describes the general working properties of Yeager's proposal as not "easy to understand, especially for economists who have not spent years in the study of monetary systems with private money provision" (445). He concedes, though, a potential efficacy of Yeager's proposal. If the medium could be redeemed in Treasury securities, so he notes, it would exhibit a working pattern that could also be "achieved with an inflation-targeting central bank, provided it incorporates a zero inflation rate as its *sole* objective and adjusts its instruments very frequently to achieve that objective" (447, emphasis in original). If central-bank policy objectives were to be reformed in this way, central banking would, in his view, come closest to achieving stability of a broad price index.

McCallum's core argument against a competitive issue of money is based on the perceived antagonism of oversight and regulation: "Some form of regulation" is needed in competitive monetary constitutions, in "which case the regulator might be faced with the same temptation to inflate as with a standard monetary authority" (McCallum 2010, 447). Instead of creating another playing field of interest groups that lobby the regulator, he suggests adopting institutions that are less subject to temptation than others and that promise to provide stability of a broad price index. In an ordo-liberal spirit, he argues for a central-bank regime and an "activist but rule-based monetary stabilization policy that emphasizes the avoidance of significant inflation and deflation" (438–39) by adopting "a clear lexicographic mandate for price stability" (448). McCallum's conclusion is broadly in line with the general central-banking advocates' perspective that a reasonably stable price level as a necessary condition for a stable and prosperous economy can be realized only by a single authority. Charles Goodhart (2003), for example, argues that the following connected conditions necessarily must be fulfilled to achieve a stable price level. First, policymakers must accept that no long-run benefit can be gained from higher inflation in terms of higher output or employment. This insight of the post-1929 debate that became common ground with the rise of monetarism is a widely shared insight among central-banking advocates. Second, and again in line with monetarism, policymakers must understand the source of inflation: excess monetary growth. Third, a stable price level can be achieved only if the institutional setup of the monopolistic monetary constitution assures independence from the political arena, an argument that is informed by the insights of monetary institutional economics and public choice.[41]

Overall, modern central-banking advocates opt for a depoliticized monetary constitution with an independent central bank that is solely aimed at achieving price stability.

Conclusion

When economists argue about policy issues—including monetary policy—they no longer operate in the domain of pure theoretical science but enter the arena of *applied* science, in which theoretical insights form the basis for recommendations on how certain problems might be dealt with, recommendations that, explicitly or implicitly, must be addressed to someone who is supposed to be interested in solving the problem in the suggested manner. Such recommendations are subject to two kinds of tests: a *validity* test and a *relevance* test. Their *validity* depends on whether or not the factual conjectures they entail actually hold, that is, on whether the recommended measures are actually capable of producing the consequences they are claimed to produce. Their *relevance* depends on whether or not their explicit or implicit addressee (provided one exists) can be assumed to be interested in seeing the predicted consequences to be brought about.

In their controversies on policy issues, economists have, quite naturally, almost exclusively focused on the *validity* of the factual claims that policy recommendations entail and have largely failed to pay systematic attention to the question of whether their recommendations pass the relevance test. But in the domain of applied science, the relevance test is no less important than the validity test if the exchange among academic peers is to avoid the danger of wandering off into a self-referential discourse that provides little, if any, help to actors in the real world who are in want of advice on how to solve the problems they care about.

The contractarian-constitutionalist perspective is very specific about the relevance test to which an economics that is true to its individualistic foundation must submit. Applied to our subject, its claim is that if the individuals involved are considered the ultimate sovereigns in organizing their common affairs—in monetary no less than in other policy matters—they must conceptually be viewed as the ultimate addressees of recommendations on how monetary regimes should be organized. And this means that in carrying out their controversies on what qualifies as a "desirable" monetary constitution, economists ought to be subject to the discipline of stating their arguments in terms that explicate the reasons why the citizens of a polity that is to choose its monetary constitution should consider a proposal as serving or not serving their common interests.

In this chapter we have made an attempt to review the modern debate on monetary regimes in light of the contractarian-constitutionalist relevance test. Because the debate has not been guided by any explicit reference to the issue of what should be considered the proper measuring rod for assessing the relative merits of alternative regime proposals—let alone by an explicit acknowledgment of the contractarian-constitutionalist standard— our ambition to systematically reconstruct and compare the various proposals along the lines intended has faced major obstacles and has produced only modest results. It may well be that many, if not most, of the authors whom we discussed tacitly presuppose that they are concerned with only the purely technical aspects of a policy issue, the normative dimension of which is essentially uncontroversial. Implicitly, even if not always explicitly, they appear to see themselves as debating which monetary regime best allows a market economy to function well, presuming that an obvious answer exists to the legitimacy question in the sense that a market economy serves people's common interests better than feasible alternative economic systems. As plausible as the latter claim may be, it does not allow one to conclude that the choice among alternative monetary regimes is a purely technical issue that monetary experts alone can decide without any further need to consult citizens' preferences.

Notes

1. Brennan and Buchanan (1981, 53ff): "What are the ultimate criteria for evaluating the basic institutions for a desirable social order? If we reject the existence of (or at least general agreement on) external ethical norms such as those sometimes claimed to be present in 'natural law' or 'revealed religion', the criteria for evaluation of institutions must in some way be *derived from individuals themselves* as the only conscious, evaluative beings.... Viewed in this light, an institution stands the test of 'legitimacy' if it can be demonstrated that it could have been, or could possibly be, *agreed* on by all persons each of whom remains unable to identify the direct impact of that institution on his private interest" (emphasis in original). The "contractarian-constitutional test" applies, as Brennan and Buchanan (54) note, to "monetary arrangements" no less than to other social institutions.

2. For a more detailed discussion see Vanberg (2007).

3. Completeness would require adding the further question of whether the proposed regime, even if it does produce the predicted outcome, is—in terms of the addressee's evaluation—preferable to other equally suitable measures. We ignore this question here because it does not add anything that is of relevance for the issue that we wish to address.

4. Horwitz (2011, 332): "We do not need a specific monetary constitution, or a monetary component to constitutions in general, to achieve the goals that Buchanan and others rightly seek. The general features of a good constitution will produce good money."

5. The new paradigm for expansive fiscal and monetary policy stimuli was also invented then. (Keynes and Henderson 1929, 37: "We conclude, therefore, that whilst an increased volume of bank-credit is probably a sine qua non of increased employment, a program of home investment which will absorb this increase is a sine qua non of the safe expansion of credit.")

6. In the United States and Switzerland, several points of this latter debate had been discussed prior to the establishment of the Federal Reserve System and the Swiss Central Bank (Smith [1936] 1990, 6).

7. We must mention that David Ricardo (1852, 408) and John Stuart Mill (1965, 682–85) already were adherents of a free-banking system if and only if the state guaranteed the redeemability of issued notes.

8. For an overview of contemporary proposals, see Vaubel (1976, 427n29).

9. This proposal has, in fact, a Mengerian origin (Mises [1912] 1924, 335). Hayek supported this proposal until he published "Monetary Nationalism" (Hayek [1937] 2011).

10. The banking vs. currency school debate of the 1930s indeed restated the classical liberal case for a free-banking system (Smith [1936] 1990; Meulen 1934). Smith and Meulen claimed that the 19th-century debate had failed to offer a systematic account of proposals for redesigning the monetary arena.

11. Rothbard's (1962, 131n) description of Hayek's proposal misses the productivity norm. The fact that Hayek regards both proposals as on an equal footing is remarkable.

12. Hayek's arguments for abandoning his previously favored proposals questioned suitability of a gold standard because of its too inflexible reaction if demand shocks occur. A commodity bundle ought to reflect the scarcity prices of input factors that fluctuate over the business cycle (Hayek [1943] 1948, 209–19).

13. Benjamin Graham includes a previously unpublished report that suggests that Keynes might have accepted a commodity standard (B. Graham 1962, 215ff).

14. As Rothbard (1962, 135) acknowledges, Henry Hazlitt also argued in numerous articles in *Newsweek* magazine (Hazlitt 2011) in favor of Mises's proposal for a gold standard with open access to money emission. According to Lawrence H. White, Mises in 1952 proposed 100 percent reserves against additional deposits created henceforth as a second-best. However, Mises defended fractional-reserve free banking from *The Theory of Money and Credit* (Mises [1912] 1924) through the last edition of *Human Action* (Mises 1966).

15. Worth mentioning is that Hayek's first encounter with stabilization policy was during his research visit in New York from 1923 to 1924. Commenting on the annual report of the Federal Reserve Board, Hayek doubted that stabilization policy could effectively fulfill the task of smoothing the business cycle (Hayek [1925] 1984). Ever since Hayek consistently doubted the efficacy of a politicized monetary policy for reasons that are broadly in line with the knowledge arguments, he later explicated in his seminal 1945 paper (Hayek [1932] 1965, [1980] 1999).

16. Friedman's distinct monetary-policy proposal was almost complete by 1959, that is, "elimination of discounting and of variable reserve requirements" while granting "open market operations as the instrument of monetary policy proper" (Friedman 1960, 50); debt management as "one major tool of monetary policy ... outside the direct control of the Federal Reserve System" (52); banking reform toward "100 percent reserves" in line with his advisers "Henry Simons and Lloyd Mints" (65; the latter three components toward banking reform were discontinued eight years later); and, finally, for international monetary policy objectives, a "system of flexible exchange rates" (84) to "define the stock of money" and "to state what the fixed rate of increase should be or how it should be determined" for internal monetary policy on an "intra-year or seasonal movements" scale (90).

17. Friedman (1967) discarded 100 percent money for various reasons. According to him, the facts as "we now know them" suggested that banking regulation was not

the main reason for the Great Depression, but monetary policy itself was (Friedman and Schwarz 1963).

18. Leland B. Yeager became an adherent of a free-banking idea because of F. A. Hayek and "other recent proponents of free choice in currency, whose writing have led him to abandon his earlier belief" (Selgin 1997, xvii). Yeager's view on how monetary policy ought to be conducted before this turning point is described in "Monetary Policy: Before and after the Freeze" ([1971] 1997). In the spirit of the 1960's monetarist status quo, Yeager wanted the central bank—in line with Friedman—to allow for a "smooth moderate growth of the domestic money supply," "worried less about maintaining so-called orderly conditions on the credit and securities markets," and aimed at securing a flexible exchange-rate regime (Yeager [1971] 1997, 322). At this time, Yeager regarded a "monetary system" that is "left entirely to private enterprise" inferior to the status quo because "satisfactory control over the quantity of money would be lacking" (Yeager [1971] 1997, 305). After his conversion, Yeager calls for a "complete withdrawal of government from money and banking" (Selgin 1997, xix).

19. BFH is an abbreviation for Fischer Black, Eugene Fama, and Robert Hall, whom Yeager and Greenfield give credit for ideas that they have incorporated in their proposal (Yeager [1983] 1997, 359n).

20. "Unlike traditional commodity standards, the BFH system separates the medium of account from the medium of settlement. The medium of account is a commodity bundle, but media of exchange (bank claims) are not redeemable for bundle commodities. Instead, the medium of exchange is redeemable for a quantity of the medium of settlement equal in value to a commodity bundle" (Cowen and Kroszner 1994, 81). This is why Cowen and Kroszner refer to this feature as "indirect convertibility."

21. The Greenfield and Yeager scheme resembles an earlier proposal for an alternative money system made by Black (1970). "Black suggests the use of shares of a portfolio of common stock as money, that is, as a generally accepted medium of exchange" (White 1984a, 710).

22. Stimulated by Hayek's *Denationalization*, Selgin was led to further explore counterarguments against the contemporary belief of economists that "money will not manage itself" (Selgin 1988, ix). He advanced the renewed free-banking debate of the late 1970s and early 1980s along with Lawrence White's studies on free banking in Britain (1984b). Selgin is in favor of nominal GDP-targeting as an alternative monetary policy objective (Selgin 2010). For a comprehensive discussion of a free banking and nominal GDP-targeting, see his blog entry http://www.freebanking. org/2013/06/19/free-banking-and-ngdp-targeting/.

23. Buchanan (1986) categorizes three basic monopolistic regimes: a central bank "i.e. a benevolent despot" (141) neither subject to constitutional nor electoral constraints, a monolithic agent subject to direct electoral pressure, and a "monolithic agent" free from "direct electoral pressure but bound by certain general constitutional rules."

24. In retrospect, Buchanan notes that his 1962 argument for predictability was "implicitly based on the contractual model" (Buchanan and Tideman [1975] 2001). While D'Amico suspects that his claim "is simply due to a distortion in retrospective autobiography … to create a theoretical continuity, even where there may be none" (D'Amico 2007, 310n24), the simultaneous publication of *The Calculus of Consent* (Buchanan and Tullock 1962) as well as references to the assessment of "the average man" as opposed to the "consensus among experts" (Buchanan 1962, 181) support Buchanan's retrospective assessment.

25. Comparing inflation with a tax on money, Brennan and Buchanan come to a twofold conclusion: first, that for individuals "there is no escape" and, second, that the "inflation tax is more closely analogous to a tax on capital assets than to a tax on any income or expenditure" (1981, 45). The latter is meant in the sense that, because capital is accumulated over time and "cannot be consumed immediately," a "tax on capital that is not anticipated long in advance can effectively confiscate capital values" (45). "As more and more people go through a learning process and come to predict the monetary issue policy of the government accurately, … incentives for government (as well as individuals) to seek ways and means of devising some sort of enforceable agreement or contract to avoid the dilemma of the monetary game are increased" (46–47). On the basis of the preceding diagnosis, Brennan and Buchanan judge "unconstrained monopoly franchises" as "illegitimate" (53) and advocate constitutional constraints as protection for citizens and taxpayers.

26. In the paper "Property as a Guarantor of Liberty," Buchanan ([1993] 2001, 249) has emphasized the "property-expanding role of monetary credibility" as an argument in favor of an "effective monetary constitution … that would guarantee stability in the value of the monetary unit" (257). Explicitly referring to individuals' interests in the liberty that private property in money can provide, he sees a major role of an "effective monetary" constitution in the "protection of the liberties of persons" (248) that it provides over and beyond "the efficiency-enhancing characteristics of predictability in the value of the monetary unit" (249).

27. Mises's regression theorem initially explains the emergence of money: "If we trace the purchasing power of money back step by step, we finally arrive at the point at which the service of the good concerned as a medium of exchange begins. At this point yesterday's exchange value is exclusively determined by the nonmonetary-industrial demand which is displayed only by those who want to use this good for other employments than that of a medium of exchange" (Mises [1949] 1966, 409). Younger followers of Mises, however, understand the regression theorem as a principle for how to set up a monetary regime and—as discussed below—submit normative reasons for the theorem.

28. In addition, Horwitz's proposal resembles Mises's plan for a banking reform: "What is needed to prevent any further credit expansion is to place the banking business under the general rules of commercial and civil laws compelling every individual and firm to fulfill all obligations in full compliance with the terms of the contract" (Mises 1966, 505).

29. Selgin and White (1996) became increasingly aware of the fact that the Rothbardian adherents such as Hans-Herman Hoppe, Jesús Huerta de Soto (1995), and Jörg Guido Hülsmann (1995) criticized their vision of a free-banking system. In countering the criticism, Selgin and White (1996) emphasize that they are opponents of fiat currency and argue for a fractional reserve system that can safeguard a stable monetary regime.

30. Yeager does not read any normative content into Mises's regression theorem. He views it as a solution to "the problem" why money is "demanded for its purchasing power" as follows: the value of money today is determined by its value yesterday, which was determined "by supply and demand in light of its value the day before, and so on back in history to the time when some commodity, valuable for its own usefulness, had not quite yet evolved into money" (Yeager [1982] 1997, 152–53). For further discussion on the regression theorem, see Yeager ([1982] 1997, 151–58) and Roger W. Garrison's dissertation, "The Austrian-Neoclassic Relation: A Study in Monetary Dynamics," mentioned in Yeager ([1983] 1997, 152n209).

31. Vanberg ([1986] 1994, 214): "If natural rights are … potentially disagreeable, then the question arises of how conflicting views of these rights are to be settled (Mises 1949, 282). At this point liberal natural rights theorists seem to face a dilemma: either, they claim that the valid interpretation of these rights is to be derived from some source independent of, and superior to, the individual's own judgments, a claim that would be incompatible with the premise that the individual's own, subjective evaluations are the ultimate source from which judgments about the 'goodness' of social states or events are to be derived. Or they consider the judgments of the persons concerned as the ultimate source from which the definition of 'natural rights' is to be derived, in which case it is hard to see how a definition of rights can be provided along any other line of argument than an individualistic-contractarian notion. That would imply, however, abandoning the claim that rights can be defined in absolute terms, independent of actual social recognition."

32. Any other monetary proposal that does not conform to this "norm" is said to eventually lead to a centrally planned system. Especially among German libertarians (Hülsmann, Hoppe, Baader, Bagus, Polleit), this deterministic outlook is widely shared.

33. (Mises [1949] 1966, 38): "In the concept of money all the theorems of monetary theory are already implied. The quantity theory does not add to our knowledge anything which is not virtually contained in the concept of money. It transforms, develops, and unfolds; it only analyzes and is therefore tautological like the theorem of Pythagoras in relation to the concept of the rectangular triangle."

34. See, in particular, Salin (1990); Reisman (1996); Huerta de Soto ([2006] 2011). See also Skousen (1996); Block (1988); Hoppe (1993, ch. 3; 1994); Hoppe, Hülsmann, and Block, (1998); special issue on "L'Or, fondement monétaire du commerce international" in *Le point de rencontre—libéral et croyant* 49 (October 1996); special issue on "Deflation and Monetary Policy" in *Quarterly Journal of Austrian Economics* 6, no. 4 (2003).

35. In retrospect, Hayek ([1980] 1999, 249) reported: "I have only succeeded in convincing economists and young people who are at the point of entering economic life of the attractions of the competitive issue of money, about which there is indeed no basic difficulty. I must admit that I have not yet persuaded a single banker that this situation is practical. They all complain that it is so completely different to what is now regarded as banking and they fear that banking of the traditional sort would disappear."

36. We limit our analysis to Hayek ([1978] 1999), White (1983), Yeager (2010) and the proposals for a depoliticized central-bank system made by Goodhart (2003) and McCallum (2010).

37. See Selgin (1999) for a discussion on price-level stabilization in Hayek's *Denationalization*.

38. The "system would provide a stable unit for pricing, invoicing, accounting, economic calculation, borrowing and lending, and writing contracts reaching into the future" (Yeager [1983] 1997, 372).

39. For a critical discussion of this argument see, for example, Selgin and White (2005). Cowen and Kroszner (1994, 148) trace this discussion back to the conflicting perspectives on the origin of money from an evolutionary (Menger) and a chartalist view (George Friedrich Knapp), highlighting the role of German nominalism in this regard.

40. Free-banking advocates, as well, have pointed to this negative aspect of denationalization. As Selgin (1999) and White (1999) argue, this could undermine and stall the advantageous effects of the evolutionary discovery process for the most appraised medium of exchange. Accordingly, they propose only one type of outside money that should be redeemable into a commodity (Selgin 1988; see discussion earlier in this

chapter). Yeager advocates a three-step approach to this problem: by completely withdrawing base money (i.e., cashless economy), by abolishing the central bank, and by defining a broad-based consumption bundle as the unit of account. Under such a regime, money would completely disappear from the citizens' wallets as tangible coins and notes and be replaced by artificial, that is, electronic deposits in the unit of account of the composite money. One can only speculate whether citizens could have a common interest in a cashless economy (Yeager), an economy without a single medium of exchange (Hayek), or one with a commodity-based money (Selgin and White).

41. For Goodhart (1989), a central feature of a monetary constitution is, in addition to central-bank independence and an externally set monetary-policy objective, that it supports the banking system by acting as a lender of last resort. Discussion of this function has been highly controversial (White 1999, 74).

References

Alesina, Alberto, and Lawrence H. Summers. 1993. "Central Bank Independence and Macroeconomic Performance: Some Comparative Evidence." *Journal of Money, Credit and Banking* 25 (2): 151–62.

Bagus, Philipp. 2009. "Monetary Reform: The Case for Button-Pushing." *New Perspectives on Political Economy* 5 (2): 111–28.

Bernholz, Peter. 2003. *Monetary Regimes and Inflation: History, Economic and Political Relationships*. Cheltenham, UK: Elgar.

Black, Fischer. 1970. "Banking and Interest Rate in a World without Money." *Journal of Bank Research* 1: 9–20.

Block, Walter. 1988. "Fractional Reserve Banking: An Interdisciplinary Perspective." In *Man, Economy, and Liberty*, edited by Walter Block and Llewellyn H. Rockwell, Jr., pp. 24–32. Auburn, AL: Ludwig von Mises Institute.

———. 2004. "Radical Libertarianism: Applying Libertarian Principles to Dealing with the Unjust Government, Part I." *Reason Papers* 27 (Fall): 113–30.

———. 2006. "Radical Libertarianism: Applying Libertarian Principles to Dealing with the Unjust Government, Part II." *Reason Papers* 28 (Fall): 85–109.

Borio, Claudio. 2008. "The Financial Turmoil of 2007–?: A Preliminary Assessment of Some Policy Recommendations." BIS Working Papers no. 251, Bank for International Settlements, Basel, Switzerland.

Brennan, Geoffrey H., and James M. Buchanan. 1981. *Monopoly in Money and Inflation: The Case for a Constitution to Discipline Government*. London: Institute of Economic Affairs.

Buchanan, James M. 1962. "Predictability: The Criterion of Monetary Constitutions." In *In Search of a Monetary Constitution*, edited by Leland B. Yeager, pp. 155–81. Cambridge, MA: Harvard University Press.

———. 1986. "Can Policy Activism Succeed? A Public Choice Perspective." In *The Monetary vs. Fiscal Policy Debate Lessons from Two Debates*, edited by R. W. Hafer, pp. 139–50. Totowa, NJ: Rowman and Allenheld.

———. 1990. "Europe's Constitutional Opportunity." In *Europe's Constitutional Future*. IEA readings series 33, pp. 1–20. London: Institute of Economic Affairs.

———. (1993) 2001. "Property as a Guarantor of Liberty." In *Federalism, Liberty and the Law: The Collected Works of James M. Buchanan*, vol. 18, pp. 216–59. Indianapolis: Liberty Fund.

———. 2010. "The Constitutionalization of Money." *Cato Journal* 30 (2): 251–58.

Buchanan, James M., and Nicolaus Tideman. (1975) 2001. "Gold, Money and the Law: The Limits of Governmental Monetary Authority." In *Gold, Money and the Law*, edited by H. G. Manne and R. L. Miller, pp. 9–69. Chicago: Aldine. Reprinted in *Federalism, Liberty and the Law, The Collected Works of James M. Buchanan*, vol. 18, pp. 385–431. Indianapolis: Liberty Fund. Citations are to *The Collected Works*.

Buchanan, James M., and Gordon Tullock. 1962. *The Calculus of Consent: Logical Foundations of Constitutional Democracy*. Ann Arbor: University of Michigan Press.

Cowen, Tyler, and Randall Kroszner. 1994. *Explorations in the New Monetary Economics*. Oxford: Blackwell.

D'Amico, Domenico. 2007. "Buchanan on Monetary Constitutions." *Constitutional Political Economy* 18 (4): 301–18.

Eucken, Walter. 1949. "Die Wettbewerbsordnung und ihre Verwirklichung." In *ORDO* 2: 1–100.

Fama, Eugene. 1980. "Banking in the Theory of Finance." *Journal of Monetary Economics* 6 (1): 39–57.

Friedman, Milton. 1948. "A Monetary and Fiscal Framework for Economic Stability." *American Economic Journal* 38 (3): 245–64.

———. 1953. "Commodity Reserve Currency." In *Essays in Positive Economics*, pp. 204–50. Chicago: Chicago University Press.

———. 1960. *A Program for Monetary Stability*. New York: Fordham University Press.

———. 1967. "The Monetary Theory and Policy of Henry Simons." *Journal of Law and Economics* 10 (2): 1–13.

———. 1968. "The Role of Monetary Policy." *American Economic Review* 58 (1): 1–17.

———. 1971. "Government Revenue from Inflation." *Journal of Political Economy* 79 (4): 846–59.

———. 2003. "The Counter-Revolution in Monetary Theory." In *Money, Inflation and the Constitutional Position of the Central Bank*, edited by Milton Friedman and Charles A. E. Goodhart, pp. 64–90. London: Institute of Economic Affairs.

Friedman, Milton, and Anna Schwartz. 1963. *A Monetary History of the United States 1867–1960*. Princeton: Princeton University Press.

Goodhart, Charles A. E. 1989. "Central Banking." In *The New Palgrave: Money*, edited by John Eatwell, Murray Milgate, and Peter Newman, pp. 88–92. New York: Norton.

———. 2003. "The Constitutional Position of the Central Bank." In *Money, Inflation and the Constitutional Position of the Central Bank*, edited by Milton Friedman and Charles A. E. Goodhart, pp. 91–108. London: Institute of Economic Affairs.

Graham, Benjamin. 1937. *Storage and Stability*. New York: McGraw-Hill.

———. 1944. *World Commodities and World Currency*. New York: McGraw-Hill.

———. 1962. "The Commodity-Reserve Currency Proposal." In *In Search of a Monetary Constitution*, edited by Leland B. Yeager, pp. 182–214. Cambridge, MA: Harvard University Press.

Graham, Frank D. 1936. "Reserve Money and the 100 Percent Proposal." *American Economic Review* 26 (3): 428–40.

———. 1942. *Social Goals and Economics Institutions*. Princeton: Princeton University Press.

Greenfield, Robert, and Leland Yeager. 1983. "A Laissez-Faire Approach to Monetary Stability." *Journal of Money, Credit and Banking* 15 (3): 302–15.

Hall, Robert. 1982. "Monetary Trends in the United States and the United Kingdom: A Review from the Perspective of New Developments in Monetary Economics." *Journal of Economic Literature* 20 (4): 1552–56.

Hayek, Friedrich A. von. (1925) 1984. "The Monetary Policy of the United States after the Recovery from the 1920s Crisis." In *Money, Capital and Fluctuations*. Chicago: University of Chicago Press.

———. (1932) 1965. *Was der Goldwährung geschehen ist.* Tübingen: Mohr.

———. (1937) 2011. "Monetärer Nationalismus und internationale Stabilität." Reprinted in *Entnationalisierung des Geldes: Schriften zur Währungspolitik und Währungsordnung*, pp. 45–119. Tübingen: Mohr Siebeck.

———. (1943) 1948. "A Commodity Reserve Currency." In *Individualism and Economic Order*, pp. 209–19. Chicago: University of Chicago Press.

———. 1960. *The Constitution of Liberty.* Chicago: University of Chicago Press.

———. 1975. "Financial Power to the People!" *The Daily Telegraph*, October 1.

———. (1976) 1999. "Choice in Currency." In *The Collected Works of F. A. Hayek, Good Money, Part II*, edited by Stephen Kresge, pp. 115–24. Indianapolis: Liberty Fund.

———. (1978) 1999. "Denationalization of Money." Reprinted in *The Collected Works of F. A. Hayek, Good Money, Part II*, edited by Stephen Kresge, pp. 128–236. Indianapolis: Liberty Fund.

———. (1979) 1999. "Toward a Free Market Monetary System." In *The Collected Works of F. A. Hayek, Good Money, Part II*, edited by Stephen Kresge, pp. 230–37. Indianapolis: Liberty Fund.

———. (1980) 1999. "The Future Value of Money." In *The Collected Works of F. A. Hayek, Good Money, Part II*, edited by Stephen Kresge, pp. 238–52. Indianapolis: Liberty Fund.

———. 1990. *Denationalization of Money: The Argument Refined.* London: Institute of Economic Affairs.

———. 1994. *Hayek on Hayek: An Autobiographical Dialogue.* Edited by Stephen Kresge and Leif Wenar. London: Routledge.

Hazlitt, Henry. 2011. *Business Tides: The Newsweek Era of Henry Hazlitt.* Edited by Marc Doolittle. Auburn, AL: Ludwig von Mises Institute.

Hicks, John R. 1935. "A Suggestion for Simplifying the Theory of Money." *Economica* 2 (5): 1–19.

Hoppe, Hans-Hermann. 1993. *The Economics and Ethics of Private Property.* Boston: Kluwer.

———. 1994. "How Is Fiat Money Possible?—or, the Devolution of Money and Credit." *Review of Austrian Economics* 7 (2): 49–74.

Hoppe, Hans-Hermann, Jörg Guido Hülsmann, and Walter Block. 1998. "Against Fiduciary Media." *Quarterly Journal of Austrian Economics* 1 (1): 19–50.

Horwitz, Steven. 2011. "Do We Need a Distinct Monetary Constitution?" *Journal of Economic Behavior and Organization* 80 (2): 331–38.

Huerta de Soto, Jesús. 1988. "Conjectural History and Beyond." *Humane Studies Review* 6 (2): 10.

———. 1995. "A Critical Analysis of Central Banks and Fractional Reserve Free Banking from the Austrian Perspective." *Review of Austrian Economics* 8 (2): 25–38.

———. (2006) 2011. *Geld, Bankkredit und Konjunkturzyklen.* Trans. Philipp Bagus. Stuttgart: Lucius & Lucius. Originally published as *Money, Bank Credit, and Economic Cycles.* Auburn, AL: Ludwig von Mises Institute.

Hülsmann, Jörg Guido. 1995. "Free Banking and the Free Bankers." *Review of Austrian Economics* 9 (1): 3–53.

———. 1998. *Logik der Währungskonkurrenz*. Essen: Management Akademie Verlag.

———. 2008. *The Ethics of Money Production*. Auburn, AL: Ludwig von Mises Institute.

Janssen, Hauke. 2006. *Milton Friedman und die "Monetaristische Revolution" in Deutschland*. Marburg: Metropolis-Verlag.

Keynes, John M. 1936. *The General Theory of Employment Interest and Money*. London: Macmillan.

Keynes, John M., and Henry D. Henderson. 1929. *Can Lloyd George Do It?* London: The Nation and Athenaeum.

Klein, Benjamin. 1974. "The Competitive Supply of Money." *Journal of Money, Credit and Banking* 6 (4): 423–53.

Köhler, Ekkehard, and Stefan Kolev. 2011. "The Conjoint Quest for a Liberal Positive Program: 'Old Chicago," Freiberg, and Hayek." HWWI Research Paper 109, Hamburg Institute of International Economics, Hamburg, Germany.

Kydland, Finn E., and Edward C. Prescott. 1977. "Rules Rather Than Discretion: The Inconsistency of Optimal Plans." *Journal of Political Economy* 85 (3): 101–21.

Lucas, Robert E. 1976. "Econometric Policy Evaluation: A Critique." *Carnegie-Rochester Conference Series on Public Policy* 1 (1): 19–46.

Lutz, Friedrich A. (1936) 1962. "Das Grundproblem der Geldverfassung." Reprinted in *Geld und Währung*, pp. 28–103. Tübingen: Mohr.

Machlup, Fritz. 1925. *Die Goldkernwährung*. Halberstadt: Meyer.

McCallum, Bennett T. 2010. "Alternatives to the Fed?" *Cato Journal* 30 (3): 439–50.

Meulen, Henry. 1934. *Free Banking—An Outline of a Policy of Individualism*. London: Macmillan.

Miksch, Leonard. 1949. "Die Geldschöpfung in der Gleichgewichtstheorie," ORDO 2, pp. 308–328.

Mill, John S. 1965. *Principles of Political Economy: with some of their Applications to Social Philosophy*. Edited with an introduction by William J. Ashley. New York: Kelly.

Mises, Ludwig von. (1912) 1924. *Theorie des Geldes und der Umlaufsmittel*. Munich and Leipzig: Duncker und Humblot.

———. 1928. *Geldwertstabilisierung und Konjunkturpolitik*. Jena, Germany: Gustav Fischer.

———. 1940. *Nationalökonomie, Theorie des Handelns und Wirtschaftens*. Geneva: Editions Union.

———. 1949. *Human Action: A Treatise on Economics*. 1st ed. New Haven: Yale University Press.

———. 1966. *Human Action: A Treatise on Economics*. 3rd ed. Chicago: Regnery.

North, Douglass C., John H. Wallis, and Barry R. Weingast. 2006. "A Conceptual Framework for Interpreting Recorded Human History." NBER Working Paper Series no. 12795, National Bureau of Economic Research, Cambridge, MA.

O'Driscoll, Gerald P. 1986. "Deregulation and Monetary Reform." In *Economic and Financial Policy Review*, Federal Reserve Bank of Dallas, pp. 19–31.

Reisman, George. 1996. *Capitalism: A Treatise on Economics*, Ottawa: Jameson Books.

Ricardo, David. 1852. "Proposals for an Economical and Secure Currency." In *The Works of David Ricardo*, edited by John R. McCulloch, pp. 395–412. London: John Murray.

Rothbard, Murray N. 1956. "Toward a Reconstruction of Utility and Welfare Economics." In *On Freedom and Free Enterprise: Essays in Honor of Ludwig von Mises*, edited by M. Sennholz, pp. 224–62. Princeton: D. van Nostrand.

————. 1962. "The Case for a 100 Percent Gold Dollar." In *In Search of a Monetary Constitution*, edited by Leland B. Yeager, pp. 94–166. Cambridge, MA: Harvard University Press.

————. 1995. "Taking Money Back." *The Freeman* 45 (9–11), September, October, and November issues.

Salin, Pascal. 1990. *La vérité sur la monnaie*. Paris: Odile Jacob.

Sechrest, Larry J. (1993) 2008. *Free Banking, Theory, History and a Laissez-Faire Model*. Auburn, AL: Ludwig von Mises Institute.

Selgin, George. 1988. *The Theory of Free Banking: Money Supply under Competitive Note Issue*. Lanham, MD: Rowman & Littlefield and Cato Institute.

————. 1997. "Introduction." In Leland B. Yeager, *The Fluttering Veil*, pp. xi–xx. Indianapolis: Liberty Fund.

————. 1999. "Hayek versus Keynes on the Price Level." *History of Political Economy* 31 (4): 699–721.

————. 2000. "Should We Let Banks Create Money?" *The Independent Review* 5 (1): 93–100.

————. 2010. "The Futility of Central Banking." *Cato Journal* 30 (3): 465–74.

Selgin, George, and Lawrence H. White. 1994. "How Would the Invisible Hand Handle Money?" *Journal of Economic Literature* 32 (4): 1718–49.

————. 1996. "In Defense of Fiduciary Media—or, We Are *Not* Devo(lutionists), We Are Misesians!" *Review of Austrian Economics* 9 (2): 83–107.

————. 2005. "Credible Currency: A Constitutional Perspective." *Constitutional Political Economy* 16 (1): 83–107.

Simons, Henry C. (1936) 1948. "Rules versus Authorities in Monetary Policy." Reprinted in Henry C. Simons (1948), *Economic Policy for a Free Society*. pp. 160–83. Chicago: University of Chicago Press.

————. 1948. *Economic Policy for a Free Society*. Chicago: University of Chicago Press.

Skousen, Mark. 1996. *Economics of a Pure Gold Standard*. 3rd ed. Irvington-on-Hudson, NY: Foundation for Economic Education.

Smith, Vera C. (1936) 1990. *The Rationale of Central Banking*. London: King. Reprint, Indianapolis: Liberty Fund.

Sumner, Scott. 1989. "Using Futures Instruments Prices to Target Nominal Income." *Bulletin of Economic Research* 41 (2) 157–62.

————. 1995. "The Impact of Futures Price Targeting on the Precision and Credibility of Monetary Policy." *Journal of Money, Credit and Banking* 27 (1): 89–106.

Tullock, Gordon. 1975. "Competing Monies." *Journal of Money, Credit and Banking* 7 (4): 492–6.

Vanberg, Viktor J. (1983) 1994. "Liberal Evolutionism and Contractarian Constitutionalism (Hayek and Buchanan compared)." In *Rules and Choice in Economics*, edited by Viktor J. Vanberg, pp. 195–207. London: Routledge.

————. (1986) 1994. "Individual Choice and Institutional Constraints: The Normative Element in Classical and Contractarian Liberalism." In *Rules and Choice in Economics*, edited by Viktor J. Vanberg, pp. 208–34. London: Routledge.

————. (1992) 1994. "Organizations as Constitutional Systems." In *Rules and Choice in Economics*, edited by Viktor J. Vanberg, pp. 125–43. London: Routledge.

————. 2007. "Democracy, Citizen Sovereignty and Constitutional Economics." In *Public Choice and the Challenges of Democracy*, edited by José Casas Pardo and Pedro Schwartz, pp. 101–20. Cheltenham, UK, and Northampton, MA: Edward Elgar.

———. 2008. *Wettbewerb und Regelordnung.* Edited by N. Goldschmidt and M. Wohlgemuth. Tübingen: Mohr Siebeck.

———. 2009. "Evolving Preferences and Policy Advice in Democratic Society." Papers on Economics and Evolution no. 0919, Max Planck Institute of Evolutionary Economics Group, Jena, Germany.

Vaubel, Roland. 1976. "Freier Wettbewerb zwischen Währungen?" *Wirtschaftsdienst* 8: 422–28.

Weber, Axel. 2008. "Financial Markets and Monetary Policy." *BIS Review* 116/2008.

White, Lawrence H. 1983. "Competitive Money, Inside and Out." *Cato Journal* 3 (1): 281–304.

———. 1984a. "Competitive Payments Systems and the Unit of Account." *American Economics Review* 74 (4): 699–712.

———. 1984b. *Free Banking in Britain: Theory, Experience and Debate, 1800–1845.* New York: Cambridge University Press.

———. 1999. *The Theory of Monetary Institutions.* Malden, MA: Blackwell.

White, William R. 2006. "Is Price Stability Enough?" BIS Working Papers no. 205, Bank for International Settlements, Basel, Switzerland.

Wood, Geoffrey E. 2003. "Introduction." In *Money, Inflation and the Constitutional Position of the Central Bank*, edited by Milton Friedman and Charles A. E. Goodhart, pp. 21–40. London: Institute of Economic Affairs.

Woodford, Michael. 2003. *Interest in Prices: Foundations of a Theory of Monetary Policy.* Princeton: Princeton University Press.

Yeager, Leland B. 1952. *An Evaluation of Freely-Fluctuating Exchange Rates.* New York: Columbia University.

———, ed. 1962a. *In Search of a Monetary Constitution.* Cambridge, MA: Harvard University Press.

———. 1962b. "Introduction." In *In Search of a Monetary Constitution*, edited by Leland B. Yeager, pp. 1–25. Cambridge, MA: Harvard University Press.

———. (1971) 1997. "Monetary Policy: Before and after the Freeze." In *The Fluttering Veil: Essays on Monetary Equilibrium*, edited by George Selgin, pp. 1–25. Indianapolis: Liberty Fund.

———. (1982) 1997. "Individual and Overall Viewpoints in Monetary Theory." In *The Fluttering Veil: Essays on Monetary Equilibrium*, edited by George Selgin, pp. 137–62. Indianapolis: Liberty Fund. Reprint with permission of Israel M. Kirzner.

———. (1983) 1997. "Stable Money and Free-Market Currencies." In *The Fluttering Veil: Essays on Monetary Equilibrium*, edited by George Selgin, pp. 337–62. Indianapolis: Liberty Fund.

———. 2009. "The Continuing Search for a Monetary Constitution." Draft paper presented at the Summer Institute for the Preservation of the History of Economic Thought, University of Richmond, VA, June 19–22.

———. 2010. "Privatizing Money." *Cato Journal* 30 (3): 417–38.

5. Monetary Regimes, Stability, Politics, and Inflation in History

Peter Bernholz

Money has been one of the most important cultural inventions during human cultural development. Without it, humanity would never have been able to reach the level of economic well-being of modern wealthy societies, connected with better health and education and longer lifespans. But the history of money has also been from its very introduction the history of its debasement and loss of value. Or as Henri Pirenne (1951, 258) expressed it for the late Middle Ages:

> The progress in the circulation of money allowed princes to use it for their profit. Having the right to mint money, they thought themselves to be entitled to handle it in the interest of their treasury without taking note that this meant their enrichment at the damage of the public. The more indispensable money became for economic life, the more it was changed by those who had the right to mint it. Especially since the 13th century, it became more and more a general practice to multiply the new issues of money with each time the purpose to diminish its value. (author's translation)

As we shall see, this instability of money brought about by political influences was not limited to medieval times. The pattern was already established in antiquity and took its highest toll only during the 20th century. Still, for our purpose, it is important to realize that the debasement of money has not taken place at a constant speed, that certain periods even enjoyed a long stability, whereas the debasement accelerated in others and took on catastrophic dimensions in many

---

A version of this chapter will also appear as an article in the journal *Procesos de Mercado*. Printed here by permission.

countries during the 20th century. In this chapter, I argue that these differences depend on the changing nature of money, on the rules or the monetary regimes by which it is governed, and on political pressures of rulers and states working in favor of inflation.

Examples of Debasement and Stability in Antiquity and the Middle Ages

Wars are one of the well-known reasons for the debasement of currencies. Athens had to replace its silver drachmas with silver-coated copper coins during the end of the Peloponnesian War, and Rome's currency suffered debasement during the Punic Wars. Debasements that extend over several decades, however, can scarcely be explained only because of war. They are usually brought about by rulers and governments financing budget deficits by debasing money without the excessive expenditures used to finance a war effort. For instance, this was the case in Ptolemaic Egypt from about the beginning of the second century BC (see Figure 5.1) and in the late Roman Empire

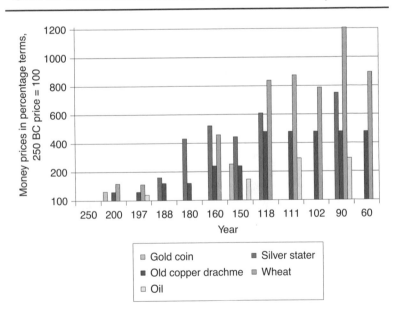

Figure 5.1
COPPER MONEY INFLATION IN PTOLEMAIC EGYPT, 250–60 BC

in the fourth century AD (see Figure 5.2). For both cases, we have a sufficient number of prices to document the ensuing inflation. Note that logarithms were taken for the Roman prices because otherwise the curves showing the development of prices would have gone through the roof. This Roman inflation seems to be the worst ever occurring on the basis of a metallic monetary standard.

Let us now look for periods of monetary stability and ask ourselves the reasons for this favorable development, given the bias of rulers to misuse their monopoly on issuing currency. Most of the Greek city-states seem to have had stable currencies for several centuries beginning at about 550 BC. Let me mention especially Athens and Corinth. Athens successfully restored its silver currency, the drachme, after the interruption caused by the Peloponnesian War shortly before

---

Figure 5.2

DEVELOPMENT OF LOG OF PRICES OF GOLD, WHEAT, AND
BARLEY IN DEBASED ROMAN CURRENCY IN EGYPT, AD 300–380

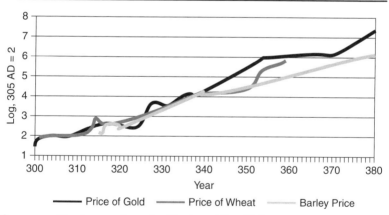

SOURCES: Prodromos-Ioannis Prodromidis (February 2006): *Another View on an Old Inflation: Environment and Policies in the Roman Empire up to Diocletian's Price Edict.* Athens: Centre of Planning and Economic Research, No. 85, www.hepe.gr/pdf/D.P/dp_85.pdf. The Figure for 311 has been taken from Rostovtzeff, Michael: (1979/1926): *Social and Economic History of the Roman Empire*, 2 vols., 2nd ed., Oxford: At the Clarendon Press, p. 471.

NOTE: The year is not given. I have taken the last year of Diocletian's reign.

400 BC. Its currency served as the first international medium of exchange in the Aegean Sea and the eastern Mediterranean. This is probably the reason for the unchanged appearance of the drachme (see Figure 5.3), which preserved its archaic style for a long time in contrast with currencies of other city-states, which were changed to the classic appearance. This recalls the unchanged appearance of the dollar bill nowadays.

Figure 5.3
ATHENIAN TETRADRACHMA

SOURCE: Athena/Eule, 460-450, Tetradrachmon, 17.14g, Durchmesser 25mm.

Corinth was an important trading city for centuries until it was destroyed by the Romans in 147 BC. The city was a keen competitor of Athens and fought it as an ally of Sparta during the Peloponnesian War. Like several other Greek city-states, it kept the silver standard that had been introduced by the island of Aegina around 600 BC even after the island had been conquered by Athens in the mid-fifth century. Table 5.1 demonstrates the long-term stability of these two currencies.

It follows that the Athenian money remained stable at least for four centuries and that of Corinth at least for 250 years. How can this stability be explained? What were the reasons? Two different hypotheses can be proposed. For Athens, and perhaps to a minor degree for Corinth, their currencies were used internationally and circulated widely outside their borders. Therefore governments had no monetary incentive to debase their currency because the profit gained from that measure was probably smaller than the seigniorage won by minting drachmas or talents not only for domestic but also for international circulation. Moreover, a debasement would have made the business of Athenian and Corinthian traders much more difficult abroad, and their trading activities were of the greatest importance for providing these cities with the necessary imports—

Table 5.1

WEIGHTS OF ATHENIAN AND CORINTHIAN SILVER COINS IN GRAMS

Athens						
Years (BC)	575–525	525–500	525–500	460–450	393–300	167–166
Didrachme	8.429	n.a.	n.a.	n.a.	n.a.	n.a.
Tetradrachme	n.a.	16.949	16.94	17.14	17.19	16.89
Corinth						
Years (BC)	570–550	515–500	525–500	460	430	320
Stater	8.55	8.61	8.66	8.67	8.59	8.61

SOURCE: Jenkins and Küthmann (1972).

NOTE: n.a. = not applicable.

especially of grain. Generally, foreign trade is much more important for small states than for bigger ones. A second reason for the stability of these moneys could be the tough foreign policy, military, and trade competition of Greek city-states. Any debasement would have damaged their reputation and led to a diversion of trade to cities with more stable currencies. This would also have implied a weakening of the relative strength of their foreign policy and military power. Obviously, both of these factors working for monetary stability were weaker in the case of Ptolemaic Egypt and practically absent in imperial Rome.

While keeping these two hypotheses concerning stability in mind, let us now turn to the Middle Ages. We know already from Pirenne (as quoted previously) that debasement was a common experience during that period. Pirenne (1951, 60; 2005, 114) thus concluded:

> Since the end of the 12th century the monetary disorder had reached a situation that a reform became necessary. It is significant that it was the biggest trading place of that period, Venice, which took the initiative. It was the Doge Henri Dandolo who issued a new type of money, the gros or matapan in 1192, which weighed a little more than two grams and was worth 12 old deniers.

This issue of the new silver coin was soon followed by the minting of the golden ducat by Venice and the golden *fiorino* by Florence. The ducat and the florin proved to be stable for several centuries. By contrast, the debasement of most other currencies went on, as shown by the exchange rates for the golden florin (Table 5.2).

If we look at the figures with base 100, we realize, for instance, that the *maravedi* of Castille fell to less than 1/46th of its value, from 1300 to 1500, and the *schilling* of Cologne to nearly 1/16th in terms of florins. Other coins also lost in value, though not as dramatically. But is there not also a loss of value for the *soldi* of Florence and of Venice? This is certainly true. However, these losses in great part may have been caused by the inability until more recent times of issuers of money to maintain fixed exchange rates between their different kinds of coins, especially as far as token money was concerned. And between gold and valuable silver coins, they faced the problem of the fluctuations of the relative price of these commodi-

Table 5.2
DEBASEMENT OF CURRENCIES IN THE LATE MIDDLE AGES AND
DEVELOPMENT OF EXCHANGE RATES FOR THE FLORIN

Country	ca. 1300	ca. 1400	ca. 1500	Currency
Castille	5.80	66.00	375.00	Maravedi
	100.00	1,137.93	6,465.52	
Cologne	6.67	42.00	112.00	Schilling
	100.00	630.00	1,680.00	
Flanders	13.13	33.50	80.00	Groot
	100.00	255.24	609.52	
Austria	2.22	5.00	11.00	Schilling
	100.00	225.00	495.00	
France	10.00	22.00	38.75	Sou
	100.00	220.00	387.50	
Hanse	8.00	10.50	31.00	Schilling (of Luebeck)
	100.00	131.25	387.50	
Rome	34.00	73.00	130.00	Soldo
	100.00	214.71	382.35	
Florence	46.50	77.92	140.00	Soldo
	100.00	167.56	301.08	
Bohemia	12.00	20.00	30.00	Groschen (of Prague)
	100.00	166.67	250.00	
Venice	74.00	93.00	124.00	Soldo
	100.00	125.68	167.57	
Aragon	11.50	12.71	16.00	Sueldo
	100.00	110.51	139.13	
England	2.67	3.00	4.58	Shilling
	100.00	112.50	171.88	

SOURCE: Spufford (1986), Table I.

NOTE: Base 100 rows show depreciations of other coins in the form of proportional amounts needed to purchase the gold florin compared to the c. 1300 base.

ties, so they could not maintain fixed exchange rates because of Gresham's law.

But what were the reasons for the long-term stability of the ducat and the florin? For both currencies, the hypotheses put forward previously seem to offer an explanation. Venice and Florence, too, were city-states with wide international trading interests and whose currencies circulated far outside their borders. And again, both states were members of a tough competitive system of Italian states and outside states.

Our hypotheses are also supported by two other examples: the Bank of Amsterdam, founded in 1606, and the Bank of Hamburg, founded 10 years later (Kindleberger 1984, 47–49). Both were deposit banks serving only merchants, and the deposits were backed 100 percent in silver. Customers could use their accounts for paying their obligations to other members or to be credited for payments received. The stability of both currencies lasted for about 180 years. Both banks were private or quasi-private institutions and supported by the leading merchants. The province to which Amsterdam belonged (Holland) was one of the rather independent constituent states of the Netherlands, and Hamburg was an independent city-state of the Holy Roman Empire. The stability of their stable giro money ended only when Hamburg was occupied by French troops under Napoleon and when the Dutch East India Company incurred losses and pressured the Bank of Amsterdam to finance them by drawing on its 100 percent silver reserve.

After the "discovery" of the new world, the Spanish silver coins, especially the *peso a ocho*, became for centuries the stable international silver coin. But this did not mean that no further debasements took place. Under Philip II, Spain had to face three government bankruptcies, but the king did not touch the value of the silver currency. Can we assume that this was a consequence of the tough system competition of Spain with other European powers?

The successors of Philip II in the 17th century were not as careful. They ruined the small Spanish silver coins circulating in Spain by substituting ever more copper for the silver they originally contained. As a first consequence, all silver coins vanished from Spain, and when Gresham's law had finished its work, inflation began. But even these successors of Philip II did not touch the internationally circulating *peso a ocho*, which was still minted with the same weight and silver content.

The Invention of Paper Money and Its Consequences for Inflation and Stability

The Chinese are well known as the first to invent paper and block printing. Not surprisingly, they also were the first to create paper money and paper-money inflation. As in other cases, this new instrument was invented privately well before AD 1000. But given the always pressing need of governments to increase their revenues, the Chinese emperors soon monopolized the use of paper money. In the beginning, the paper notes issued were in most cases convertible into copper coin, but later they were overissued, lost their convertibility, and led to inflation. Finally in all Chinese imperial dynasties, which were not conquered before, paper money was driven out by copper coins or silver bullion, quite in accordance with what I have called Thiers' Law. This was especially the case during the Mongol Yuan and the Chinese Ming dynasties overthrowing it. After these experiences, the Chinese preferred not to use paper money for several centuries.

As an example of these developments, let us look at the Ming dynasty (Figure 5.4).

The invention of paper money, that is, of a pure credit money, obviously lent much more leverage to rulers and politicians manipulating the value of currencies than had been possible by debasing metal coins. In the Ming case, the devaluation amounted to an average annual rate of inflation of 12.7 percent for rice between 1375 and 1402, or 15.5 percent between 1386 and 1402 (Bernholz 2003, 57, Table 4.1). This rate was higher than the worst inflation caused by debasement in Rome of about 8.125 percent per annum, representing a bad harbinger of events to come.

European paper money, too, was invented and developed privately. One of the first convertible notes was issued by the Swedish banker Palmstruck (Figure 5.5). But soon rulers and governments grasped the new opportunity to increase their revenues by monopolizing and overissuing paper notes. The first paper-money inflations in Europe occurred in France with the experiment managed by the Scottish economist John Law. Law undertook to save the regent, the Duke of Orleans, from the unbearable debt left to him by Louis XIV at his death in 1715 as a consequence of his many wars and his luxurious royal court. The next paper-money inflation took place in Sweden during the Seven Years' War, again

Figure 5.4
PAPER MONEY OF THE MING DYNASTY

after the earlier convertibility into silver had been abolished. During the French Revolution and the Napoleonic Wars, nearly all European states abolished convertibility into gold or silver and thus introduced a pure paper-money standard, including France's assignat paper money. During this time, too, the earliest hyperinflation in history occurred in revolutionary France from 1789 to 1795, with monthly rates of inflation for the first time climbing above 50 percent.

In the United States, several states experienced sizable paper-money inflations from the beginning of the 18th century, whereas the War of Independence nearly produced a hyperinflation of the continental currency created by the new federation. "Not worth a continental" is still a well-known expression in America.

Figure 5.5
EARLIEST SWEDISH DALER NOTE

The Big Contrast: Gold and Silver Standards versus Fiat Paper-Money Standard

Probably because of the bad experiences with inconvertible paper money during the French Revolution and the Napoleonic Wars, most important countries returned to stable currencies—with bank or government notes convertible into gold or silver—in the beginning of the 19th century. Of the great powers, only Russia and Austria (later Austria-Hungary) went again and again from silver convertibility to inconvertible paper money. This situation was mostly caused by rising government expenditures because of wars. Both countries finally joined the gold standard in the 1890s.

The stability reached after 1815 with the introduction of these stable monetary constitutions contrasts sharply with the instability of the fiat paper-money regimes after the breakdown of the gold standard in the beginning of World War I and finally during the Great Depression (Figure 5.6).

The developments shown in Figure 5.6 are those of the prices in the most stable countries. As can be seen, no upward trend of prices but only long-term swings occurred during the time of the gold standard. This pattern changed dramatically after adoption of a discretionary fiat paper-money regime. Note that natural logarithms had to be used; otherwise these later developments would have moved through the roof.

What were the reasons for this striking difference? Apart from the new technological possibilities provided by paper money, one obvious fact suggests itself. Under the gold standard both the hands of politicians and of central bankers were bound. This was no longer true after the convertibility of banknotes into gold at a fixed parity had been abolished. Interestingly, the dangers of a fiat paper-money standard were clearly perceived by some leading monetary economists during the time of metallic standards. The German economist Adolph Wagner (1868, 46–48) wrote in 1866:

> Experiences with paper money until now prove at least that it is possible … to give value to a paper money, which cannot be exchanged at will into another money. This may not necessarily and not easily be at a permanently equal value with some metal money; but this would not by itself result in a disadvantage.… The obstacle for an equal value, i.e., for maintaining an equal general purchasing power …

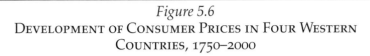

Figure 5.6
DEVELOPMENT OF CONSUMER PRICES IN FOUR WESTERN
COUNTRIES, 1750–2000

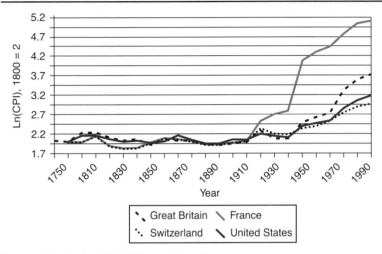

SOURCE: Bernholz (2003), Figure 2.1, p. 3.

is the impossibility to fulfill the requirements necessary for the strength of this belief. One would have to institute the most reliable guarantees to prevent that paper money would ever be used for financial purposes to create artificial purchasing power for the issuing agency without labor out of nothing; and to secure that it would be increased only according to the true necessity of the economy.... Men would have first to be capable of unlimited self-discipline to resist any temptation to increase money arbitrarily, even if their very existence, or that of the state, were at stake.... A somewhat greater security against the abuse of the right to issue money might be perhaps provided by one or the other constitutional rule. But this certainly does not amount to a big difference.

Similar thoughts were put forward by the English economist William Stanley Jevons (1898, 229–30):

There is plenty of evidence to prove that an inconvertible paper money, if carefully limited in quantity, can retain its

117

full value.... The principal objections to an inconvertible
paper currency are two in number:

1. The great temptations which it offers to over issue and
   consequent depreciation.
2. The impossibility of varying its amount in accordance
   with the requirements of trade....

Italy, Austria, and the United States, countries where the
highest economical intelligence might be expected to guide
the governments, endure the evils of an inconvertible paper
money.

Finally, Ludwig von Mises (1912, 288) in his book on money states:

As soon as only the principle has been adopted that the
state is allowed and has to influence the value of money, be
it even only to guarantee its internal stability, then the danger of mistakes and exaggerations at once again emerges.
These possibilities and the memories of the financial and
inflationary experiments of the recent past have pushed into
the background the unrealizable ideal of a money with an
unchangeable intrinsic value as compared to the postulate:
that at least the state should refrain from influencing in any
way the intrinsic value of money.

But even after the gold standard had been abolished in favor of fiat
paper-money standards, the question remains: Did the kind of monetary regime governing the behavior of central banks not amount to
a difference? This was indeed the case, as can be seen by looking at
Figure 5.7.

Until 1971–73, a weakened gold standard with fixed exchange
rates to the dollar prevailed, apart from a few reevaluations or
devaluations of some currencies. This so-called Bretton Woods
system implied gold convertibility of dollar notes—but only for
monetary authorities. Because, however, the U.S. Federal Reserve
System neglected the development of U.S. gold reserves, the rates
of inflation of all the countries considered were mainly determined
by its monetary policies. And the Federal Reserve System was a
relatively independent central bank. So not surprisingly, the rates
of inflation were similar and lower than in the following period.

Figure 5.7
DEVELOPMENT OF THE COST OF LIVING IN SEVEN WESTERN COUNTRIES, 1950–2000

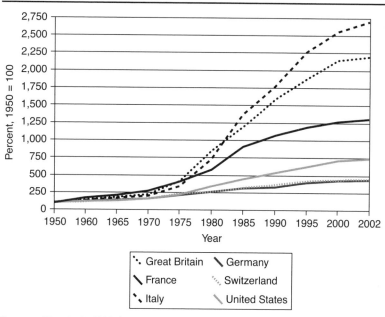

SOURCE: Bernholz (2003), Figure 2.2, p. 4.

With the breakdown of the Bretton Woods system and the move of the major countries toward flexible exchange rates, the situation changed dramatically. Now the monetary policies of the national central banks mainly determined the development of national price levels. As a consequence, sizable differences in the increases of consumer prices developed. In countries with central banks dependent on their treasuries and thus on politics, such as Italy, France, and the United Kingdom, prices rose much more strongly than in countries with independent central banks, such as Switzerland, Germany, and the United States. This confirms our hypothesis that the less the hands of politicians, governments, and rulers are bound, the less monetary stability is guaranteed. But still, compared to the gold standard, an inflationary bias caused by a fiat paper-money regime remained, as can be seen by looking at Figure 5.7. Even independent central-bank governors are human beings exposed to political and psychological pressure.

The dangers of fiat monetary regimes turn out to be much more pronounced if not only the relatively stable countries are considered. Except for during the French Revolution, all hyperinflations in history with monthly inflations of more than 50 percent occurred after the breakdown of the gold standard (Table 5.3).

Before turning to the lessons to be drawn from our analysis, a short comment on the pretended necessity of a monopoly of central banks to issue banknotes recommends itself. Monopolistic central banks are a rather recent phenomenon. They all follow the example of the Bank of England, which started as a private bank in 1694 and slowly developed into a monopoly central bank during the 18th and 19th centuries. In the beginning, the English government granted the Bank of England a monopoly on issuing banknotes for the London region in exchange for a war loan given to the Crown. Helped by the instability and numerous bankruptcies of private note-issuing banks in other parts of England, the Bank Charter Act of 1844 restricted the power of other banks to issue rival notes.

The central banks in other nations were founded much later than the Bank of England: the Banque de France privately in 1800, the German Reichsbank in 1873, the Swiss National Bank in 1907, and the Federal Reserve System in 1913. In these cases, the monopoly to issue banknotes evolved over time (Banque de France) or was established at once. The granting of the monopoly was mainly motivated because of the necessity of a lender of last resort helping restore the financial system in cases of banking crises.

By contrast, evidence exists here that note-issuing banks that are well-organized, competitive, and private worked quite well when not hindered by inadequate government regulations. This was especially the case in Scotland (White 1984; Selgin 1987) as well as in Switzerland (Nedwed 1992). Both systems worked well and maintained convertibility during the time of the gold standard.

Lessons of History Concerning the Introduction and Abolishment of Stable Monetary Regimes

The hypothetical results of the preceding analysis can be summarized as follows:

Table 5.3
HYPERINFLATIONARY EPISODES IN WORLD HISTORY

	Country	Year	Highest inflation per month (%)		Country	Year	Highest inflation per month (%)
1	Argentina	1989/90	197	16	Hungary	1945/46	12.95 quatrillion
2	Armenia	1993/94	438	17	Kazakhstan	1994	57
3	Austria	1921/22	124	18	Kyrgyzstan	1992	157
4	Azerbaijan	1991/94	118	19	Nicaragua	1986/89	127
5	Belarus	1994	53	20	Peru	1988/90	114
6	Bolivia	1984/86	120	21	Poland	1921/24	188
7	Brazil	1989/93	84	22	Poland	1989/90	77
8	Bulgaria	1997	243	23	Serbia	1992/94	309,000,000
9	China	1947/49	4,209	24	Soviet Union	1922/24	279
10	Congo (Zaire)	1991/94	225	25	Taiwan	1945/49	399
11	France	1789/96	143	26	Tajikistan	1995	78
12	Georgia	1993/94	197	27	Turkmenistan	1993/96	63
13	Germany	1920/23	29,526	28	Ukraine	1992/94	249
14	Greece	1942/45	11,288	29	Yugoslavia	1990	59
15	Hungary	1923/24	82	30	Zimbabwe	2008	8.97 septillion

SOURCES: Bernholz (2003); Hanke and Kwok (2009).

- Rulers, states, and politicians have a bias in favor of budget deficits and their financing by excessive money creation.

- They are therefore inclined to favor a public monopoly for creating money, a tendency that is furthered by the attractions of a unified currency for daily transactions.

- Governments and politicians are usually in favor of removing restrictions for themselves in directing monetary policies such as a gold standard or independent central banks whenever they feel able to do so.

- These tendencies are reinforced by technical developments moving money more and more into the direction of fiat and credit money.

- Inflation-stable monetary regimes had a greater chance to emerge if competition of smaller states for international trade was present or if the seigniorage and mercantile advantages from providing an internationally circulating currency were deemed greater than those from debasing or devaluating the currency, or both.

Let us now look more closely at the historical circumstances in which it was possible to introduce stable monetary regimes in spite of the inflationary bias of rulers and politicians. As I stated at a conference at the Cato Institute in Washington, D.C., 15 years ago, the following conditions are helpful in this respect (Bernholz 1987):

- Hyperinflations or very high inflations (10–17 historical cases)
- Restoration of a sound monetary constitution at the old (gold, silver, or foreign exchange) parity following periods of war or government bankruptcy, during which convertibility at a fixed parity has been abolished (14 historical cases)
- The introduction or reintroduction of a stable monetary constitution at a lower parity following moderate inflation and favored by a decreasing undervaluation (7 historical cases)
- The introduction of stable monetary constitutions following the examples of other countries

Here again, systems competition seems to play a role.

Because of lack of space, I have to refer you to the above-mentioned paper for the individual historical cases in question. For I still want to analyze the conditions under which it was possible for rulers and politicians to erode or abolish sound monetary constitutions. In doing so, I will have to limit myself to examples taken from the past centuries (Table 5.4).

All these events refer to financial crises that have often arisen with the outbreak of wars when ordinary government revenues could not be adapted to the needs of war finance. Not by chance did all European governments except Albania abolish the gold standard at the beginning of World War I. Similar events occurred during the French Revolution and the Napoleonic Wars. Even Britain suspended the gold standard at that time, though the country returned to it at the old parity afterward. Specie payments were suspended by an Order in Council in February 1797, that is, not by an act of Parliament. Even in earlier times

Table 5.4
EMERGENCIES LEADING TO AN EROSION OF STABLE MONETARY REGIMES (INCOMPLETE)

Country	Period	Cause	Kind of Erosion
European countries	1790–1817	French Revolution, Napoleonic Wars	Abolishment of silver or gold convertibility
Austria (Austria-Hungary), Russia	Several times in 19th century	Wars leading to overindebtedness	Abolishment of silver convertibility
Italy	1866	War with Austria	Abolishment of silver and gold convertibility
Greece	1886	Government bankruptcy	Abolishment of gold convertibility
Argentina	1890	Government bankruptcy	Abolishment of gold convertibility
European countries	1914	World War I	Abolishment of gold convertibility
Most countries	1931–36	Great Depression	Abolishment of gold convertibility
United States	1933	Great Depression	Devaluation of dollar against gold, prohibition of owning gold
United Kingdom, France, Italy	1958–73	Deficits of balance of payments, too expansive policies	Devaluations of pound, franc, and lira in Bretton Woods System
United States, worldwide	1971–73	Too expansive U.S. monetary and fiscal policies	End of Bretton Woods System with fixed exchange rates

when paper notes played no or only a minor role, wars were an important cause of debasement. Frederick II of Prussia debased Prussia's silver currency during the Seven Years' War. And more than 2000 years earlier, Athens debased its silver currency during the Peloponnesian War, and Rome did the same during the chaotic periods of the fourth century AD with its many civil and international wars. But financial crises are not limited to wars. Thus the Great Depression not surprisingly brought about the final end of the gold standard. In Executive Order 6102, President Franklin D. Roosevelt pronounced on April 5, 1933, "All persons are hereby required to deliver on or before May 1, 1933, to a Federal Reserve Bank or branch or agency thereof or to any member bank of the Federal Reserve System all gold coin, gold bullion, and gold certificates."

But the problems are even more fundamental. For we have to ask what caused the financial crises. Here we have first to mention the politicians and rulers who were responsible themselves for the outbreak of wars or who during peacetime accumulated ever-higher government debt that finally could no longer be financed in capital markets. But we must also mention the regular economic crises (Kindleberger 1978) typical of developed capitalist countries that provided occasions or excuses to governments and central banks to step in to help stabilize the situation, often by massively increasing their deficits. Given the inflationary bias of governments and politicians, we should not be surprised that they grasp any situation they can declare to be an emergency to erode or abolish the factual or constitutional limits on their control of the currency. For only in emergencies do important changes seem to be warranted. As Carl Schmitt ([1922] 1993, 13), a well-known German professor of public and constitutional law who was an early adherent of the Nazi movement, once pointed out, *Souverän ist, wer über den Ausnahmezustand entscheidet,* which can be translated as "Sovereign is he who decides on the state of emergency," that is, when laws can be changed and even constitutional rules be suspended because an emergency can be declared. Thus the real power in a state is revealed by answering the question, who has the power to suspend and perhaps even to change the constitution in an emergency? Actually, two subquestions emerge: First, who has the right or the power to declare an emergency? Second, who has the right or power to take the actions foreseen by or to break the constitution?

My hypothesis is that constitutions binding the hands of politicians and governments in normal times can be undermined in times of emergency. Indeed, as has been shown, overwhelming support exists for this hypothesis in terms of empirical evidence. And since nowadays no budget constraint stops central banks from being on a fiat paper-money standard, it cannot come as a surprise that politicians strive to gain control of central banks to remove the budget constraint for their government spending.

References

Bernholz, Peter. 1987. "The Implementation and Maintenance of a Monetary Constitution." In *The Search for Stable Money: Essays on Monetary Reform*, edited by James A. Dorn and Anna J. Schwartz, pp. 83–117. Chicago and London: University of Chicago Press.

———. 2003. *Monetary Regimes and Inflation: History, Economic and Political Relationships*. Cheltenham, UK: Edward Elgar.

———. 2011. "Understanding Early Monetary Developments by Applying Economic Laws: The Monetary Approach to the Balance of Payments, Gresham's and Thiers' Laws," University of Basel working paper.

Hanke, Steve H., and Alex K. F. Kwok. 2009. "On the Measurement of Zimbabwe's Hyperinflation." *Cato Journal* 29 (2): 353–64.

Jenkins, G. K., and Harald Küthmann. 1972. *Münzen der Griechen*. Munich: Ernst Battenberg.

Jevons, William Stanley. 1898. *Money and the Mechanism of Exchange*. New York: Appleton.

Kindleberger, Charles P. 1978. *Manias, Panics and Crashes: A History of Financial Crises*. New York: Basic Books.

———. 1984. *A Financial History of Western Europe*. London: George Allen & Unwin.

Nedwed, Harald. 1992. "Notenbankenfreiheit: Theoretische Analyse und historische Erfahrungen aus der Schweiz im 19. Jahrhundert." Basler Dissertation, Druckerei Ganzmann AG, Basel, Switzerland.

Mises, Ludwig von. 1912. *Theorie des Geldes und der Umlaufmittel*. Munich and Leipzig: Duncker und Humblot.

Pirenne, Henri. 1951. *Histoire économique de l'Occident médiéval*. Bruges: Desclée de Brouwer.

———. 2005. *Economic and Social History of Medieval Europe*. London: Routledge.

Schmitt, Carl. (1922) 1993. *Politische Theologie*. 6th ed. Berlin: Duncker & Humblot.

Selgin, George. 1987. *The Theory of Free Banking*. Totowa, NJ: Rowman and Littlefield.

Spufford, Peter. 1986. *Handbook of Medieval Exchange*. Royal Historical Society Guides and Handbook no. 13. London: Royal Historical Society.

Wagner, Adolph. 1868. *Die russische Papierwährung*. Riga: N. Kymmel.

White, Lawrence H. 1984. *Free Banking in Britain. Theory, Experience and Debate 1800–1845*. Cambridge, UK: Cambridge University Press.

6. Index Futures Targeting and Monetary Disequilibrium

W. William Woolsey

This chapter explores index futures targeting and the closely related proposal for index futures convertibility, which have recently received popular attention in combination with nominal gross domestic product (GDP)–level targeting because of the work of Scott Sumner (1989, 1995, 2011). Nominal GDP–level targeting aims to provide a macroeconomic environment for effective microeconomic coordination. It is a monetary regime that helps avoid undesirable shifts in the price level and real output caused by imbalances between the quantity of money and the demand to hold money. It dampens and rapidly reverses shifts in real output and the price level caused by "demand shocks," while allowing some adjustment in the price level to avoid, or at least limit, any exacerbation of shifts in real output arising from "supply shocks."

Of course, nominal GDP is directly determined by the production and pricing decisions of a multitude of firms as well as a variety of governmental units. It is less an "instrument" of monetary policy than M1, M2, or MZM. A conventional approach to nominal GDP targeting would involve adjusting something more closely controlled by a central bank, either the quantity of base money or some policy interest rate, so that nominal GDP is expected to be on target. Index futures targeting and index futures convertibility are approaches to bridging the gap between changes in current monetary conditions and the future level of nominal GDP.

The author thanks Scott Sumner, Russell Sobel, and participants at the 2013 annual meetings of the Western Economics Association for helpful corrections and comments.

The first section reviews the concept of monetary disequilibrium. The next section introduces Sumner's proposal for index futures targeting and the related proposal for index futures convertibility in the context of nominal GDP–level targeting. The following section considers the relationship between free banking and index futures targeting and index futures convertibility.

Monetary Disequilibrium

Monetary disequilibrium is an imbalance between the quantity of money and the demand to hold money. A key criterion for evaluating a monetary regime should be to determine how monetary disequilibrium might arise and what market process brings the quantity of money and the demand to hold money back into equilibrium.

Suppose the nominal quantity of money is fixed. Such a monetary regime has at least one advantage—no problems can occur because of an undesirable change in the quantity of money. For example, if the demand to hold money was not changing at some particular point in time, the regime would prohibit changes in the quantity of money that would cause a shortage or surplus of money.

Unfortunately, a monetary regime that fixes the quantity of money requires that a change in the demand to hold money be equilibrated by an adjustment in the prices of all goods and services, including resource prices such as wages, to bring the real quantity of money in line with the demand to hold it. Such changes in prices are inevitably disruptive to microeconomic coordination. Most important, if prices and wages adjust only gradually, the reduction in expenditure on currently produced goods and services results in reduced output and employment of resources such as labor. The demand to hold money is choked off by waste and poverty. Further, even if prices and wages were perfectly and instantly flexible, the resulting shift in wealth between creditors and debtors makes every nominal contract a speculation on the demand to hold money.

A central bank with discretionary authority to adjust the quantity of fiat money is the most common monetary regime today. Conceptually, such an institution could adjust the quantity of money so that it remains equal to the demand to hold money. Unfortunately, avoiding monetary disequilibrium by making appropriate changes in the quantity of money is easier said than done.

Given the quantity of money, adjustments in the price level are necessary to bring the real quantity of money in line with the demand. This suggests that avoiding such changes in the price level would be a reasonable approach to avoiding monetary disequilibrium. Adjust the quantity of money such that no changes in the price level are needed.[1]

Unfortunately, the price level can change because of shifts in the supply of particular goods or services. For example, a decrease in the supply of oil tends to raise the price of oil and, as a matter of arithmetic, the average level of prices. Contracting the quantity of money to force down other prices, so that the price remains at some targeted level, creates money disequilibrium. Forcing other prices down needlessly disrupts production and employment in other markets, when the initial increase in the price of oil was all that was needed to signal appropriate adjustments to the reduced availability of oil.[2]

The actual practice of central banks—periodic adjustments in a policy interest rate aimed at stabilizing inflation and avoiding output gaps—might be rationalized as the least bad way of avoiding, or reversing, imbalances between the quantity of money and the demand to hold it. Unfortunately, the entire framework of minimizing some social loss function rationalizes the generation of monetary disequilibrium. Worse, the earliest central banks were developed to help finance governments. Inflationary default and simply creating money for politicians to spend are always serious threats. Furthermore, creditor interests pressuring a central bank into allowing a deflationary policy to strip debtors of their net worth is not outside the realm of possibility.

A nominal GDP–level target is an alternative approach to avoiding monetary disequilibrium. Because excess supplies or demands for money affect the price level through changes in expenditures on output, a monetary regime that targets the level of nominal GDP must reverse, or better yet, preempt any surplus or shortage of money. In other words, the quantity of money must adjust to the demand to hold it.

Further, nominal GDP–level targeting allows shifts in the supplies of particular goods and services to change both the prices of those goods and the price level without necessarily causing monetary disequilibrium, and at the very least reducing the disruption caused by efforts to stabilize the price level.[3]

Index Futures Targeting and Index Futures Convertibility

Index futures targeting and index futures convertibility are closely related alternative monetary regimes where the issuer or issuers of money are required to buy and sell an index futures contract on some macroeconomic statistic. Sumner has described and advocated index futures targeting in the context of a central bank obligated to buy and sell index futures on the consumer price index (CPI) or nominal GDP. Because one of the earliest proposals was for nominal GDP targeting (Sumner 1989), and Sumner has emphasized nominal GDP targeting since the beginning of the Great Recession (2009; 2011, 91–94), that approach is emphasized here.

The basic proposal is for a central bank to issue base money, both hand-to-hand currency and reserve balances for banks. The quantity of base money would be adjusted by conventional open market operations using government bonds such as Treasury bills (T-bills). However, the changes in the quantity of base money would be determined by trades of a futures contract on nominal GDP. Sumner advocates targeting the growth path of nominal GDP, and he usually proposes a 5 percent growth rate. This amounts to a series of quarterly target levels for nominal GDP, with each target level 1.25 (5/4) percent above the previous quarter's target.[4]

Table 6.1 shows a hypothetical target growth path for nominal GDP (in billions of dollars) that starts in January 2012 at approximately where nominal GDP would have been if it had continued growing along the trend of the Great Moderation. The target levels then increase at an annual rate of 5 percent. The target for April 2012 is 1.25 percent greater than the target for January of 2012. If nominal GDP is on target, then an implicit target exists for the growth rate of nominal GDP—a 5 percent annual rate. However, the actual target for any quarter is the level shown in the table. If nominal GDP is not on target, then the implicit target growth rate for any future date would necessarily be different from 5 percent.

Figure 6.1 shows the same target growth path for nominal GDP in natural logs as a solid line. Nominal GDP remains on target until the first quarter of 2013, when it begins to fall at a 2 percent annual rate. When the recession ends during the first quarter of 2014, nominal GDP has fallen slightly more than 5 percent below target. Nominal GDP returns to target by the fourth quarter of 2015.

Table 6.1
GROWTH PATH FOR NOMINAL GDP,
JANUARY 2012–OCTOBER 2015

Quarter	Target nominal GDP ($billions)
January 2012	18,900
April 2012	19,136
July 2012	19,375
October 2012	19,618
January 2013	19,863
April 2013	20,111
July 2013	20,363
October 2013	20,617
January 2014	20,875
April 2014	21,136
July 2014	21,400
October 2014	21,667
January 2015	21,938
April 2015	22,212
July 2015	22,490
October 2015	22,771

The growth rate over that one year of recovery is approximately 11 percent. Of course, the average growth rate over the two-year period from the first quarter of 2013 to the first quarter of 2015 would be 5 percent.

The best scenario would be for nominal GDP to remain on target. Further, if the recovery had begun after the second quarter of 2013, the shortfall of nominal GDP from target would have been much lower. In this example, nominal GDP would have been approximately 2 percent below target, and with a one-year recovery, the growth rate during the recovery would be 5.5 percent—only slightly higher than what would have occurred if nominal GDP had remained on target.

Figure 6.1
Targeted Growth Path for Nominal GDP, January 2012–October 2015

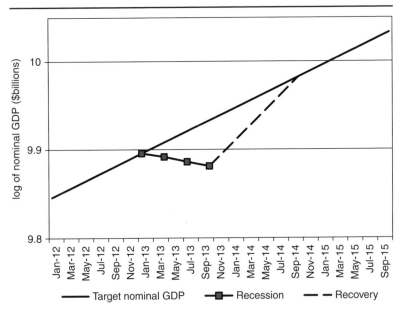

Defining the Index Futures Contract

The regime requires that the central bank create an index futures contract on nominal GDP. For example, an index value can be calculated by dividing the actual value of nominal GDP for a quarter by the targeted level. The central bank then multiplies the index by an arbitrary dollar amount to define a settlement value for the index futures contract. For example, suppose the central bank uses $1,000.

$$Pt = \frac{NGDP_t}{NGDP_t^*} \times \$1,000$$

where P_t is the settlement value of the futures contract, $NGDP_t$ is the value of nominal GDP at time t, and $NGDP_t^*$ is the target level at time t.

If nominal GDP rises 1 percent above its targeted value, then the settlement value is $1,010. If nominal GDP should instead fall 2 percent below its targeted value, the settlement value of the contract would be $980. In other words, the settlement value of the contract is $10 for every 1 percent deviation of nominal GDP from target.

Using the scenario illustrated by Figure 6.1, in the first quarter of 2013, the target for nominal GDP is $19,683 billion, and nominal GDP is on target. Dividing nominal GDP by the target, the result is 1. Multiply by $1,000, and the settlement value of the contract is $1,000.

In the second quarter of 2012, nominal GDP had fallen to $19,764 billion while the target is $20,111 billion. Dividing the value of nominal GDP by the target, we get the result 0.98. Multiply by $1,000, and the settlement value of the contract is $980. Nominal GDP is 2 percent below target, and the settlement value of the contract is $20 less than $1,000—$10 for every 1 percent deviation.

The central bank buys and sells the contracts at a price of $1,000. Sumner often advocates having the central bank trade the contracts one year in the future (2006, 12; also see Sumner 2009). For example, from January 1, 2012, to March 31, 2012, the central bank would buy or sell the contract for the first quarter of 2013. When nominal GDP for the first quarter of 2013 is calculated, late in the second quarter of 2013, it would be on target. The settlement value would be calculated. It would be $1,000, the price for which the central bank bought and sold the contract during the first quarter of 2012. The contract would expire without any payments being made.

From April 1, 2012, to June 30, 2012, the central bank would trade the futures contract for the second quarter of 2013. The calculation for nominal GDP for the second quarter of 2013 would be complete near the end of the third quarter of 2013. Given the preceding example, nominal GDP fell 2 percent below target. The settlement value of the contract would be $980, $20 less than the price for which the central bank traded the contract more than one year before.

Those who sold the contract in the second quarter of 2012 for $1,000 receive $20 per contract sold, the difference between the price at which the central bank traded the contract and the $980 settlement value of the contract. Those who purchased the contract for $1,000 would pay $20 per contract they bought. These payments would occur near the end of the third quarter of 2013—once the settlement value of the contract is determined.

If nominal GDP were above target, then those who purchased the futures contract would receive payments, whereas those who sold the contract would make payments. If nominal GDP were 1 percent above target, then those who bought the contracts would receive $10 per contract. Those who sold contracts would pay $10 per contract.

The trades of the futures contract have no direct effect on the quantity of money. The contracts are promises to make payments at the time of settlement. When a speculator purchases a $1,000 futures contract, no money is paid immediately. And when a speculator sells a $1,000 futures contract, no money is immediately received.

In the preceding example, no money would change hands when the contracts trade in the second quarter of 2012. Money would change hands only sometime late in the third quarter of 2013, after nominal GDP for the second quarter was found to be 2 percent below target.[5]

In most futures markets, both buyer and seller must deposit and maintain a margin account to cover losses on the contract. The monetary implications of margin accounts would at best be ambiguous and sometimes perverse. Although a central bank could develop a special sort of deposit account for required margins, having speculators post a bond of securities suitable as collateral would probably be simpler.[6]

Parallel Open-Market Operations with T-Bills

The changes in the quantity of base money occur through ordinary open-market operations with securities such as T-bills, so the trades of index futures contracts generate changes only in base money because of some rule imposed on the central bank. Although Sumner's view on what rule is most appropriate has evolved, review of the earlier, more intuitive rules is instructive. One simple rule would require open-market operations in parallel with trades of the futures contract (Sumner 2006, 9). For every $1,000 futures contract the central bank buys, it must buy T-bills with a market value of $1,000. For every $1,000 futures contract the central bank sells, it must sell T-bills with a market value of $1,000.[7] The open-market operations using T-bills would cause base money to change in the usual way.

For every $1,000 futures contract sold by a speculator to the central bank, base money increases by $1,000. The speculator selling the futures contract isn't paid $1,000 by the central bank. Rather, whoever owned the government bonds purchased by the central bank receives the $1,000. The speculator who sold the futures contract receives a promise to be paid $10 for every 1 percent that nominal GDP one year in the future is below target and in exchange promises to pay $10 for every 1 percent that nominal GDP one year in the future is above target.

Decreases in the quantity of base money require that speculators purchase futures contracts from the central bank. The central bank sells the futures contracts at the fixed price of $1,000 per contract and simultaneously sells $1,000 worth of T-bills in an ordinary open-market sale. Base money does not decrease because the speculators pay the central bank for the futures contracts. They are receiving a promise of $10 for every percent by which nominal GDP in one year exceeds the target in exchange for a promise to pay $10 for every percent by which nominal GDP falls below the target. The decrease in the quantity of base money occurs through the sale of T-bills, and those buying the T-bills from the central bank are the ones who have less money.

Like those who are selling, those buying the futures contracts must provide a performance bond. Although this inevitably involves tying up some kind of funds as collateral, it would likely be only a small fraction of the value of the futures contracts sold.

Changes in Base Money According to the Central Bank's Position on the Futures Contract

Because sales of futures contracts by speculators expand the quantity of base money and purchases by them decrease it, their net long or short position on the contract is what changes base money. With the central bank trading the contract at a fixed price, this is the opposite of its own position on the contract. For example, if some speculators sell more contracts than other speculators buy, then the central bank must buy the difference. The market is short on the

135

contract, and the central bank takes the matching long position. There is no point in having the central bank make offsetting open-market purchases and sales of T-bills, so the rule for parallel trades can be simplified by a requirement that the central bank make open-market purchases of securities and expand base money by an amount equal to its long position on the contract.

Sumner recognizes the absurdity of requiring a strict one-for-one matching of the quantity of base money with the amount of futures sold by speculators (2006, 15). This would require that the level of base money be reset to zero at the beginning of each quarter and that speculators obtain a new, vast, and growing short position on the contract. The $868 billion level of base money in the third quarter of 2008 would have required an $868 billion short position for speculators and an $868 billion long position for the central bank.

A more plausible approach would require *changes* in base money to be matched by trades of the futures contract. On the first day of each new quarter, base money would be where it was at the end of the previous quarter. If no one trades the futures contract during the quarter, base money would remain the same and begin the subsequent quarter at the level of the previous quarter.

With the usual monetarist assumptions, the demand for base money would have a trend growth rate equal to the trend growth rate for the target for nominal GDP. So for the typical quarter, the central bank would need to have a long position on the contract sufficient to generate the needed expansion in base money. For the decade leading up to 2008, the increases in base money averaged $8 billion each quarter. For that to occur, speculators would need to sell contracts worth $8 billion more than what they purchased, leaving them with an $8 billion short position. The central bank would buy the contracts, have the matching $8 billion long position, and purchase $8 billion worth of T-bills. That would generate the needed $8 billion increase in base money per quarter.

Quarters with decreases in base money were rare during the decade before 2008. For example, a $2 billion decrease occurred in the first quarter of 1991 and a $7 billion decrease in the second quarter of 2000. For that to happen, speculators would need to buy $7 billion more futures contracts than they sell, leaving them with a $7 billion long position. The central bank would sell the difference, accepting the matching $7 billion short position. It would make a $7 billion sale of securities, causing the needed $7 billion decrease in base money.

Some existing futures contracts have a multibillion-dollar open interest, so transactions of these sizes are not entirely unrealistic. However, since 2008, quarters have occurred with base money increasing over $500 billion. Some large decreases have taken place, including $53 billion in the second quarter of 2010. These would be very large positions for speculators to take.

Tentative Targets for Base Money

More recently, Sumner (2006, 15) has proposed that the central bank be given discretion to make whatever adjustment in base money it sees fit, announce that tentative target, and then make adjustments according to speculators' trades of the contract. For example, if the central bank forecasts that a 5 percent annual growth rate in base money is appropriate, and base money is currently $800 billion, the central bank could announce a tentative target for the quarter of $810 billion. Speculators would then buy and sell the contracts for $1,000. If the speculators were short on the contract, the central bank would increase its target for base money by the amount of its matching long position. For example, if the central bank's long position was $2 billion, the central bank would make open-market purchases of $12 billion. That would be the initial $10 billion tentative target plus the added $2 billion adjustment caused by the central bank's long position. As a result, base money would increase to $812 billion.

Conversely, if speculators were long on the contract, the central bank would take the matching short position. If the amount of the central bank's short position was $3 billion, then it would reduce its target to $807 billion and make open-market purchases of $7 billion. If speculators went very long on the contract, buying $12 billion more than they sold, the central bank would have a $12 billion short position, so it would reduce its target for base money from $810 billion to $798 billion. It would then make an open-market sale of $2 billion.

Creating and Trading Daily Futures Contracts

Sumner (2006, 16) has proposed that the central bank develop a nominal GDP index futures contract that trades for a single day.[8]

The daily target would increase by the targeted annual growth rate. The value of nominal GDP for any particular day would be interpolated between quarterly measurements. For example, when nominal GDP for the first quarter of 2013 is calculated, sometime late in the second quarter, a value for each day of the first quarter would be calculated.[9] It would be divided by the daily target value and then multiplied by $1,000, as before.

On any particular day, the central bank trades only the contract for that day one year in the future. So on September 24, 2012, the central bank trades the futures contract for September 24, 2013. First, the central bank provides a tentative target for base money for that day, and speculators trade the contract. The central bank then adjusts its target for base money by the long or short position on the daily contract. If the central bank is long, it raises its tentative target by the long position. If the central bank is short on the contract, it reduces its tentative target by the short position. The central bank then uses regular open-market operations to change base money so that it equals the adjusted target.

The key rationale for daily contracts is to create an incentive for speculators to trade the contract before the end of the quarter. In an early version of index futures targeting, Sumner (1995, 92) proposed that the central bank trade index futures contracts during the current month on the next month's CPI. Changes in base money each month matched the central bank's long or short position on the contract. Garrison and White criticized the proposal, among other reasons, by arguing that speculators would wait until the last day of the month to trade the contract, so that too little time would remain for the changes in the quantity of money to affect the CPI (Garrison and White 1997, 537). Calculating a daily CPI by interpolation and trading futures for each day appears to answer that criticism.

Unfortunately, interpolation still makes trading at the end of the period more profitable. Returning to nominal GDP targeting, if nominal GDP deviates from target for one quarter, the extrapolated deviation calculated for each day will become larger as the end of the quarter approaches.

For example, suppose nominal GDP for the fourth quarter of 2012 is on target and then rises 1 percent above target in the first quarter of 2013. The interpolated deviation will be near zero for January 1,

2013, and it will be approximately 1 percent on March 31, 2013. If nominal GDP returns to target in the second quarter of 2013, then the interpolated deviation will be approximately 1 percent on April 1, 2013, falling back to near zero on June 30, 2013.

For those trading the futures contract in early 2012, the greatest return would be on the last day of the first quarter, March 31, 2012, and the first day of the second quarter, April 1, 2012. A contract purchased on January 1, 2012, will have a settlement value of $89/90 \times \$1,000 + 1/90 \times \$1,010 = \$1,000.11$. Because the central bank sells contracts for $1,000, the payoff is 11 cents. If the contract were purchased on February 1, then the settlement value is $32/90 \times \$1000 + 58/90 \times \$1,010 = \$1,003.56$, for a payoff of $3.56. And on March 31, the value of the contract is $1/90 \times \$1000 + 89/90 \times \$1010 = \$1009.89$, for a payoff of $9.89.

If the futures contract traded in the current quarter is for one year in the future, little reason for worry exists that any change in the quantity of money would occur too late to impact spending on output one year in the future. Further, if the central bank has discretion to create a tentative target, necessary changes in base money can occur even without trades of the contract. Given these modifications in the proposal and the incentive created to trade on the first and last day of each quarter, little reason exists to create and trade a daily contract.

Speculation and Expectations of Nominal GDP

Given the tentative target for base money, those speculators who expect nominal GDP will be above target in one year have an incentive to purchase the futures contract. When the contract is settled, for every percentage point nominal GDP exceeds the target, they expect to earn $10.

Those speculators who expect that nominal GDP will be below target in one year have an incentive to sell the futures contract. When the contract is settled, for every percentage point nominal GDP falls short of the target, they expect to earn $10.

The central bank buys and sells the contracts for $1,000, so no change occurs in the price of the contract. The central bank's position on the contract shows a market estimate of whether nominal GDP in one year will be above or below target conditional on its tentative target for base money.

If, on one hand, speculators anticipating that nominal GDP will be above target purchased more contracts than those expecting that it will be below target sold, the market would have a long position on the contract and the central bank would have the matching short position. If, on the other hand, speculators anticipating that nominal GDP will be below the target sold more contracts than those expecting it to be above target bought, the market would have a short position on the contract and the central bank would have the matching long position.

The rule for the central bank is to adjust its tentative target for base money according to its position on the contract. If the central bank is short on the contract, it must reduce its tentative target for base money by an amount equal to the short position. If the central bank is long on the contract, it must raise its tentative target for base money by an amount equal to the long position.

For example, suppose base money is $990 billion and the monetary authority provides a tentative target for base money of $1,000 billion—a $10 billion increase. Speculators buy $600 million worth of contracts and sell $100 million worth of contracts. The market would be $500 million long on the contract, with the central bank taking the matching $500 million short position. The central bank would reduce its tentative target by $500 million to $999.5 billion, and the targeted increase to $9.5 billion. The central bank's open-market desk would purchase securities, such as T-bills, worth $9.5 billion. The central bank's final target has been determined by market speculators.

Sumner argues that these adjustments in the tentative target for base money would keep the market expectation for nominal GDP on target. The argument is simple. For example, suppose the market expectation is for nominal GDP to be above target, and speculation on the contract reveals that expectation with a long position. The central bank would respond to its matching short position by reducing its target for the quantity of base money. Ceteris paribus, this would reduce nominal GDP in a year. However, if the market expectation remained that nominal GDP will be above target, buying the contract would still yield profits. This would generate a long position on the contract and a short position for the central bank, which would further reduce its target for base money. That would decrease the expected value of nominal GDP. The process would stop only when the difference between the expected value of nominal GDP and the target was no greater than the transaction costs for the speculators, the opportunity cost of funds tied up in margin accounts, and compensation for risk.

If the market expects nominal GDP to be below target, then speculators would have an incentive to sell futures contracts. That would generate a short position for the market, revealing the market expectation. The central bank would have the matching long position and increase its target for base money. Ceteris paribus, the increase in base money would raise expected nominal GDP. However, if expected nominal GDP remained below target, profits would remain from selling the futures contract. This would generate an additional expansion in the quantity of base money. Ceteris paribus, that would increase nominal GDP. This process would continue until the difference between nominal GDP and the target is so small that speculators would no longer be motivated to sell the futures contract—because of the transaction costs for speculators, the opportunity cost of funds tied up in margin accounts, and compensation for risk.

To the degree index futures targeting caused any change in base money, both the central bank and speculators would take a risk of loss. Because the central bank must adjust its position to that of the speculators, changes in the quantity of base money resulting from trades imply that, on net, the speculators expect to gain at the expense of the central bank.

Index Futures Convertibility

Index futures convertibility involves a slight modification of index futures targeting. The central bank has full discretion to adjust the quantity of money subject to the constraint that it buy and sell the index futures contracts on the policy target at a fixed price.[10]

Unlike Sumner's index futures targeting, no rule requires changes in base money parallel to trades in the futures contract. For example, a central bank restrained by index futures convertibility could follow a conservative policy and adjust current monetary conditions, presumably through ordinary open-market operations, to keep its net position on the contract equal to zero. The purchases of those speculators who expect nominal GDP to be above target would be exactly matched by the sales by those speculators who expect nominal GDP to be below target. The market as a whole, and thus the central bank, would have neither a long nor a short position on the contract. The central bank would be fully hedged against any deviation of nominal GDP from target and would simply transfer funds between speculators who have bought and speculators who have sold the contract if any deviation occurred. Of course, if nominal GDP remained on target, no settlement payments would be made.

In contrast, the central bank could follow a more activist policy and take a position on the contract. For example, if the central bank chose a long position on the contract, this would imply a short position by the market—some speculators selling more than other speculators purchased. "The market" would be expecting nominal GDP to fall below target. The central bank, then, would be speculating that nominal GDP would be above target, agreeing with those speculators who bought and disagreeing with those speculators who sold. If the central bank turned out to be wrong, then it, along with all the speculators who were long on the contract, would make payments to those speculators who had sold contracts. Conversely, if the central bank turned out to be right, then it, along with all the speculators who also bought the contract, would earn money from the speculators who were short.

Possibly no one would trade the futures contract at all. The central bank would still be committed to a policy rule for nominal GDP and would adjust current monetary conditions as it sees best to keep nominal GDP on target one year in the future. However, such a scenario is unlikely. At least some speculators, with expectations very different from those of the central bank, would trade the contract. A conservative central bank could make very modest changes in current monetary conditions to make sure that its position is hedged.

Therefore, an "activist" policy would generally amount to ignoring a small net position on the contract based upon the trades of those speculators with the most divergent expectations. However, if events created broader expectations of changes in nominal GDP, then trading on the contract would increase. The central bank would likely also observe the same developments and make an adjustment in current monetary conditions. But those speculators who found the central bank's response excessive or inadequate would trade the contract. If the market expectation for nominal GDP diverged greatly from the target, the central bank would develop a large position on the contract. That would compel it to determine whether to make adjustments in current monetary conditions based upon market sentiment to bring market purchases and sales closer into balance.

The alternative would be to maintain a large short or long position on the contract. Although such a position on the contract would create an opportunity for significant profit by the central bank, it would be at the expense of a chance of heavy losses.

Index Futures Targeting and Index Futures Convertibility Contrasted

The key difference between Sumner's version of index futures targeting and index futures convertibility involves the role of central-bank discretion. With Sumner's approach, the central bank can determine a tentative target for base money each quarter, and that tentative target is adjusted according to trades of the contract. However, as the adjustments in the target for base money bring expected nominal GDP to the target, both the speculators and the central bank are left with a position on the contract that exposes them to risk of loss and little expected gain. If the speculators make offsetting trades to reverse their position, the central bank must adjust its target for base money, pushing expected nominal GDP away from target.

With index futures convertibility, the central bank is free to make adjustments to current monetary conditions, perhaps by making adjustments to a formal target for base money, so that it reduces risk of loss. In the limit, it is fully hedged and bears no risk of loss. As those adjustments are made, any speculator can make offsetting transactions, closing out any existing position on the contract. That would be a means by which the central bank would reverse and hedge its position on the contract. However, this implies that speculators bear transaction costs to trade a futures contract knowing that after the central bank responds, they may find it advantageous to reverse their trades and close out their position on the contract. This possibility shows that the reason why any individual speculator would actually trade the contract is because he or she expects someone, either the central bank or some other speculator, to be willing to hold the opposite position.

For example, suppose some speculators expect that nominal GDP will rise above target. They could profit by purchasing the contract. If the central bank has an activist policy and has confidence that current monetary conditions are appropriate, it would sell the contract. It would have a short position matching the speculators' long positions. Their expectations would be to profit at the expense of the central bank. However, suppose the central bank follows a conservative policy and so would seek to reduce its short position, perhaps to zero, so that it was fully hedged. Given this monetary contraction, some of those who did not previously expect nominal GDP to be above target would expect it to be below target because of the change in current monetary conditions. So they would sell contracts. The speculators initially purchasing the contract would only do so to the degree that they expected either the central bank or else some other market speculators to disagree with their assessment. They would purchase the contract only to the degree that they expected nominal GDP to remain above target after any consequent tightening by the central bank.

Paradoxically, if some adjustment in current monetary conditions were seen as necessary and appropriate by everyone, then no one would have an incentive to trade the futures contract. However, if this perception were truly universal, then no such trades would be necessary because the central bank, sharing this same perception, would make the necessary adjustment in current monetary conditions. It is divergent expectations that would generate trades of the futures contract, which would reveal those expectations. A central bank could then make adjustments according to the market expectation. If the central bank failed to fully hedge its position, then its profits or losses would provide a signal of the quality of its judgment relative to the judgment of the market.

Index Futures and Free Banking

Sumner's proposal for index futures targeting is in the context of a conventional money and banking system. The central bank issues base money that takes the form of hand-to-hand currency and reserve balances for banks. Commercial banks, and perhaps other financial institutions, issue a variety of monetary instruments, but they are all redeemable in base money. Because the prices of private monetary instruments are fixed in terms of base money, their issue is limited by the demand to hold them. As long as the central bank adjusts the quantity of base money to meet the demand, including the derived demand based upon a perhaps unmet demand to hold checkable deposits or other monetary liabilities, monetary disequilibrium can be avoided.

Is index futures targeting or convertibility consistent with free banking? Free banking has three elements. First is the *constitutional* element of free banking, as outlined by F. A. Hayek (1976, 1990). This element allows households and firms to use any alternative moneys, with actual or potential competition between alternative moneys constraining any issuer from abuse.

Given such a rule, "central bank" could issue monetary "base money" subject to index futures targeting or convertibility. Households, firms, and other banks would then use that money or alternatives as they choose. To the degree this reduces the demand to hold the central bank's liabilities, it would have to issue less. Further, if some of those in the area where nominal GDP was being targeted quote prices in terms of other moneys, the exchange rate with those other moneys would partly determine nominal GDP in terms of the central bank's money. As the proportion of prices quoted in other moneys increases, any system of nominal GDP targeting would become an exercise in controlling the exchange rate on the central bank's currency rather than influencing the expectations of those setting prices and planning production.

Second, index futures targeting or convertibility is consistent with the *microeconomic* elements of free banking. In particular, it is consistent with allowing banks to issue hand-to-hand currency redeemable in base money. Further, reserve requirements are not needed. If banks can persuade their customers to use banknotes for hand-to-hand currency rather than base money, the monetary regime would reduce the quantity of base money to reflect the reduced demand for it as hand-to-hand currency. Similarly, if banks choose to hold fewer reserves, tending to result in an expansion in bank credit and deposits, the regime would reduce the quantity of base money to reflect the reduced demand for it for use as bank reserves.

To the degree that deposit insurance is aimed at preventing the adverse consequence of a large, sudden increase in the demand for base money, index futures targeting and convertibility would accommodate any such increases in the demand for base money and avoid the consequent decrease in nominal expenditures and deflation of prices. By making that benefit of deposit insurance superfluous, perhaps it could be removed. Since the moral hazard created by deposit insurance is the key rationale for capital requirements, by

145

making deposit insurance unnecessary, index futures targeting and convertibility would reduce the need for capital regulation as well.

Third, index futures targeting or convertibility appears inconsistent with the *macroeconomic* element of free banking, in particular, the absence of a central bank implementing a monetary policy. With index futures targeting, the central bank determines a tentative target for base money and then adjusts it according to the speculators' trades of the futures contract. With index futures convertibility, the central bank adjusts current monetary conditions as it sees fit, subject to the constraint that it stand ready to trade the index futures contract.[11]

A Competitive Banking System and Index Futures Convertibility

Multiple competing banks providing tentative targets for their monetary liabilities and then adjusting them according to trades of an index futures contract is a situation difficult to imagine. However, index futures convertibility is a more plausible candidate for a rule that could be applied to competing private banks.[12] Each bank has discretion to operate as it sees fit, subject to the constraint that it buy or sell futures contracts on nominal GDP at a fixed price.

Although an individual bank could hardly do anything to affect nominal GDP and could only conceivably vary its exchange rates relative to other moneys so that nominal GDP calculated in its money is on target, the banking system could affect nominal GDP. For a system of competing banks to provide a convenient payments system, each bank needs to accept the other banks' checks, electronic payments, and hand-to-hand currency for deposit and then settle net clearing balances. If all of those banks are subject to index futures convertibility on nominal GDP, then the most likely scenario would be for checks, electronic payments, and banknotes to be accepted for deposit at par, creating what amounts to a jointly produced money supply.

Having each bank commit to buy or sell unlimited quantities of index futures contracts with each other bank is hardly practical. Any one bank could hedge by trading futures with another bank. But the other bank could simply reverse the trades. For example, a bank with a short position on the contract, could hedge its position by buying contracts from another bank, leaving that other bank with the short position. But that other bank could then buy contracts from the first bank.

To avoid what would amount to a pointless "arms race," a simple rule tying positions on the contract to interbank clearings would solve the problem. Banks with favorable clearings buy the contract, and banks with adverse clearings sell the contract.

If an individual bank expected nominal GDP to be above target, it would profit from buying the contract, which it could do by developing favorable net clearings. Raising the interest rate it pays on monetary and other deposits and selling securities and raising the interest rates it charges on loans would accomplish this. To the degree other banks agreed with this assessment or else wanted to avoid risk, they could reverse their positions by also raising their interest rates and restricting credit. Because these transactions by the banks would mostly generate offsetting gross clearings, the typical bank would be unsuccessful in its effort to buy the contract. However, the resulting tightening in current monetary conditions would tend to reduce the expected value of nominal GDP.

If, on the other hand, an individual bank expected nominal GDP to be below target, it would profit from selling the contract, which it could do by developing adverse net clearings. This could be accomplished by lowering the interest rates paid on monetary and other deposits while purchasing securities and lowering the interest rates charged on loans. Again, if other banks shared this assessment, or simply wanted to avoid the risk involved in a long position on the contract, they could also take action to obtain adverse clearings. Again, if all banks attempt to obtain adverse net clearings, the result is largely offsetting gross clearings. The typical bank would not succeed in selling the contract. Yet the resulting decrease in the demand to hold money because of the decrease in the interest rates paid on money and increase in the quantity of money from the purchases of securities and lowered interest rates on loans would tend to raise the expected value of nominal GDP, bringing it to equilibrium.

If nominal GDP was expected to remain on target, and banks did not want to bear the risk of taking positions on the contract, then each bank would seek to avoid adverse or favorable net clearings and so would seek to attract deposits sufficient to match loans. In an economy with a growing demand for money, this would involve plans by each bank to attract a growing quantity of deposits matched by a growing asset portfolio. Each bank would seek to set the interest rate it charges on loans and the interest rate it pays on deposits such

147

that the growing quantity of credit demanded by borrowers would match the quantity of monetary and nonmonetary bank liabilities demanded by depositors.

Other speculators could trade with banks. If a bank was unwilling to take the opposite position of the speculator, it could hedge by shifting its position to other banks through generating a change in its net clearing balance. For example, a speculator expecting nominal GDP to rise above target could purchase the futures contract from a bank. The bank, not wanting to be short on the contract, could raise the interest rate it pays on deposits and sell securities and raise the interest rate it charges on loans. This would generate favorable net clearings that would allow the bank to hedge its position by "purchasing" the futures contract from the other banks with matching adverse net clearings. The other banks, of course, either would accept the resulting short position on the contract or also contract monetary conditions to obtain favorable clearings. In equilibrium, either the initial speculator would sell a futures contract, no longer expecting nominal GDP to rise above target, or else some other speculator, which could be a bank, must be willing to hold the matching short position on the contract, expecting nominal GDP to be below target.

With a free-banking version of nominal GDP targeting, the zero bound on nominal interest rate would not exist in the usual sense. If nominal interest rates, especially on short and safe assets, were driven down to very low levels, perhaps even below zero, then issuing hand-to-hand currency would become unprofitable. If it became too unattractive, then banks would cease issuing it. Money in the form of deposits, perhaps with negative nominal interest rates, would still be issued in whatever amount was necessary to keep the expected value of nominal GDP on target.

Conclusion

Index futures targeting and index futures convertibility provide a mechanism for harnessing market forces to the goal of avoiding monetary disequilibrium. By targeting the growth path of nominal GDP, market speculators are given an incentive and the ability to influence current monetary conditions such that the shifts in spending in output due to monetary disequilibrium are anticipated and avoided.

Sumner's version of index futures targeting requires a central bank to make a tentative target for base money and then modify that target according to the trades of the contract by speculators. Although these trades should leave expected nominal GDP near the target, they also leave both the speculators and the central bank with a position on the contract and a risk of loss.

Index futures convertibility allows a central bank discretion to adjust current monetary conditions subject to the constraint that it trade the index futures contract. If no one trades the contract, then the central bank adjusts current monetary conditions in the usual way but aims at a policy target for nominal GDP. If speculators disagree with the central bank, they will trade the contract. A central bank with a conservative policy adjusts current monetary conditions to hedge all trades of the futures contract, so that the market expects nominal GDP to be on target. A central bank with an activist policy takes a position on the contract, at least partly offsetting what it considers errors by the speculators. A central bank with an activist policy has the opportunity to earn profit but bears the risk of loss. These profits or losses would provide a signal of the effectiveness of the central bank relative to the market.

Although Sumner's index futures targeting was developed in a context of a central bank with a monopoly on the issue of base money, the related system of index futures convertibility makes it possible to combine a forward-looking target for nominal spending on output with a laissez faire approach to the payments system. Competing banks can seek maximum profits from issuing deposits and purchasing earning assets, but if each bank is constrained to buy and sell index futures contracts, the banking system will tend to create monetary conditions such that nominal GDP is expected to remain on target.

Notes

1. See Yeager ([1956] 1997, [1968] 1997, and [1973] 1997) for a detailed discussion of the key role of monetary disequilibrium in macroeconomic disturbances.

2. George Selgin (1997) explains how price-level changes are the least disruptive response to changes in productivity. Much of his analysis focuses on the scenario where the trend growth rate of nominal expenditure is less than the trend growth rate of productive capacity, so that the change in the price level is in the context of a deflationary trend for output prices.

3. See Woolsey (2012, 234–35) for a discussion of the conditions necessary for a nominal GDP target to avoid monetary disequilibrium in the face of supply shocks.

4. The 5 percent growth rate is the sum of the 3 percent trend growth rate of real output in the United States plus the 2 percent inflation target pursued by many central banks. A 3 percent growth rate would be consistent with a stable price level on average. A slower growth rate would result in a mild trend deflation.

5. The payments for settlement of the contract, which occur more than a year after the contracts trade, would have ambiguous monetary consequences and should be sterilized. In other words, if settlement of the contracts increases base money, the central bank should sell government bonds so the settlement has no effect on the quantity of base money. If, in contrast, the settlement of the contracts reduces the quantity of base money, the central bank should buy government bonds, offsetting that change.

6. Sumner has advocated special margin accounts paying higher-than-market rates of interest. The goal would be to subsidize trading the futures contract. Such subsidies are especially important if base money can change only in response to trades of the futures contracts (Sumner 2006, 16).

7. The open-market operations could possibly be a multiple of the trades of the futures contract. For example, if the central bank buys a $1,000 contract, it would be required to buy $10,000 worth of T-bills.

8. Sumner is following Dowd's proposal for convertibility with "quasi-futures" contracts (Dowd 1994, 2000), which also limits trading to a single day.

9. The interpolation would be $\alpha \text{NGDP}_t + (1 - \alpha)\text{NGDP}_{t-1}$, where α is the proportion of the quarter that has been completed. For example, September 24 will be the 85th day of the quarter, so 85/89, or 95.5 percent, of the quarter will be completed. The daily value for nominal GDP would be 95.5 percent of nominal GDP for the third quarter of 2013 plus 4.5 percent of nominal GDP for the second quarter of 2013.

10. Although other targets are possible, the system is analyzed using nominal GDP one year in the future.

11. Much of the literature on free banking focuses on historical banking systems that combine the microeconomic and macroeconomic elements of free banking. Although the general concept is for banking to be subject to no special rules, the absence of restrictions on branching, the issue of banknotes, and reserve requirements are emphasized. The assumption, consistent with historical experience, is that bank liabilities are redeemable in some base money, such as gold. That the quantity of base money (or interest rates) is not managed by a central bank or anyone else and that the resulting monetary order is consistent with macroeconomic stability are also emphasized. See Dowd (1992), Selgin (1988), and White (1984, 1989, 1999).

12. See Woolsey (1994) for a discussion of index futures convertibility and free banking in the context of stabilizing a price index. David Glasner (1989, 230–41) proposes free banking combined with a version of index futures convertibility. He follows Thompson (1982) in proposing to stabilize an index of wages.

References

Dowd, Kevin. 1992. *The Experience of Free Banking*. London: Routledge.

———. 1994. "A Proposal to End Inflation." *Economic Journal* 10 (425): 828–40.

———. 2000. "Using Futures Prices to Control Inflation: Reply to Garrison and White." *Journal of Money, Credit and Banking* 32 (1): 142–45.

Garrison, Roger, and Lawrence White. 1997. "Can Monetary Stabilization Policy Be Improved by CPI Futures Targeting?" *Journal of Money, Credit and Banking* 29 (4): 535–41.

Glasner, David. 1989. *Free Banking and Monetary Reform.* Cambridge, UK: Cambridge University Press.

Hayek, Friedrich A. von. 1976. *Choice in Currency.* London: Institute for Economic Affairs.

———. 1990. *Denationalization of Money: The Argument Refined.* London: Institute of Economic Affairs.

Selgin, George. 1988. *Theory of Free Banking.* Lanham, MD: Rowman and Littlefield.

———. 1997. *Less Than Zero: The Case for a Falling Price Level in a Growing Economy.* London: Institute for Economic Affairs.

Sumner, Scott. 1989. "Using Futures Instrument Prices to Target Nominal Income." *Bulletin of Economic Research* 41 (2): 157–62.

———. 1995. "The Impact of Futures Price Targeting on the Precision and Credibility of Monetary Policy." *Journal of Money, Credit, and Banking* 27 (1): 89–106.

———. 2006. "Let a Thousand Models Bloom: The Advantages of Making the FOMC a Truly 'Open Market.'" *B.E. Journal of Macroeconomics* 6 (1): 1–27.

———. 2009. "The Real Problem Was Nominal." *Cato Unbound*, September 14. http://www.cato-unbound.org/2009/09/14/scott-sumner/the-real-problem-was -nominal/.

———. 2011. "Retargeting the Fed." *National Affairs* 9 (Fall): 79–96.

Thompson, Earl. 1982. "Free Banking under a Labor Standard: The Perfect Monetary System." Paper prepared for the U.S. Gold Commission. http://www.econ.ucla .edu/thompson/25-1.pdf.

White, Lawrence H. 1984. *Free Banking in Britain.* Cambridge, UK: Cambridge University Press.

———. 1989. *Competition in Currency.* New York: New York University Press.

———. 1999. *The Theory of Monetary Institutions.* Oxford: Basil Blackwell.

Woolsey, W. William. 1994. "Stabilizing the Expected Price Level in a BFH Payments System." *Contemporary Economic Policy* 12 (2): 46–54.

———. 2012. "The Great Recession and Monetary Disequilibrium." In *Boom and Bust Banking: Leaning with the Wind,* edited by David Beckworth, pp. 211–38. San Francisco: Independent Institute.

Yeager, Leland B. (1956) 1997. "A Cash Balance Interpretation of Depression." In *The Fluttering Veil: Essays on Monetary Disequilibrium,* edited by George Selgin, pp. 3–19. Indianapolis: Liberty Fund.

———. (1968) 1997. "The Essential Properties of the Medium of Exchange." In *The Fluttering Veil: Essays on Monetary Disequilibrium,* edited by George Selgin, pp. 87–110. Indianapolis: Liberty Fund.

———. (1973) 1997. "The Keynesian Diversion." In *The Fluttering Veil: Essays on Monetary Disequilibrium,* edited by George Selgin, pp. 199–216. Indianapolis: Liberty Fund.

7. Recent Issues Concerning Monetary Policy Reform

Bennett T. McCallum

Recent discussions on monetary policy reform, by writers who presume that we will continue to live in a world of central banks, have been dominated by topics raised by the financial crisis of 2008–2009 and the subsequent recession.[1] These topics, moreover, have for the most part not actually concerned "monetary policy reform" in any fundamental sense but have instead focused on problems involving (a) operating procedures for situations in which the zero lower bound on nominal interest rates is binding or (b) the reform of financial market regulations. The principal (partial) exception to this statement involves the proposal—made prominent by the paper of Blanchard, Dell'Aricca, and Mauro (2010)—that central banks should raise their inflation rate targets to avoid difficulties associated with the zero lower bound. Accordingly, I begin in the next section with a review of the issues on that topic, one that follows my recent overview paper (McCallum 2011). Next, I discuss another basic analytical topic that has been prominent, namely, the validity or invalidity of monetary policy procedures and analyses that presume that the central bank is using an interest rate instrument and paying little or no attention to monetary aggregates. In the following section, I briefly introduce a troublesome issue raised by the fact that most current analytical models used to study monetary policy provide a multiplicity of solutions. The final section provides a brief conclusion.

I am grateful to Lawrence H. White for helpful suggestions.

153

Should Central Banks Raise Their Inflation Targets?

Should central banks, because of the zero-lower-bound problem, raise their inflation-rate targets? Several relevant arguments are reviewed and considered in a recent paper of mine (McCallum 2011), which is drawn upon heavily in the subsections that follow.

In the absence of the zero lower bound (ZLB) on nominal interest rates, the optimal steady-state inflation rate, according to standard New Keynesian (NK) reasoning, lies between the Friedman-rule value of deflation at the steady-state real interest rate (e.g., 3 percent per year), designed to satiate agents with the transaction-facilitating services of the medium of exchange, and the Calvo-model value of zero, which eliminates an inefficiency stemming from different selling prices among suppliers with similar production costs.[2] Extensive and sophisticated calibration studies reported by Schmitt-Grohé and Uribe (2011) indicate that a larger weight should be given to the latter.

An attractive modification of the Calvo pricing equation, however, would specify that those sellers who cannot reoptimize in a given period would have their prices rise automatically at a trend rate that had been determined in the past. This modification would imply that the weight on the second of the two preceding values should be zero—that is, that the Friedman-rule value would be optimal (see, e.g., McCallum 2011).

Some scope may exist for activist monetary policy to be effective even when the one-period interest rate is at the ZLB. In an example offered by Svensson (2001, 2003) and McCallum (2000), monetary demand management can be conducted effectively under ZLB conditions by appropriate exchange-rate policies. The idea is that one-period risk-free bonds and foreign exchange are not perfect substitutes, presumably for reasons stressed in the "portfolio balance" literature of the 1970s (see, e.g., Dornbusch 1980). Central-bank purchases of foreign exchange will, accordingly, tend to depreciate a country's exchange rate.[3] The central bank could then exploit that relationship to manage the (nominal) exchange rate in accordance with a policy rule expressed in terms of an exchange-rate instrument—with the rate of exchange-rate appreciation appearing in place of the policy interest rate in a Taylor (1993)–style rule. Simulations reported by McCallum (2003) and Coenen and Wieland (2003) indicate that substantial stabilization could be effected in this manner. It must be admitted, nevertheless, that professional disagreement exists on that point—and that the approach would be most appropriate for small open economies.

Present institutional arrangements are not immutable. In particular, is it actually the case that zero represents an inescapable lower bound on nominal interest rates? Of course the precise lower bound may be slightly negative because of the cost of storing money, but this magnitude is small enough to be neglected. Instead our concern now is the validity of the argument, developed by Goodfriend (2000, 2001) and Buiter (2003, 2010), that with modern technology, institutions can be designed to permit payment of negative nominal interest on all forms of money, thereby making it possible to have negative (as well as positive) values for the central bank's policy rate, and thereby *eliminating*—rather than surmounting—the putative problem of the ZLB. In this regard, Citi Research (2010, 5), presumably influenced strongly by Buiter (2010), states that "there are at least three administratively and technically feasible ways to eliminate the zero lower bound on nominal interest rates completely.... The first is to abolish currency. The second is to ... start paying interest, positive or negative, on currency. The third is to ... end the fixed exchange rate ... between currency and bank reserves or deposits with the central bank."

The abolishment of currency seems like an extremely radical step—almost unimaginable—until one contemplates it somewhat calmly. My own attitude has been influenced by a rather trivial aspect of my own routine—lunch each day at my university. Only a few years ago, my regular lunch companions and I used cash to pay for our lunches at the Carnegie Mellon Faculty Club, and I was annoyed when someone in line ahead of us chose to pay by credit card and thereby slowed the process noticeably. Then a new system for accepting credit-card payments was adopted by the cashier, and the time needed for a credit-card transaction decreased sharply. Next, a couple of years ago, I realized that one of my companions had adopted a routine of paying by credit card—and that this apparently involved no extra time at all. Finally, several months ago, I realized that all of my regular companions had switched to credit-card payment as their usual mode of transaction—and that each of them was taking less of the cashier's time (and that of other customers) than I was imposing each day with my cash transaction! A second recognition was that taxicabs now typically have facilities for accepting credit-card payments, thereby eliminating an example that I used to mention in undergraduate classes as transactions for which one needed to carry cash.

In addition, one may be impressed by the point that approximately 75 percent (by value) of U.S. currency outstanding consists of $100 bills. These are notes of the largest denomination available, of course, which are of greatest use to "the underground economy, the criminal community, that is, those engaged in tax evasion, money laundering and the financing of terrorism, and those wishing to store the proceeds from crime and the means to commit further crimes out of sight and reach of the authorities" (Buiter 2010, 224). In the case of Europe, 59 percent of the value of euro notes outstanding in April 2009 was in the denominations of 100, 200, or 500 euros, whereas less than 10 percent of the stock value was in the form of 5, 10, and 20 euro notes (Buiter 2010, 223). Partly on the basis of these facts, Buiter develops a strong argument for the elimination of (government) currency. An important part of the argument is the suggestion, made in Goodfriend (2000), that the central bank make available free transaction accounts for all legal residents, accounts that could be administered through "commercial banks, post offices, and other retail facilities" (2000, 224). In that case, it would not be true that the institutional change would be devastating for the poorer members of the (legal) population.

A second approach would involve taxation of currency. Buiter (2010) stresses, however, that the administration of positive tax rates (i.e., negative interest rates) on negotiable bearer instruments entails inherent problems that sharply reduce the attractiveness of this approach.[4] A third approach of Buiter's is to unbundle—divorce—the medium of exchange (MOE) and the medium of account (MOA). The MOE consists in part of currency and claims to currency; the MOA is the entity in terms of which prices are quoted.[5] Governments do not invariably have full control over either of these but can retain control over the MOE if government currency is not issued to excess. And by requiring that transactions with the government must be denominated in terms of an appointed MOA, the government can most likely gain acceptance for its choice of the latter. Then in each period it could specify interest rates for both, with the MOE interest rate kept nonnegative but with no such stipulation for the MOA rate, by issuing bonds in terms of both media. Then the central bank can conduct policy in terms of its instrument, the MOA interest rate.

If prices in terms of this MOA are the prices that are relevant for market supplies and demands, then the central bank will continue to be able to influence aggregate demand by variations in the policy interest rate even when the MOE rate is immobilized at zero.

Buiter (2010) devotes many words to analysis of this third approach, but his preference seems probably for the abolition of currency. Actually, Buiter and Goodfriend have the abolition of a government-issued currency in mind. Both evidently would favor regulations that would not rule out the possibility of private issuers attempting to put their own currency-like vehicles into circulation.

Increasing target inflation for the purpose of avoiding occasional ZLB difficulties would tend to undermine the rationale for central-bank independence—to be able to take a longer-term view of monetary policy than that of elected political officials—and would constitute an additional movement away from policy recognition of the economic necessity for intertemporal discipline.[6]

Monetary Policy Analysis in Models without Money?

In recent years most academic analysis of monetary policy has been conducted in NK models in which there is no "money supply," that is, no variable represents any monetary aggregate. Monetary policy is represented by a policy rule reflecting the manner in which the central bank is managing a short-term interest rate, such as the federal funds rate in the United States. In this regard, one must distinguish two different issues. One is whether it is desirable for central banks to conduct policy by means of periodic adjustments of such an interest rate; the second is whether in economies, in which policy is in fact conducted in this manner, it is analytically legitimate to use for policy analysis a model that includes no monetary variable. Here I discuss the second issue; the first is a major topic that has been prominent for many years and will perhaps continue to be so for many to come.[7]

A standard three-equation NK model might be written as

$$(7.1) \quad y_t = b_0 + b_1(R_t - E_t p_{t+1}) + E_t y_{t+1} + v_t \qquad b_1 < 0$$

$$(7.2) \quad \pi_t = \beta E_t \pi_{t+1} + \kappa(y_t - \bar{y}_t) + u_t \qquad \kappa > 0$$

$$(7.3) \quad R_t = \mu_0 + (1 + \mu_1)\pi_t + \mu_2(y_t - \bar{y}_t) + e_t \qquad \mu_1 > 0$$

where the variables are y_t = output, π_t = inflation rate, and R_t = nominal one-period interest rate, all expressed in terms of fractional deviations from steady-state values. $E_t\pi_{t+1}$ represents the expected value at date t of the period $t+1$ inflation rate, and similarly for $E_t y_{t+1}$, while $\bar{y}_t$ represents flexible-price output, so that $(y_t - \bar{y}_t)$ is the output gap. Here (7.1) is an "expectational IS equation" that combines the intertemporal Euler equation (for a typical infinite-lived household with standard time-separable preferences) with a linearized overall resource constraint plus the assumption that the economy-wide capital stock is fixed. Equation (7.2) is the basic Calvo model of imperfectly flexible price setting, and (7.3) is the central bank's policy rule that specifies settings of the interest instrument R_t in response to current values of inflation and the output gap. With $\mu_1 > 0$, the Taylor principle (changes in the R_t target should more than match changes in π_t) will be satisfied even if $\mu_2 = 0$. The exogenous shocks in this system—v_t, u_t, and e_t—are, respectively, shocks pertaining to (a) time-preference plus natural-rate of output plus government consumption fluctuations, (b) price-setting behavior, and (c) monetary policy behavior. This is a simplified setup but is highly representative of current mainstream analysis.

The model (7.1)–(7.3) is often interpreted as pertaining to a "cashless economy," in which no medium of exchange exists, that is, no money. That is not a necessary interpretation, however; instead one can take this to be a model in which an MOE provides transaction-facilitating services and a resulting money demand function of the form[8]

$$(7.4) \quad m_t - p_t = \gamma_0 + \gamma_1 y_t + \gamma_2 R_t + \zeta_t$$

where $\gamma_1 > 0$, $\gamma_2 < 0$, and the disturbance ζ_t is presumably related to the other shock processes in the model (7.1)–(7.3). Then *if* the central bank conducts policy by choosing R_t as specified by (7.3), this relation (7.4) will serve only to specify how much money the central bank has to supply each period to implement its policy as specified in (7.3); relation (7.4) will have no effect on the behavior of either y_t or p_t and may therefore not need to be considered at all.

Of course, a money demand function of the form in (7.4) is a special case that will come about only if the way in which money affects transaction costs, in the (implicit) model that underlies (7.1)–(7.2), involves a transaction-cost function that is *separable*. And that is a special and quite unlikely form for the transaction-cost function to assume. But my own attempt to estimate the magnitude of the effect on the model's properties of specifying a more realistic transaction-cost function led to the conclusion that the quantitative effects of this correction are negligible.[9]

Accordingly, the standard analytical approach of the NK[10] mainstream of recent years does not seem to be fundamentally flawed, in the sense that it can be applicable to an economy in which in fact a tangible medium of exchange exists. Also, it is in my opinion appropriate that this analysis includes a price-adjustment relationship (that is, "Phillips curve") that involves some sluggishness in prices, thereby imparting a nontrivial effect of monetary policy on the cyclical behavior of real output and employment.[11] Whether the details of the usual Calvo-type adjustment relationship are adequately understood to permit central banks to successfully conduct activist countercyclical policy in a desirable manner is much less clear. The best thing that central banks can do to enhance output and employment may well be to keep inflation low and steady. No analysis of these issues has been attempted here.

Determinacy

A continuing issue of fundamental importance in the analysis of monetary policy concerns the unfortunate fact that, while most formal analysis of various policy rules and regimes is conducted in dynamic structural models with rational expectations, such models almost always have a multiplicity of rational expectation solutions. Therefore, some additional criterion is needed to determine which of the various rational expectation solutions is being predicted by the analysis (and, accordingly, to provide the analyst's message concerning the behavior of the actual economy being modeled). Without some such criterion, the model does not provide the outcomes of a specified policy rule.

In monetary economics in particular, one criterion has, in fact, been rather widely accepted. It is the criterion of a single stable solution (SSS), that is, that among the multiple solutions that satisfy all of the model's relationships plus the orthogonality implications of rational expectations, one and only one is dynamically stable (nonexplosive). This criterion is in practice often referred to as "determinacy," as if the SSS requirement was equivalent to the desired condition—namely, that the model at hand provides a unique prediction as to the behavior of the (model) economy. A unique prediction is what "determinacy" is supposed to mean, however, so using this word as a synonym for the SSS condition is highly unsatisfactory. This point has been made implicitly but effectively by John Cochrane (2007), who has argued that in a wide class of NK models (which have been the centerpiece of monetary analysis over the past two decades), policy behavior satisfying the Taylor principle leads to satisfaction of the SSS requirement but nevertheless features the existence of a dynamically explosive path for inflation that is not ruled out by any transversality condition or any other generally accepted economic principle. Thus the SSS does not provide a unique prediction as to the behavior of the model economy, leading Cochrane to argue that NK analysis is fundamentally flawed. In a previous paper (McCallum 2009a), I have agreed with Cochrane's analytical point regarding the explosive path but have shown that the SSS does, and Cochrane's explosive solution does not, satisfy the criterion of "least-squares learnability." Furthermore, I have argued, this type of learnability should be considered as a *necessary* condition for a solution to be viewed as a plausible contender for the unique prediction of behavior provided by the model at hand. Accordingly, Cochrane's analysis does not provide any logical justification for his criticism of NK models. In a comment, Cochrane (2009) contends, however, that the analysis in McCallum (2009a) is flawed in three ways. In response to this, I (McCallum 2009b) explain very briefly that Cochrane's objections are analytically incorrect or inapplicable.

Conclusion

The foregoing sections have identified three distinct issues relating to monetary policy that have been prominent in the recent literature. The first issue concerns the suggestion that central banks should raise their inflation targets to make ZLB difficulties rarer, that is, situations in which a central bank cannot provide (temporary) output or employment stimulus by the usual step of reducing short-term nominal interest rates. My survey of this controversy will probably be interpreted as reflecting opposition to increasing the inflation-rate target—if not, I should do some rewriting.

The second set of issues concerns the use of models of the NK type in which there is no recognition of medium-of-exchange money. My suggestion is that these models would be better thought of as ones in which a medium of exchange exists, and that *if* policy is conducted by means of interest-rate manipulation, then use of such a model will probably not lead the researcher seriously astray. Portions of NK models may be seriously misspecified, but this particular departure from monetarist approaches is probably not highly damaging.

The third set concerns issues of "determinacy." The proper meaning of this term pertains to whether or not a model yields a unique solution or prediction concerning economic behavior. But to presume that having a single solution that is dynamically stable implies that true determinacy prevails, and attaches to this solution, is not justified.

Notes

1. Here "recession" refers to the situation of higher-than-normal unemployment of recent years, which has continued long after the "official" recession in the United States ended according to the National Bureau of Economic Research business-cycle dating committee.

2. The Friedman rule was made famous by Friedman (1969), but its logic was developed much earlier, in Friedman (1960). The widely used Calvo model of slow price adjustments was introduced in Calvo (1983).

3. This need not imply "beggar-thy-neighbor" effects on other economies; the positive effect on domestic demand will under plausible parameterizations result in increased imports.

4. Goodfriend (2000, 1016) has suggested that "a carry tax could be imposed on currency by imbedding a magnetic strip in each bill. The magnetic strip could visibly record when a bill was last withdrawn from the banking system ... [with a tax] deducted from each bill upon deposit according to how long the bill was in circulation since last withdrawn." Perhaps such a system could become viable in the future, but with today's technology it would appear excessively expensive.

5. Similarities but also (crucial) differences exist between Buiter's third approach and what I would term the Yeager-Greenfield system. The latter has been developed in a number of papers by Leland Yeager (1983, 1992), plus others that are coauthored with Robert Greenfield (Greenfield and Yeager 1983). One major difference is that the Yeager-Greenfield system was originally designed as one intended to eliminate, or reduce as far as possible, governmental influence on monetary affairs. A second is that a major objective of the Yeager-Greenfield system is to achieve "stability," in the sense of constancy through time, of the price level, whereas Buiter's approach is more concerned with avoidance of recessions.

6. For more discussion on this point, see McCallum (2011).

7. In this regard it should be noted that the first issue can be expressed in a manner that seems to downplay its importance: in both cases the actual monetary actions are typically open-market purchases or sales; the difference is just which of the variables the central bank looks at to decide when to stop making these purchases or sales. That choice can, however, be of great importance.

8. Here, m_t denotes the relevant money stock, and p_t the price level, expressed in fractional deviation units.

9. See McCallum (2001). A similar exercise was independently conducted by Woodford (2003, 111–23) with results that were extremely close to mine. Ireland (2004) took a different approach but obtained similar conclusions.

10. The term "New Keynesian," when applied to the mainstream analytical approach of the past 20 years, is perhaps a misnomer. This approach seems closer to the "monetarist" position of Friedman, Schwartz, Brunner, Meltzer, Laidler, and Parkin during the Keynesian vs. monetarist debates of the 1970s than to the "Keynesian" position of Tobin, Modigliani, Samuelson, Solow, Gordon, Okun, and Klein.

11. To exclude any such relationship would be to imply that an extreme tight money episode engineered by the central bank would not induce a recession—thereby suggesting that the Volcker disinflation was just an accident.

References

Blanchard, Olivier J., Giovanni Dell'Aricca, and Paolo Mauro. 2010. "Rethinking Macroeconomic Policy." IMF Staff Position Note, International Monetary Fund, Washington, DC. Reprinted in *Journal of Money, Credit and Banking* 42 (S1): 199–215.

Buiter, Willem H. 2003. "Helicopter Money: Irredeemable Fiat Money and the Liquidity Trap." NBER Working Paper 10163, National Bureau of Economic Research, Cambridge, MA.

———. 2010. "Negative Nominal Interest Rates: Three Ways to Overcome the Zero Lower Bound." *North American Journal of Economics and Finance* 20 (3): 213–38.

Calvo, Guillermo. 1983. "Staggered Prices in a Utility-Maximizing Framework." *Journal of Monetary Economics* 12 (3): 383–98.

Citi Research. 2010. "The Case for Raising the Inflation Target." Citigroup Global Markets, Global Macro View, (March 5). http://bx.businessweek.com/global-busi-ness/global-macro-view-05-march-2010-by-citi-research/6234371355931297299-fd3b1bf6b0e527571bc3eda957053c32/.

Cochrane, John H. 2007. "Inflation Determination with Taylor Rules: A Critical Review." NBER Working Paper 13409, National Bureau of Economic Research, Cambridge, MA. (Note that current online version of WP 13409 is a revised 2010 version in which much of the relevant material has been removed.)

———. 2009. "Can Learnability Save New-Keynesian Models?" *Journal of Monetary Economics* 56 (8): 1109–13.

Coenen, Guenter, and Volker Wieland. 2003. "The Zero-Interest-Rate Bound and the Role of the Exchange Rate for Monetary Policy in Japan." *Journal of Monetary Economics* 50 (5): 1071–101.

Dornbusch, Rudiger. 1980. "Exchange Rate Economics: Where Do We Stand?" Brookings Papers on Economic Activity, vol. 1, pp. 143–85. Washington, DC: The Brookings Institution.

Friedman, Milton. 1960. *A Program for Monetary Stability.* New York: Fordham University Press.

———. 1969. "The Optimum Quantity of Money." In *The Optimum Quantity of Money and Other Essays*, pp. 1–50. Chicago: Aldine.

Goodfriend, Marvin. 2000. "Overcoming the Zero Bound on Interest Rate Policy." *Journal of Money, Credit and Banking* 32 (4): 1007–35.

———. 2001. "Financial Stability, Deflation, and Monetary Policy." *Bank of Japan Monetary and Economic Studies* 19 (S-1): 143–67.

Greenfield, Robert L., and Leland B. Yeager. 1983. "A Laissez-Faire Approach to Monetary Stability." *Journal of Money, Credit and Banking* 27 (3): 302–15.

Ireland, Peter N. 2004. "Money's Role in the Business Cycle." *Journal of Money, Credit and Banking* 36 (6): 969–83.

McCallum, Bennett T. 2000. "Theoretical Analysis Regarding a Zero Lower Bound on Nominal Interest Rates." *Journal of Money, Credit and Banking* 32 (4): 870–904.

———. 2001. "Monetary Policy Analysis in Models without Money." *Federal Reserve Bank of St. Louis Review* 83 (4): 145–60.

———. 2003. "Multiple-Solution Indeterminacies in Monetary Policy Analysis." *Journal of Monetary Economics* 50 (5): 1153–75.

———. 2009a. "Inflation Determination with Taylor Rules: Is New-Keynesian Analysis Critically Flawed?" *Journal of Monetary Economics* 56 (8): 1101–108.

———. 2009b. "Rejoinder to Cochrane." *Journal of Monetary Economics* 56 (8): 1114–15.

———. 2011. "Should Central Banks Raise Their Inflation Targets? Some Relevant Issues." *Federal Reserve Bank of Richmond Economic Quarterly* 97 (2): 111–31.

Schmitt-Grohé, Stephanie, and Martín Uribe. 2011. "The Optimal Rate of Inflation." In Benjamin M. Friedman and Michael Woodford, eds., *Handbook of Monetary Economics*, vol. 3B, pp. 653–722. San Diego: Elsevier.

Svensson, Lars E. O. 2001. "The Zero Bound in an Open Economy: A Foolproof Way of Escaping from a Liquidity Trap." *Bank of Japan, Monetary and Economic Studies* 19 (S-1): 277–312.

———. 2003. "Escaping from a Liquidity Trap and Deflation: The Foolproof Way and Others." *Journal of Economic Perspectives* 17 (4): 145–66.

Taylor, John B. 1993. "Discretion versus Policy Rules in Practice." *Carnegie-Rochester Conference Series on Public Policy* 39 (1): 195–214.

Woodford, Michael. 2003. *Interest and Prices: Foundations for a Theory of Monetary Policy.* Princeton: Princeton University Press.

Yeager, Leland B. 1983. "Stable Money and Free-Market Currencies." *Cato Journal* 3: 305–26.

———. 1992. "Towards Forecast-Free Monetary Institutions." *Cato Journal* 12: 53–73.

163

8. Monetary Reform in a World of Central Banks

Gunther Schnabl

The wavelike movement affecting the economic system, the recurrence of periods of boom which are followed by periods of depression, is the unavoidable outcome of the attempts, repeated again and again, to lower the gross market rate of interest by means of credit expansion.

—Ludwig von Mises (1949, 572)

The desirable behavior of the total quantity of money [...] can never legitimately be applied to the situation of a single country which is part of an international economic system, and that any attempt to do so is likely in the long run and for the world as a whole to be an additional source of instability.

—Friedrich August von Hayek (1937, 93)

Since the mid-1980s, the global monetary system has suffered from a swelling wave of wandering bubbles that has cumulated into a series of crisis events and excessive monetary easing (Schnabl and Hoffmann 2008). Whereas monetary easing has originated in the large industrial countries with independent central banks, boom-and-bust periods have emerged in both the industrialized and the emerging world. Given that monetary policy rates in the industrialized countries have approached the zero bound, and rising government debt levels herald further pressure on central banks toward

I thank Andreas Hoffmann and the participants of the April 2012 Liberty Fund Conference in Freiburg, "In the Search for a Monetary Constitution Revisited," for very useful comments.

monetizing government debt, doubts concerning the sustainability of the current world monetary system—which is based on fiat money and the discretionary use of monetary policy for business-cycle stabilization—are growing (Selgin, Lastrapes, and White 2012; Polleit 2011).

Although few doubts can exist that, given the current scope of monetary expansion, price, financial, economic, and political stability are at risk, very little action has been taken toward monetary policy reform so far. Policymakers, central bankers, and economists seem absorbed by day-to-day crisis management rather than reflecting on the roots of financial fragility and crisis. The imminent threat of financial meltdown and rising unemployment is argued to make further monetary easing pressing, with monetary policy success supposedly to be ensured by moderate consumer price inflation (Bernanke 2011; Draghi and Constâncio 2012).

To create a basis for the discussion of monetary policy reform, this chapter uses the Austrian monetary-business-cycle theories as put forward by Wicksell (1898), Mises (1912), and Hayek ([1929] 1976) as a theoretical framework. This allows it to identify monetary policy mistakes in the form of "benign neglect" toward monetary policy reform, which is argued to have led to a vicious circle of financial crisis and monetary expansion and therefore into what is dubbed a low-interest-rate and high-government-debt trap. To identify the appropriate toehold for monetary policy reform, the stability of non-exit equilibria and monetary policy–based redistribution chains in favor of the current world monetary hegemon are derived. To solve the current dilemma of a hysteresis of a low-interest-rate and high-government-debt environment, currency competition between the dollar and the euro, with China as a referee, is proposed.

The Failure of Monetary Policy Rules and the Supremacy of Keynes over Hayek

Since the mid-1980s, starting with a too-loose monetary policy in Japan, the world has experienced a pendulum of monetary expansion and financial market boom and bust (Schnabl and Hoffmann 2008). The outcome has been a crisis of unprecedented scope, triggered by an unprecedented scale of monetary expansion, which has been justified by contained consumer price inflation.

The monetary overinvestment[1] theories by Wicksell (1898), Mises (1912), and Hayek ([1929] 1976) provide a valuable framework to understand the interaction dynamics between monetary expansion, boom and bust on financial markets, and benign neglect toward monetary policy reform. Given a higher weight of financial markets for economic activity, goods market–based monetary rules, which were originally designed to depoliticize monetary policy, became the gateway toward a revival of Keynesian macroeconomic fine-tuning based on monetary policy.

Monetary Policy Failure from a Wicksell-Hayek-Mises Perspective

Although the monetary overinvestment theories by Wicksell (1898), Hayek ([1929] 1976), and Mises (1912) were designed to model real business cycles—with the impact on financial markets playing only a second-order role—they provide a useful starting point to understand the most recent boom-and-bust cycle in financial markets and the failure of monetary reform. Whereas in the seminal overinvestment theories, undue monetary expansion triggers (real) investment booms that are followed by rising consumption, inflation, and rising stock market prices, nowadays financial-market booms (preferably in stock and real estate markets) are followed by consumption and investment booms. The move into recessions is triggered by financial-market crisis rather than by rising inflation, as in the seminal overinvestment theories.

To describe a Wickell-Hayek-Mises-type overinvestment boom, four interest rates are distinguished. First, the *internal interest rate* is assumed to reflect the expected returns of investment projects. Second, the *natural interest rate* is defined to balance supply (saving) and demand (investment) on domestic capital markets (I = S). Third, the *central-bank interest rate* is the policy rate set by the central bank. It represents the interest rate that commercial banks are charged by the central bank for refinancing operations. Fourth, the *capital-market interest rate* is defined as the interest rate set by the private banking (financial) sector for credit provided to private enterprises (Hoffmann and Schnabl 2011a). Following the interest rate concept of Wicksell (1898), Mises (1912), and Hayek ([1929] 1976, [1935] 1967), the saving-investment decisions in an economy

167

are in equilibrium when the *natural rate of interest* is equal to the *central-bank* and *capital-market interest rate*.[2]

An upswing in a closed economy starts, for instance, because positive expectations caused by real or financial innovation (Schumpeter 1911; Hayek [1929] 1976) increase the internal interest rate of investment. Given rising investment, the natural rate of interest increases. In the endogenous business-cycle models of Mises (1912) and Hayek ([1929] 1976, [1935] 1967), a credit and overinvestment cycle emerges as the central bank keeps the policy rate constant during the upswing, thereby allowing for too easy refinancing conditions. Alternatively, because of competition for market shares, commercial banks hold capital-market rates low by expanding credit lines (Hayek [1929] 1976). Additional investment projects with lower marginal efficiency are financed that are not backed by rising saving, as the interest rate remains low. An unsustainable disequilibrium between saving and investment is constituted.

According to Hayek ([1935] 1967), excessive lending at constant capital-market rates during the upswing distorts the production structure of the economy. As capital-market rates stay low despite higher investment, the credit expansion falsely signals to investors that saving (preferences of households to forgo present consumption) has increased. With consumption being expected to decline in the present and to increase in the future, high future returns on investment of capital goods (goods aimed at producing future consumer goods) are expected. Unemployed capacities and labor are drawn into the production of investment goods. More consumption is induced by rising employment, wages, and income. The demand for consumer goods rises as well, thus providing an incentive to further increase capacities (Garrison 2004).

The positive expectations can be transmitted to the asset markets, where speculation may set in. According to Schumpeter (1911, 237), price expectations of stocks and other real assets can be disconnected from real economic development. A speculative mania may emerge, in which speculative price projections set in and "the symptoms of prosperity themselves finally become, in the well-known manner, a factor of prosperity" (Schumpeter 1911, 226).

Investment and consumption can comove upward as long as an unemployed workforce and idle capacities exist. At some point, labor becomes scarce and capacity limits are reached. Resources are bound in the capital goods sectors, whereas the consumption goods sector is unable to satisfy increasing demand. The overemployment of capital and labor cannot be sustained to keep up the production level. Consumer price inflation accelerates. The central bank increases the interest rate to fight inflation (Mises 1912; Hayek [1929] 1976, [1935] 1967), or commercial banks reassess the credit risk, or both. Investment projects turn unprofitable and cannot be finished because of scarce resources (Hayek [1935] 1967). Central-bank policy rates and capital-market rates rise, and credit is restricted.

The boom turns into bust. Investment projects with an internal interest rate below the increased interest rate have to be dismantled. Asset prices burst, which worsens the equity positions and creditworthiness of firms. Investment falls further, which pulls the natural interest rate below the central-bank or the capital-market rate or both. A saving overhang emerges because saving is more lucrative at relatively higher interest rates, whereas investment is less profitable. This leads to further disinvestment. Production declines, unemployment rises, and wages fall. Because of falling consumption (at higher interest rates), prices start to deflate. As the central bank or commercial banks hold the interest rate above the natural interest rate, the downturn is amplified.

The Natural Interest Rate and Monetary Policy Rules

Although the Austrian business-cycle theories aimed to model real business cycles, they can be used as a framework for classifying and identifying monetary policy mistakes. Based on the Austrian concept of the natural interest rate—which balances saving and investment—two types of monetary policy mistakes can be defined.

First, during an economic upswing, the central bank keeps the interest rate below the natural interest rate (for too long) (monetary policy mistake of type 1). This triggers an overinvestment boom as described above, which inevitably leads into crisis and recession. Second, during recessions the central bank keeps the central-bank rate above the natural interest rate (for too long), thereby aggravating the downturn (monetary policy mistake of type 2).

The policy implication arising from the monetary overinvestment theories is that central banks should keep central-bank rates close to the natural interest rate both in boom and recession to smooth business cycles (Hayek [1929] 1976). Although the natural interest rate remains a theoretical concept and therefore unknown to policymakers, it should be the task of central banks to gain sufficient information to keep the central-bank rate close to the natural interest rate. In this spirit, Taylor (1993) provided an inflation-targeting rule. It aims to isolate independent central banks from producing Philips-curve type short-term employment effects (Kydland and Prescott 1977). White (2010) characterizes such a constitutional constraint on monetary policymakers as "rule of law" rather than "rule by authorities."

However, since the 1990s, inflation targeting regimes as frameworks to contain inflationary pressure and economic stability failed for two reasons. First, given the fall of the iron curtain and the integration of a large set of low-wage countries (in particular, China) into the world economy, money supply in large industrial countries could grow without any visible impact on domestic consumer price inflation (Hoffmann and Schnabl 2011b).

Second, the gradual growth of international financial markets allowed money-supply growth to be absorbed by capital markets rather than goods markets. Easing monetary conditions showed up in rising asset prices rather than goods prices. With national monetary expansion in the large industrialized countries being absorbed by foreign goods and domestic and foreign financial markets, monetary expansion could assume a Keynesian discretionary stimulus function without violating consumer-inflation-based monetary policy rules.

During a period that was dubbed the Great Moderation (Bernanke 2004), central banks could keep interest rates low for long periods during booms because the impact of monetary expansion on consumer price inflation was postponed via a loop way through emerging market economies and financial markets. Easing monetary conditions fueled bubbles in emerging and financial markets, which only made inflation rise with a significant lag when the wealth effects of rising asset prices made economic agents indulge in consumption.

In the large countries issuing the large international currencies, these loop ways are particularly extended, as they take their ways through fast-growing emerging-market economies (Hoffmann and Schnabl 2011b). For instance, monetary expansion in the United States stimulated capital outflows to China, where the resulting growth impulses helped absorb the additional money supply, and the government embarked on nonmarket-based sterilization policies to keep dollar export prices low (McKinnon and Schnabl

2012). Only to the extent that Chinese monetary authorities allow domestic inflation to rise and the exchange rate to appreciate, the inflationary effects of U.S. monetary expansion have feedback effects on the United States itself, through U.S. price inflation over imports from China (McKinnon and Schnabl 2009).

Second, the fast growth of emerging markets and financial markets allowed persistently low consumer price inflation caused by an asymmetric attitude toward monetary policy mistakes of type 1 and type 2. The monetary policies as observed since the mid-1980s in the large countries (Japan, United States, Germany and euro area) became mainly subject to a monetary policy mistake of type 1: interest rates set by central banks tended to be kept too low for too long during economic upswings, in the United States after 2001 under Alan Greenspan, for instance, below the Taylor (1993) target. In contrast, during recessions, central banks tended to slash interest rates immediately to avoid monetary policy mistakes of type 2.

Keynes's Supremacy over Hayek

The consequence has been the supremacy of Keynes over Hayek in a world where central-bank independence and monetary policy rules seemed to thrive. Monetary policy reform toward a symmetric use of monetary policy over the business cycle (to avoid monetary policy mistakes of type 2 *and* type 1) with a larger role of financial markets for monetary policy did not occur, as central banks were thought to be unable to spot or to tame bubbles. Alan Greenspan pioneered a central-bank system, which felt obliged to stabilize financial markets in times of crisis (the so-called Greenspan Put) but which remained inactive in boom periods. In the so-called Jackson Hole consensus, U.S. central bankers agreed that central banks do not have sufficient information to spot bubbles but should intervene in times of financial turmoil.

Whereas in the monetary overinvestment models, central-bank mistakes were modeled symmetrically to explain business-cycle fluctuations, realized monetary policy patterns in the large industrial countries since the mid-1980s were asymmetric. Monetary policy mistakes of type 1 prevailed, as the impact of expansionary monetary policies on asset price inflation (and volatility) was proclaimed to be outside the responsibility of central banks during boom phases. In contrast, monetary policy mistakes of type 2 were decisively avoided to prevent central banks from worsening recessions by too tight monetary policy stances. Given a rising sensibility of central banks concerning financial stability during crisis, they even tended to transform policy mistakes of type 2 into policy mistakes of type 1 during recessions, which further amplified the degree of asymmetry in monetary policymaking. The ultimate outcome has been the convergence of central-bank interest rates toward zero and the advent of unconventional monetary policy.

Three possible reasons exist for a too expansionary monetary policy during crisis, that is, a decline of the central-bank rate below the natural interest rate: first, in times of financial panic, the central bank has incomplete information concerning the degree of financial instability and assumes the natural interest rate to be lower than it actually is. Second, central banks make a correct assessment of the natural interest rate, but no clear institutional separation exists between the financial sector and the central bank. The central bank sets interest rates too low to minimize the losses of the financial sector. Third, the central bank is dependent on the government and increases the probability of reelection by minimizing unemployment and government deficits. For instance, Buchanan and Wagner (2000, 120) argue "that the actions of the Federal Reserve Board have not been independent of the financing needs of the federal government. Our hypothesis is that political pressures also impinge on the decisions of monetary authorities."

The outcome has been the supremacy of Keynes over Hayek in monetary policymaking. Monetary policy, gradually and covertly, took over the role of providing a growth stimulus, both in recession and in boom, instead of remaining solely obliged to price stability in a wider sense, that is, stability of goods *and* asset prices. Two types of justifications exist for the return of Keynesian monetary policymaking despite the apparent success of central-bank independence and monetary policy rules. First, during recessions, against the background of the fears of the world economic crisis, monetary expansion was justified as the way to avoid a Wicksell-Hayek-Mises monetary policy mistake of type 2 (Bernanke 2011). Yet, in practice, monetary policy mistakes of type 2 tended to be transformed into monetary policy mistakes of type 1.

Second, during booms central banks tended to remain inactive despite financial market exuberance, which can be characterized as discretionary benign neglect toward necessary monetary policy reforms behind the fig leaf of outdated monetary policy rules. Central banks did not curtail excessive money supply growth because domestic inflation remained contained and any impact of monetary expansion on future economic stability was claimed to be outside predefined rules. In Europe, where the monetary pillar of the European Central Bank monetary policy strategy provided sufficient room to incorporate the impact of expansionary monetary policy on asset price inflation, the monetary pillar came under attack (De Grauwe 2006). The reference value for money supply growth became widely ignored.

The Global Move into the Low-Interest-Rate and High-Debt Trap

Since the monetary counterrevolution of the early 1980s, which marked the return toward a high weight of price stability for monetary policy, interest rate levels in the large industrial countries (Japan, United States, Germany, and euro area) gradually declined toward zero. Whereas in the United States and the euro area, the exit from the zero or historical low-interest-rate policy may be perceived to be only temporarily postponed, the zero-interest-rate policy in Japan has persisted since 1999 (Krugman 2012). It will be shown how the structural decline of monetary policy rates below the natural interest rate—and the resulting erosion of the signaling and allocation function of the interest rate—interacted with fiscal policy to further postpone monetary policy reform.

The Global Structural Decline of Interest Rates

The structural decline of both the nominal and real-world interest levels began in Japan in the mid-1980s, driven by an asymmetric exchange-rate policy. Because the dynamic export sector is the main pillar of growth, yen appreciation constitutes a painful drag on growth. Japanese monetary authorities intervened in foreign exchange markets in times of yen appreciation to soften appreciation pressure, whereas they remained widely inactive when the yen depreciated.

Given this asymmetric intervention pattern, the Japanese foreign-exchange reserves rose by then to unprecedented levels. Although Japanese foreign currency purchases were sterilized in the first place to neutralize effects on domestic monetary conditions, interest rates fell during appreciation phases more than they were raised during yen depreciation phases. As a result, Japanese short-term interest rates fell in waves, often linked to crisis events, from approximately 11 percent in 1980 to nil in 1999. Since then Japan remains stuck in a zero-interest-rate environment (Schnabl 2013).

A similar scenario emerged in the United States under Alan Greenspan with respect to stock markets, as monetary policy tended to respond to bear markets (1987 stock market crash, burst of the dot-com bubble, subprime crisis) while it refrained from intervening in the bull markets of the dot-com or the subprime booms (Hoffmann 2009). The key interest rate fell more quickly in recessions than it rose during booms, from more than 18 percent in 1980 to close to nil in 2009.

The European Economic and Monetary Union experienced a less pronounced development than in Japan or the United States because the German notion that monetary policy should be solely committed to price stability to some extent prevailed. The institutional framework of the European System of Central Banks sets an explicit inflation target and—based on the second pillar of the monetary policy strategy—pays attention to monetary aggregates. The growth of money supply M3 far beyond the reference value of 4.5 percent may have given information that inflationary pressure—in goods or financial markets—had emerged. Yet, the euro area did not remain isolated from foreign monetary trends because of appreciation pressure on the euro, which affected in particular the economic performance of former weak currency countries. During the most recent crisis, euro area interest rate levels declined to a historical low of 0.5 percent, accompanied by unconventional monetary policy measures such as outright government bond purchases.

Figure 8.1 summarizes the structural decline of nominal and real interest levels in the large industrialized countries since the early 1980s close to and below zero.

The Monetary Policy–Induced Increase of Public Debt Levels

The structural decline of interest levels, which reflects a gradual monetary expansion in the large industrial countries, was followed by a growing wave of boom-and-bust cycles, as described by Hoffmann and Schnabl (2011a). Both the boom and the bust periods contributed to a (partially hidden) gradual increase of government

Figure 8.1
NOMINAL AND REAL MONEY MARKET INTEREST RATES IN
JAPAN, THE UNITED STATES, AND GERMANY AND THE EURO
AREA

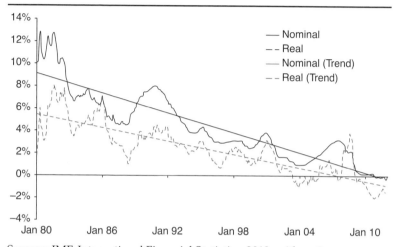

SOURCE: IMF, International Financial Statistics, 2013, arithmetic averages.

debt levels, as politicians around the world exhibited a benign neglect toward the Keynesian postulate of symmetric countercyclical fiscal policies. The gradual rise of government debt in the euro area could not be prevented by the Maastricht rules on fiscal sustainability.

During boom periods, when monetary expansion and financial market exuberance inflated tax revenues—often to the surprise of policymakers—policymakers could not resist the temptation to raise expenditures instead of reducing already considerable public debt levels. The pro-cyclical fiscal policy mistakes during upswings increasingly driven by the financial market had two dimensions. First, politicians did not behave anti-cyclically during the boom because additional tax revenues were not completely saved and spending was not cut (fiscal policy mistake of type 1).

Second, although the statistical concept of cyclically adjusted fiscal balances existed, the calculation of cyclically adjusted fiscal balances—and thereby the target values for fiscal contraction during booms—did not incorporate the fact that during overinvestment (or speculation) booms, tax revenues were inflated beyond the scope

175

of conventional upswings (fiscal policy mistake of type 2). For instance, in Ireland and Spain unsustainable financial market and real estate booms made public budgets look sound, although the rising imbalances set the stage for immense upcoming burdens on public finances.

The two types of fiscal policy mistakes become visible during financial crisis, when the burst of financial or real estate bubbles leads to a sharp decline of tax revenues and to extraordinary expenditures to stabilize financial markets. The consequences of fiscal policy mistakes of types 1 and 2 can be hidden during crisis through monetary expansion as long as interest rates are high enough to embark on monetary expansion. Hoffmann and Schnabl (2011a) dub this phenomenon the "fiscal honeymoon." Yet when monetary policy rates approach the zero bound, public debt levels start to strongly increase as the effectiveness of unconventional monetary policy expansion remains limited. Where, as in the European Monetary Union, debt levels are constrained by institutionalized rules, these rules tend to be abandoned due to extraordinary circumstances.

The hike in public debt levels during crisis in the low-interest-rate environment has four dimensions:

- First, the declining effectiveness of monetary policy
- Second, the extraordinary need for fiscal stimulus during extraordinary crisis
- Third, the lack of anti-cyclical saving during the boom in the Keynesian sense
- Fourth, the lack of anti-cyclical public saving in the Hayekian sense, which is linked to the inability of policymakers to spot bubbles and to anticipate the fiscal consequences

Figure 8.2 shows the resulting structural increase of public debt levels in the large industrial countries, which with the most recent crisis have reached historical peaks in the postwar period.

The Hysteresis of the Low-Interest-Rate Trap

Once countries have entered the low-interest-rate trap and public debt levels continue to increase, the situation is likely to persist. The hysteresis of the low-interest-rate trap is caused by the fear of

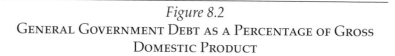

Figure 8.2
GENERAL GOVERNMENT DEBT AS A PERCENTAGE OF GROSS
DOMESTIC PRODUCT

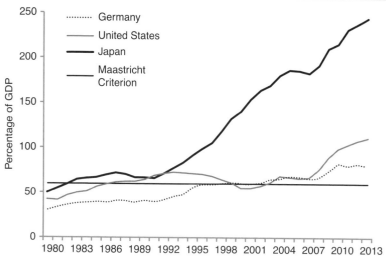

SOURCE: International Monetary Fund, World Economic Outlook database.

structural adjustment after the boom has turned into bust. The usual adjustment process of the private sector, according to the monetary and real overinvestment theories of Wicksell (1898), Hayek ([1929] 1976), and Schumpeter (1911), is the dismantling of investment projects that were started when the interest rate was kept too low for too long and that have turned out to be unprofitable once credit conditions were tightened.

In the real sector, without policy intervention, enterprises faced by declining demand and declining prices exit from the market, consolidate their business activities, or struggle to survive on a lower level of production. Schumpeter (1911, 360–69) regards this "cleansing effect" of recessions as an essential part of a market economy for four reasons (Maurel and Schnabl 2012): speculative investment is to be abandoned; inefficient enterprises have to leave the market; the efficiency of the remaining enterprises is strengthened (as wages decline and productivity rises); and new enterprises, products, and production processes emerge at the cost of old ones.

177

To prevent such an adjustment process and the resulting rise in unemployment, central banks will tend to keep policy rates low for long periods. This implies in the low-interest-rate trap "the persistence of the unadapted and unlivable" (Schumpeter 1911, 367). The marginal efficiency of private investment will tend to decline as the allocation function of the interest rate is lost, and (speculative) investment projects with a very low marginal efficiency will persist.

From a financial-market perspective, the zero-interest-rate policy of the central bank provides incentives for commercial banks to postpone the restructuring of the credit portfolio (Schnabl 2013). Investment projects with low marginal efficiency will continue to be financed and—as the average marginal efficiency of the financed investment projects declines—commercial banks become more vulnerable to a tightening of monetary conditions. The central bank will feel motivated to keep interest rates low to preserve financial stability.

From the government perspective, the pressure on the central bank to keep interest rates low results from the signaling function of the interest rate concerning the soundness of public debt levels. Under free-market conditions, rising default risk caused by rising debt levels is reflected in higher risk premiums. For instance, for the countries affected by the current European crisis since the turn of the millennium, rising (potential) debt levels would have led to rising risk premiums. Yet expansionary monetary policies, following the burst of the dot-com bubble, compressed the risk premiums on the demand and the supply sides of the government bond market. On the supply side, buoyant capital inflows into the later crisis economy created the illusion of lasting increases in tax revenues, which stimulated further bond sales. On the demand side, during credit booms the improving macroeconomic performance and rising tax revenues created the illusion of rising debtworthiness of governments.

The upshot is that in the low-interest-rate trap, after government debt levels have substantially increased, governments will only be able to circumvent painful spending cuts if the central bank compresses risk premiums on government debt. They do this by keeping interest rates low and by conducting unconventional monetary policy measures such as outright government bond purchases.

During the downward path of interest rates since the early 1980s, central banks provided an incentive to increase government debt levels through a price and an income effect. The price effect results from reduced financing costs for government debt, which allow increasing debt levels without a major impact on the interest rate burden (as a share of expenditure). During the busts, the deleveraging of private agents (because of increased risk exposure) creates a negative income effect, which urges governments to raise expenditure.

With debt levels increasing, the central bank must keep interest rates low because of the inverse income and price effects: rising interest rates would increase the share of the interest rate burden in the public budgets, which would force the government into tax increases or spending cuts. The austerity measures would aggravate the recession, which is unpopular among voters and policymakers. Therefore the most likely outcome is that the fiscal consolidation keeps being postponed, thereby preventing the exit from the zero-interest-rate policies.

The Failure of Monetary Policy Reform

Because the hysteresis of ultra-low interest rates and high public debt levels is linked to loss of the allocation and signaling function of the interest rate, structural decline of the marginal efficiency of investment, and growing structural distortions in the world economy, reforms of the world monetary system are pressing. The question of how the world can return to a free-market-based system with a sound macroeconomic environment can be addressed at two levels: (a) the exit strategy from ultra-low interest rates and high debt and (b) the constitution of an alternative world monetary system that impedes central banks of large countries from embarking on undue monetary expansion.

The Exit Dilemma

The prevalent institutional monetary policy framework, based on central-bank independence and monetary policy rules, still seems to be widely accepted among policymakers, central bankers, and academics. Given this status quo, monetary policy reform in a world of central banks would focus on the exit from low-interest-rate and high-debt policies rather than changing the fundament of the world monetary system. Exit from the low-interest-rate and high-debt traps has a macroeconomic policy dimension, which refers to the coordination of the monetary exit with the fiscal exit concerning the timing, and a country dimension, which refers to the monetary policy stance of other countries versus the United States as the global monetary hegemon.

The overinvestment theories as discussed above stand for the monetary exit moving first. Because decisionmaking, implementation, and transmission of fiscal tightening is slow, any approach that regards fiscal consolidation as a prerequisite for monetary consolidation would be equivalent to a postponed monetary policy exit. Boom-and-bust cycles, crisis, and structural distortions would be perpetuated, and the scale of future structural adjustment would increase.

In contrast, moving timely toward monetary consolidation, that is, gradually pushing the central-bank rate toward the natural interest rate, would create a clear incentive to policymakers to consolidate public expenditure and public debt levels. The reconstitution of the signaling and allocation function of interest rates would render redundant all current attempts to substitute the signaling function of interest rates with fiscal policy rules.[3] The cleansing effect (Schumpeter 1911) would trigger—after a painful restructuring process—a sustainable upswing on the back of a gradual increase of the marginal efficiency of investment. Yet short-term-oriented policymakers would be inclined to circumvent creative destruction by urging the central bank to keep interest rates low.

From an international perspective, a credible exit from low-interest -rate policies hinges on the United States as the hegemon in the world monetary system, because any move toward monetary expansion in the United States implies an inherent pressure on other central banks to follow (McKinnon 2010; Hoffmann and Schnabl 2011b; Loeffler, Schnabl, and Schobert 2013). With the Federal Reserve having announced that the federal funds rate will remain close to zero at least until 2014, a restriction is set on the exit from low-interest-rate policies for all members of the informal dollar standard (McKinnon 2010) as well as the European Monetary Union.

The transatlantic transmission of the nonexit from the low-interest-rate trap works through the euro/dollar exchange rate, economic heterogeneity, and crisis in the euro area. As U.S. monetary policy expands, the euro—ceteris paribus—appreciates. The resulting moderation in inflation opens the door for further monetary expansion in the euro area, while capital inflows from the United States and declining interest rates encourage risk taking in financial markets. The multinational European Central Bank decisionmaking body will be inclined to embark on monetary expansion as the heterogeneity between countries with weak and strong economic performance in the monetary union is amplified.

Global Imbalances and Redistribution as Impediments to Monetary Reform

For this reason the efforts toward monetary policy reform should be focused on a mechanism to control the monetary hegemon against monetary expansion. Hayek (1937, 93) argued that "a really rational monetary policy could only be carried out by an international monetary authority, or at any rate by the closest cooperation of the national authorities and with the common aim of making the circulation of each country behave as nearly as possible as if it were part of an intelligently regulated international system."

Although Hayek's proposition addresses the core flaw of the current fiat-money-based international monetary system, it suggests that any monetary policy reform strongly hinges on the willingness of the United States as the prevailing monetary hegemon. The monetary expansion in large industrial countries not only has inflated asset market prices on a global level but also has caused imbalances in current accounts. This sets the stage for systematic international redistribution processes, which reinforce the benign neglect toward monetary policy reforms by the global monetary hegemon.

The structural decline of interest rates has encouraged rising debt and consumption levels of households, enterprises, and government, as interest rate cuts have kept the interest burden as a share of income constant. The outcome has been growing shares of consumption, government spending, government debt, and current account deficits as a percentage of gross domestic product, with the last having led to a growing net nominal international liability position.

At the periphery of the informal world dollar standard, countries are forced into rising current account surpluses based on their attempts to cope with buoyant capital inflows and spiking raw material prices (see McKinnon and Schnabl [2012] for China; Loeffler, Schnabl, and Schobert [2013] for East Asia). Given declining U.S. interest rates, carry trades are encouraged to hunt for yield in a rising number of emerging markets where growth perspectives are inflated by capital inflows in a self-fulfilling manner.

Because both goods and capital markets of emerging-market economies are less developed than in industrial countries, the absorption capacity for capital inflows and monetary expansion without inflationary and asset market pressure is comparatively low. This has forced the emerging markets at the periphery of the informal dollar standard into relatively restrictive monetary policies—in the form of nominal exchange-rate stabilization and non-market-based sterilization—and thereby into the financing of U.S. current account deficits (Schnabl and Freitag 2012).

Similarly, in Europe the divergence of current account balances between Germany and many European periphery countries since the turn of the millennium has been driven by divergent fiscal policy stances (Schnabl and Wollmershäuser 2013). Whereas in Germany serious attempts were made to consolidate public finances and the competitiveness of the enterprise sector based on wage austerity, many countries at the periphery of the European (Monetary) Union embarked on expansionary fiscal and wage policies. The resulting rise of current account deficits at the periphery of the European (Monetary) Union was financed by capital inflows from countries with tighter fiscal policy stances, such as Germany. The divergence in intra-European current account imbalances, international assets, and liability positions was amplified by a low interest rate policy of the European Central Bank after the dot-com bubble burst in 2000, which compressed risk premiums on interest rates.

The rising divergence of international asset positions within the informal dollar standard and within the European (Monetary) Union has become the breeding ground of redistribution schemes, which erode the incentive of international debtor economies to initiate monetary policy reform. In the informal world dollar standard, the supremacy of the United States over monetary policy decisions is linked to the exorbitant privilege of the dollar as an international currency, which provides the United States with a quasi-unlimited line of credit (McKinnon 2010). Given the structural characteristics of underdeveloped goods and capital markets, the countries at the periphery of the world dollar standard are inevitably forced into accumulation of dollar reserves.[4]

The outcome has been an unprecedented surge of foreign (dollar) reserves in the balance sheets of the dollar-periphery countries' central banks. This provides an incentive for the United States to embark on further monetary expansion, as any additional U.S. monetary expansion is equivalent to a real devaluation of the foreign dollar assets. In the case of fixed exchange rates, international assets are devalued in real terms because of imported inflation. In the case of flexible exchange rates, international dollar assets are devalued in nominal and real terms through dollar depreciation.

This redistribution process from dollar-periphery central banks to the U.S. government is not linked to crisis because it takes place among the public sectors, with losses being realized by periphery central banks. The upshot is that any move toward monetary reform by the United States is equivalent to a move away from the United States' exorbitant privilege of providing an international currency and therefore unlikely at the current time, particularly because U.S. government debt is to a large extent held by foreign rather than domestic agents.

An incentive for the United States to move toward monetary policy reform could be created by a stability-oriented monetary policy stance in Europe, which would enhance the international role of the euro and thereby would undermine the widely unchallenged exorbitant privilege to issue the leading international currency. However, in Europe as well, the move toward a tighter monetary policy stance is unlikely given the current economic instability in the southern part of the euro area.

Conclusion: Checks and Balances in the International Monetary System

Hayek (1937) argued that national monetary policies themselves bear the danger of international (economic) instability if they aim to stimulate domestic growth without taking into account the international repercussions. It has been shown that the temptation by monetary hegemons to stimulate growth based on consumption, debt, and redistribution has led into an unprecedented scale of U.S. monetary expansion. The outcome is an unprecedented scale of monetary expansion on a global level, which has triggered financial and economic instability.

Accepting the current central-bank-based international monetary system as a given, any monetary reform with the aim of nudging central-bank interest rates back toward the natural interest rate presupposes a disciplining mechanism on the world monetary hegemon. Because this hegemon is unlikely at the current time to impose any constraint on monetary policymaking by itself, the constraint has to come from outside, that is, from the periphery countries of the world dollar standard.

Such an external constraint could be achieved based on a credible commitment of the East Asian countries, specifically China, to gradually repeg their currencies from the dollar to the euro. Although this would entail significant revaluation losses for China and other East Asian countries on their dollar-denominated foreign assets, future accumulation of foreign assets would be protected against (real) devaluation. The euro could serve as a more credible anchor currency, as the resulting seigniorage gains of the European Central Bank could be used to solve the current crisis and would allow for a reconstitution of stability-oriented monetary policy. The prevalent two-pillar monetary policy strategy would allow, based on the second monetary pillar, placing more weight on the impact of money supply growth on financial market exuberance and crisis.

In this environment of enhanced competition for the privileges of an international currency, East Asia (in particular China) could assume the role of a mediator. A stronger diversification of East Asian foreign reserve holdings and exchange-rate stabilization based on dollar- and euro-based currency baskets with changing weights could create a disciplining mechanism concerning undue monetary expansion in the United States and the euro area. This system of monetary checks and balances could lead the way toward credible monetary reform to create more global financial, economic, and political stability.

Notes

1. Alternatively, "malinvestment."

2. Usually, the capital-market interest rate is assumed to follow the central-bank interest rate. For the (temporary) divergence of capital-market interest rates and central-bank interest rates during crisis, see Hoffmann and Schnabl (2011b).

3. This approach would be even more appealing because nonautomatic fiscal policy rules in the European Union have proved to be weak.

4. This phenomenon is independent from the exchange-rate regime (Schnabl and Freitag 2012). Given fixed exchange rates such as in Hong Kong and many oil-exporting countries, U.S. monetary expansion is directly translated into domestic monetary expansion. Given more flexible exchange-rate regimes, the threat of inflation and

asset price bubbles, sterilization costs (which erode central-bank indepen-dence) or revaluation losses on foreign currency denominated reserves provide an inherent incentive to intervene against appreciation pressure on domestic currencies (Loeffler, Schnabl, and Schobert 2013).

References

Bernanke, Ben S. 2004. "The Great Moderation: Remarks by Governor Ben S. Bern-anke at the Meetings of the Eastern Economic Association." Washington, DC, February 20.

———. 2011. "The Effects of the Great Recession on Central Bank Doctrine and Practice." Speech at the Federal Reserve Bank of Boston 56th Economic Conference, Boston, MA, October 18.

Buchanan, James M., and Richard E. Wagner. 2000. *Democracy in Deficit: The Political Legacy of Lord Keynes*. Indianapolis: Liberty Fund.

De Grauwe, Paul. 2006. "Flaws in the Design of the Eurosystem." *International Finance* 9 (1): 137–44.

Draghi, Mario, and Vitor Constâncio. 2012. "Introductory Statement to the Press Conference." European Central Bank, October 4. http://www.ecb.europa.eu/press/pressconf/2012/html/is121004.en.html.

Garrison, Roger. 2004. "Overconsumption and Forced Saving in the Mises-Hayek Theory of the Business Cycle." *History of Political Economy* 36 (2): 323–49.

Hayek, Friedrich A. (1929) 1976. *Geldtheorie und Konjunkturtheorie*. Reprint, Salzburg: Philosophia Verlag.

———. (1935) 1967. *Prices and Production*. 2nd ed. New York: Augustus M. Kelley.

———. 1937. *Monetary Nationalism and International Stability*. London: Longmans, Green.

Hoffmann, Andreas. 2009. "Asymmetric Monetary Policy with Respect to Asset Markets." *Oxonomics* 4 (2): 26–31.

Hoffmann Andreas, and Gunther Schnabl. 2011a. "A Vicious Cycle of Manias, Crises and Asymmetric Policy Responses: An Overinvestment View." *World Economy* 34 (3): 382–403.

———. 2011b. "National Monetary Policy, International Economic Instability and Feedback Effects: An Overinvestment View." Global Financial Markets Working Paper 19, Friedrich-Schiller-University, Jena.

Krugman, Paul. 2012. *End This Depression Now*. New York and London: W. Norton & Company.

Kydland, Finn E., and Edward C. Prescott. 1977. "Rules Rather Than Discretion: The Inconsistency of Optimal Plans." *Journal of Political Economy* 85 (3): 473–92.

Loeffler, Axel, Gunther Schnabl, and Franziska Schobert. 2013. "Limits of Monetary Policy Autonomy and Exchange Rate Flexibility by East Asian Debtor Central Banks." Working paper no. 122, Universitat Leipzig, Faculty of Economics and Management Science.

Maurel, Mathilde, and Gunther Schnabl. 2012. "Keynesian and Austrian Perspectives on Crisis, Shock Adjustment, Exchange Rate Regime and (Long-Term) Growth." *Open Economies Review* 23 (5): 847–68.

McKinnon, Ronald. 2010. "Trapped by the International Dollar Standard." *Journal of Policy Modeling* 27 (4): 477–85.

McKinnon, Ronald, and Gunther Schnabl. 2009. "The Case for Stabilizing China's Exchange Rate: Setting the Stage for Fiscal Expansion." *China and World Economy* 17 (1): 1–32.

———. 2012. "China and Its Dollar Exchange Rate: A Worldwide Stabilizing Influence?" *World Economy* 35 (6): 667–93.

Mises, Ludwig von. 1912. *Die Theorie des Geldes und der Umlaufmittel*. Leipzig: Duncker und Humblot.

———. 1949. *Human Action*. New Haven, CT: Yale University Press.

Polleit, Thorsten. 2011. *Der Fluch des Papiergeldes*. Munich: Finanzbuchverlag.

Schnabl, Gunther. 2013. "The Macroeconomic Policy Challenges of Balance Sheet Recession: Lessons from Japan for the European Crisis." CESifo Working Paper 4249, Center for Economic Studies and Ifo Institute, Munich.

Schnabl Gunther, and Stephan Freitag. 2012. "Reverse Causality in Global Current Accounts." *Review of International Economics* 20 (4): 674–90.

Schnabl, Gunther, and Andreas Hoffmann. 2008. "Monetary Policy, Vagabonding Liquidity and Bursting Bubbles in New and Emerging Markets: An Overinvestment View." *World Economy* 31 (9): 1226–52.

Schnabl, Gunther, and Timo Wollmershäuser. 2013. "Fiscal Divergence and Current Account Imbalances in Europe." CESifo Working Paper 4108, Center for Economic Studies and Ifo Institute, Munich.

Schumpeter, Jochen. 1911. *Theorie der wirtschaftlichen Entwicklung*. Leipzig: Duncker und Humblot.

Selgin, George, William Lastrapes, and Lawrence White. 2012. "Has the Fed Been a Failure?" *Journal of Macroeconomics* 34 (3): 569–96.

Taylor, John. 1993. "Discretion versus Policy Rules in Practice." *Carnegie-Rochester Conference Series on Public Policy* 39 (1): 195–214.

White, Lawrence. 2010. "The Rule of Law or the Rule of Central Bankers?" *Cato Journal* 30 (3): 451–63.

Wicksell, Knut. 1898. *Geldzins und Güterpreise*. Frankfurt: Verlag Gustav Fischer.

9. Free Banking in History and Theory

Lawrence H. White

In 1962, when Leland B. Yeager assembled *In Search of a Monetary Constitution*, support for a genuine gold standard (where gold rather than a national central-bank unit provides the medium of account and medium of redemption and the international distribution of money is allowed to regulate itself without interference) was rare (Yeager 1962). It had nearly disappeared under "the Keynesian Avalanche."[1] Only two writers in the Yeager volume, Murray N. Rothbard and Arthur Kemp, advocated a strict gold standard. Support for free banking—or any laissez faire monetary system without a central bank—was even rarer. Milton Friedman had explicitly rejected it in his *Program for Monetary Stability* (1960) on the grounds that wildcat bankers, history showed us, would find it profitable to issue more currency than they intended to redeem. Wrote Friedman (1960, 6):

> A fiduciary currency ostensibly convertible into the mon-
> etary commodity is therefore likely to become over-issued
> from time to time and convertibility is likely to become
> impossible. Historically, this is what happened under
> so-called 'free banking' in the United States and under simi-
> lar circumstances in other countries.

Subsequent research on free-banking episodes (and on so-called free banking in the United States) later convinced Friedman (and coauthor Anna Schwartz) that his 1960 historical judgment had been too hasty (Friedman and Schwartz 1986).

In his introduction to the volume, Yeager (1962, 23) considered the idea of free banking. He noted that it would eliminate statutory reserve requirements and thereby the problems of "institutional instability" and a "rubbery" money multiplier created by incentives to innovate around reserve requirements. But he worried that under free banking "a loose linkage between basic currency and the total money supply could prove troublesome" (Later free-banking theorists would argue that the money multiplier will vary to accommodate shifts in the demand to hold bank-issued money and will thereby actually serve as a stabilizing force [Selgin 1988]). Rothbard acknowledged that, under a specie (coined gold or silver) standard, free banking would restrain credit creation more strictly than discretionary central banking (Yeager 1962, 110). But he strongly preferred mandatory 100 percent reserve requirements on banknotes and demand deposits as an even stricter restraint on credit creation and as supposedly the only legally legitimate arrangement to boot (Yeager 1962, 114–17).

Since 1962, Keynesian central-banking policies have performed poorly, and legally restricted commercial banking systems have exhibited instability. Alternatives to Keynesian macroeconomic theories have been developed, most notably under the rubric of "new classical" economics. Theorists and policymakers have emphasized the "time-consistency" problem with discretionary monetary policy. The view of free banking as a self-regulating currency system has been rehabilitated and theoretically extended in interesting directions. But at the same time, the sharply contrasting view that laissez faire banking is inherently unstable, rationalizing government deposit insurance as a low-cost remedy, has been formalized in various ways (Diamond and Dybvig 1983). These real-world and theoretical developments have sparked new interest in reexamining the actual historical performances of the gold standard and of banking systems close to laissez faire.

In accounting for these developments in monetary economics, Friedman and Schwartz—who were prominent among those reexamining government's role in money—emphasized the development of the "rational expectations" approach. The Lucas critique of Keynesian forecasting and "the explicit modeling of the role of expectations," as they noted, had "a major impact on the profession's thinking and, incidentally, have promoted greater attention to institutional structures as compared with current policy formation" (Friedman and Schwartz 1986, 38). To this account I would explicitly add Kydland and Prescott's (1977) critique of the discretionary optimal-control approach to policymaking and their case for "rules," in the sense of enforceable precommitments, to constrain monetary policy.

To explain the new interest in free banking, Friedman and Schwartz (1986, 39) proposed:

> Even granted the market failures that we and many other economists had attributed to a strictly laissez-faire policy in money and banking, the course of events encouraged the view that turning to government as an alternative was a cure that was worse than the disease, at least with existing government policies and institutions. Government failure might be worse than market failure.

The Orthodox Case for the Gold Standard and to Some Extent for Free Banking[2]

As the label "new classical economics" suggests, the escape from Keynesian thinking in some ways meant recapturing older insights using up-to-date modeling techniques.

Most mainstream economists up to World War I accepted the theory, built on the work of David Hume and Adam Smith, that a specie standard automatically regulates a nation's or a region's money stock, including its specie-redeemable bank-issued money. Adam Smith (1982, 507) restated Hume's price-specie-flow theory in his own *Lectures on Jurisprudence* and then, in the *Wealth of Nations* (Book II, Chapter 2), extended the analysis to the case of a currency consisting of specie plus redeemable paper currency notes issued by competing commercial banks (A. Smith [1776] 1981). Smith asserted that the quantity of mixed currency is also self-regulating when a country participates in an international specie standard because any excess notes would be redeemed for specie, and that specie would flow out of the country. An economy with a given volume of annual produce, he proposed, requires only a certain amount of money to circulate that produce. If the banks issue any greater amount of notes, the "channel of circulation ... must overflow" with the excess. The excess "cannot be employed at home," so it goes abroad in purchases of goods and services (A. Smith [1776] 1981, 293). Smith's analysis here was a bit sketchy and, as Henry Thornton noted in 1802, failed to mention the "price" part of Hume's price-specie-flow mechanism. Smith failed to explain why the excess money wouldn't or couldn't initially be spent domestically, bidding up domestic prices, in the manner Hume spelled out. Smith skipped the Humean equilibrating process and went straight to the long-run result.

The introduction of banknotes enhanced the nation's wealth, Adam Smith ([1776] 1981, 293–95) argued, precisely because they will displace specie, and "the greater part" of the gold and silver sent abroad will "almost unavoidabl[y]" be used to "purchase an additional stock of materials, tools, and provisions" that is "destined for the employment of industry." Banknotes thus enabled the nation to exchange much of its "dead stock" of gold and silver for productive capital goods.

Defenders of competitive note issue in Britain, particularly the members of the free-banking school, who opposed monopoly privileges for the Bank of England in the debates of the 1830s and 1840s, followed in Smith's footsteps. They amplified his policy position favoring free competition in banking by spelling out how the clearing system among multiple issuing banks would see to it that any overissuing bank would quickly lose reserves to its rival banks. Competition would restrain any overissue more effectively than monopoly in note issue by a central bank. The currency school, by contrast, denied the Smithian argument and called for nationalization of banknote issue so that the central authority could make the quantity of money conform to its prescription.[3]

The passage of Peel's Bank Charter Act of 1844 signaled the political triumph of the currency school and the failure of the free-banking school to carry the day in the policy arena. Free banking was little discussed in the eight decades thereafter (Selgin and White, 1990; Dowd 1992d). Although orthodox economists continued to accept the Humean-Smithian theory of monetary self-regulation under a gold standard, they neglected the free-banking school's qualifier that the redemption process works *promptly and rigorously* only when an issuer is surrounded by competitors. For example Bonamy Price ([1869] 2000, 214–16), professor of political economy at Oxford, in an 1869 lecture affirmed:

> The quantity of banknotes in circulation is subject to the same rule as that which governs the quantity of coin. It is regulated by the demand of the public; and that demand is determined by the quantity which the public can find use for—the quantity which is actually employed in making purchases and payments, including the reserves of bankers. [Any issue of banknotes beyond that quantity demanded] will be rendered abortive by the public immediately sending back the excess to the bank for payment.

He made no mention of whether this return of excess notes would work as well under monopolistic as under competitive issue.

By failing to distinguish the rapid correction of overissue (via the clearinghouse) under competitive note issue from the sluggish correction (via the price-specie-flow mechanism only) under nationally monopolized or cartelized note issue, Price and others suggested that even the Bank of England with its near monopoly on English note issue was barred from issuing excess banknotes even in the short run. Like the banking school of John Fullarton and Thomas Tooke, they became indifferent to the question of monopoly versus competition in the currency-issuing system. Having thus intellectually disarmed themselves, liberal economists who supported the gold standard had little reason to object to legislative acts that gave national monopolies of issue to central banks.

Once central banks became self-consciously important players on the scene, beginning gradually with the Bank of England in the 1830s, the gold standard no longer operated automatically in central-banking countries. As the free-banking school writers perceived in the 1830s (but the banking school denied in the 1840s, and were followed in this respect by later subscribers to the real bills doctrine), self-regulation of the volume of redeemable money no longer ruled in the short to medium run with a single institution in charge of issuing currency and holding gold reserves. To the extent that the central bank could speed up, slow down, or even reverse the nation's gold flows by altering interest rates or by sterilizing the effect of gold flows on bank reserves, the quantity of money in circulation became contingent on central-bank policy.

The Development of Free-Banking Thought, 1912 to the Present

Ludwig von Mises's *The Theory of Money and Credit* of 1912 was a watershed in free-banking thought, developing the arguments with far greater sophistication. Mises did not see at first much political traction for the idea. But in the second edition, in light of the German hyperinflation, Mises ([1924] 1990, 434–35) suggested a revival of the free-banking versus central-banking debate:

> The events of recent years reopen questions that have long been regarded as closed. The question of the freedom of the banks is one of these. It is no longer possible to consider it

completely settled as it must have been considered for decades now. Unfortunate experiences with banknotes that had become valueless because they were no longer actually redeemable led once to the restriction of the right of note issue to a few privileged institutions. Yet experience of state regulation of banks-of-issue has been incomparably more unfavorable than experience of uncontrolled private enterprise. What do all the failures of banks-of-issue and clearing banks known to history matter in comparison with the complete collapse of the banking system in Germany? Everything that has been said in favor of control of the banking system pales into insignificance beside the objections that can nowadays be advanced against state regulation of the issue of notes. The etatistic arguments, that were once brought forward against the freedom of the note issue, no longer carry conviction; in the sphere of banking, as everywhere else, etatism has been a failure.

The reopening of the debate was unfortunately not very wide. Shortly after Mises's book was published in English translation in 1934, Vera Smith critically reviewed the historical free-banking versus central-banking debates in her book *The Rationale of Central Banking* ([1936] 1990). F. A. Hayek, who was Smith's dissertation adviser, weighed the idea of free banking in his *Monetary Nationalism and International Stability* (1937, 77). Lionel Robbins discussed free banking favorably in *Economic Planning and International Order* (1937, 269–305).[4]

The topic of free banking then faded from public view. A few noteworthy contributions went almost unnoticed. In 1956, Gary Becker wrote a paper titled "Free Banking" that took issue with the inefficient legal restrictions on banks proposed by Milton Friedman. The paper went unpublished, however, until 1993 (see Becker [1956] 1993). In contributions to edited volumes, Rondo E. Cameron (1967, 1972) lauded Scotland's free-banking system for its contribution to the country's economic development. And in a journal article that was not noticed until Eugene Fama cited it 10 years after its publication, Fisher Black (1970) considered "The Effects of Uncontrolled Banking."

The topic of free banking returned to visibility in the mid-1970s as the combined result of the independent efforts of three authors: Hugh Rockoff produced a doctoral dissertation (written under Robert

Fogel) and subsequent articles on the American "free-banking" experience, Benjamin Klein (inspired by Friedman's "optimum quantity of money" theory) offered a theory of the perfectly competitive supply of irredeemable monies, and F. A. Hayek (bemoaning the double-digit inflation rates produced by national central banks) proposed the denationalization of money as a reform program. Following their leads, the present author, George Selgin, Kurt Schuler, Kevin Dowd, Steven Horwitz, and others in the 1980s and 1990s reexamined Scottish free banking and other historical episodes relatively close to laissez faire and developed the theory of free banking.

A Google N-gram (Figure 9.1) shows that the relative appearance of the phrase "free banking" in English-language books began trending upward in 1979 and peaked in 1993–95. By 2005, it had returned to the low levels of the 1960s and 1970s.[5]

Figure 9.1

GOOGLE N-GRAM SHOWING THE FREQUENCY OF THE PHRASE "FREE BANKING" IN ENGLISH-LANGUAGE BOOKS, THREE-YEAR SMOOTHING

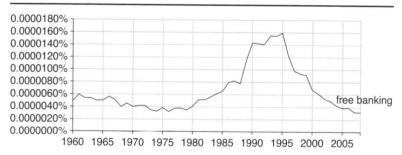

SOURCE: http://books.google.com/ngrams.

A second point in favor of an automatic gold standard, from the orthodox viewpoint, was the constraint that it placed on government borrowing. When government bonds must be repaid in gold—and not in something the government or its central bank can print—government borrowing is limited to what can credibly be repaid by future surpluses (net of debt service). Thus Joseph Schumpeter (1954, 405–6) wrote that "An 'automatic' gold currency ... is extremely sensitive to government expenditure .... This is the reason why gold is so unpopular now and also why it was so popular in a bourgeois era. It imposes restrictions on governments or bureaucracies." If we add that a gold standard is automatic only with free banking, then Schumpeter provides a fiscal explanation for the decline in the popularity of free banking and the advent of central banking with the decline in the popularity of restraining the state.[6] In light of today's sovereign debt crises in Europe and the threat of the same in the United States, Schumpeter's view also suggests an opening for a revival of interest in free banking on a commodity standard as the system that offers the most credible of precommitments against the sacrifice of sound money to the central state's desire for debt monetization and seigniorage.

The Historical Record of Free Banking

Kurt Schuler has identified some 60 episodes of plural private note issue in the 19th century. His contribution leads off a volume edited by Kevin Dowd that includes case studies of nine episodes (Schuler 1992; see also Dowd 1992a, 2). Ignacio Briones and Hugh Rockoff (2005) have helpfully surveyed a variety of economists' assessments of six episodes: Scotland, the United States, Canada, Sweden, Switzerland, and Chile. Because none of the six systems they review enjoyed complete freedom from legal restrictions, they suggest that "lightly regulated banking" is a more accurate label than "free banking." Scotland, for example, had two restrictions imposed on its banks after 1765, namely a ban on banknotes below £1 and a ban on "option clauses" in notes that gave the issuing bank an option to delay repayment under exigent circumstances. These six episodes, like all others that fall under the "free-banking" rubric, involved competing notes denominated in and redeemable for a common specie standard. Schuler's larger set of episodes, in Kevin Dowd's (1992a, 2) words, all involve "at least a certain amount of bank freedom, multiple note issuers, and the absence of any government- sponsored 'lender of last resort.'"

I first review the Briones-Rockoff findings and then comment on the additional episodes detailed in the Dowd volume. Briones and Rockoff (2005, 291) issue an appropriate disclaimer about the danger of confirmation bias in the literature:

> Historical cases of free banking, moreover, tend to attract students with strong ideological priors. It is probably true

194

that free banking has attracted more scholars predisposed to free markets than to regulation. In part, this may reflect the interest of Hayek and other leading free market scholars in free banking. The attraction of this issue may also reflect the relative success of a number of free-banking systems. Advocates of free markets, like advocates of regulation, are drawn to cases that appear to confirm their priors.

Scotland. The Scottish free-banking system of 1716 to 1845 combined stability with competitive performance. To quote my own earlier work on it, there were "many competing banks, most of them were well capitalized," while in its heyday after 1810 "none were disproportionately large, all but a few were extensively branched," and "all offered a narrow spread between deposit and discount rates of interest" (White 1995, 32). Briones and Rockoff (2005, 295–96) find "considerable agreement that lightly regulated banking was a success in Scotland." They note that some writers have given at least partial credit to "unlimited liability, or the presence of large privileged banks acting as quasi-central banks." After 1810, however, the three chartered banks (the only banks with limited liability) were no larger than the noncharted banks (which had unlimited liability) and did not play any special supervisory roles, while the system continued to perform successfully. Scottish banking exhibited economies of scale but not natural monopoly, and the banks mutually accepted one another's notes at par. A few writers have expressed doubt that Scotland was a good example of free banking on the grounds that the Bank of England backstopped the system. I have elsewhere tried to show that such claims are mistaken (White 1995, ch. 3).

United States. Banking restrictions differed dramatically among states in the antebellum United States. The least restricted, most openly competitive, and best-behaved system was in the New England states, where the Suffolk Bank of Boston, succeeded by the Bank for Mutual Redemption, operated a banknote clearinghouse that kept most notes at par throughout the region. Many other states, led by New York, enacted what were called "free-banking" laws. These acts opened up entry to all qualifying comers (in contrast to chartering systems that required a special act of the state legislature), but also imposed collateral restrictions on note issue and maintained geographical branching restrictions. Briones and Rockoff (2005, 302) reiterate a point that Rockoff emphasized in his own pioneering work on the state free-banking systems, namely that these legal restrictions were more than light. The less successful experiences in some states "appear to have been the result of restrictions imposed on the American free banks—restrictions on branch banking and the peculiar bond security system—rather than the result of freedom of entry." On the positive side, freer entry enhanced competition, and the "stories about wildcat banking" that some historians took to be the natural consequence, "although not baseless, were exaggerated." In New York and some other early-adopting states, the system "worked well," which explains why it spread to more and more states.

Canada. The Canadian system, Briones and Rockoff (2005, 304) note, "like the Scottish system and parts of the American system, was clearly a successful case of lightly regulated banking." Canada did not suffer the financial panics that the United States did in the late 19th century. Its banks did not even fail in the Great Depression. The Canadian banking system "did so well that a central bank was not established until 1935," and even then the reason was not dissatisfaction with the existing banking system but some combination of nationalism and wishful thinking about what a central bank could do to end the Great Depression.[7]

Sweden. Sweden had a system of competitive private note issue by "Enskilda" banks while at the same time having the official Riksbank as banker to the state. The Enskilda banks' record for safety was remarkable. Briones and Rockoff (2005, 306–7) report that, "Although one could debate the relative contributions of the Riksbank and the Enskilda banks, it is clear that the combination of the two maintained convertibility and provided an efficient means of payment for the Swedish economy."

Switzerland. Switzerland's system ended in a crisis, but Briones and Rockoff (2005, 310) doubt that this reflects poorly on lightly regulated banking because, "at least after the federal banking law of 1881, the Swiss experience seems to have been less free than other experiences in many important dimensions such as the existence of privileged cantonal banks and restrictive collateral requirements for private banks." Moreover, the law diminished "the capacity of the public for differentiating notes," which created a common-pool problem, weakening the effectiveness of the clearing system against overissue.[8]

Chile. Briones and Rockoff (2005, 314) also consider Chile's experience a poor test because the system was skewed by government favoritism: "With a small ruling elite and concentrated economic power, Chile had great difficulty creating note-issuing banks that were completely independent of the government." Nonetheless what was called a free-banking law was "successful in developing the financial and banking industry."[9]

Australia. Operating with few restrictions, Australian banks were large, widely branched, and competitive, and they practiced mutual par acceptance, making the system resemble Scotland's. The Australian episode is of special interest for suffering the worst financial crisis known under a free-banking system. After a decade-long real estate boom came to an end in 1891, some building societies and land banks failed, after which 13 of 26 trading banks suspended payments in early 1893. George Selgin (1992a, 182–83) finds that the banks' reserve ratios do not indicate any overexpansion of bank liabilities during the boom, though some banks clearly made bad loans. The boom was rather financed by British capital inflows, which suddenly stopped after the Baring crisis of 1890. Kevin Dowd (1992b, 49, 70–71) adds that the banks were not undercapitalized. He argues that "misguided government intervention" in the first failed institutions "needlessly undermined public confidence" in other banks, while other interventions boosted the number of suspensions (all but one of the suspended banks soon reopened) by providing favorable reorganization terms for banks in suspension.[10]

Colombia. The free-banking era in Colombia lasted only 15 years, from 1871 to 1886, during the period of a classical liberal constitution. Thirty-nine banks were created, two of which did about half the business. The system survived a civil war in 1875 with only a few months' suspension and appears to have been otherwise free of trouble. It ended when the government created its own bank and gave it a monopoly of note issue for seigniorage purposes (Meisel 1992).

Foochow, China. George Selgin (1992b) reports that the banking system in the city of Foochow (or Fuzhao) in southeastern China operated under complete laissez faire in the 19th and early 20th centuries, being left alone by the national ruling dynasty. The successful results resembled those of free banking in Scotland or Sweden. Banknotes were widely used and circulated at par, bank failures were rare, and the system provided efficient intermediation of loanable funds.

Postrevolutionary France. The end of the French Revolution, the economist Jean-Gustave Courcelle-Seneuil later wrote, "left France under the regime of freedom for banks." New banks began issuing redeemable banknotes in 1796. In Courcelle-Seneuil's evaluation, the banks operated "freely, smoothly and to the high satisfaction of the public." After only seven years, in 1803, Napoleon Bonaparte took power and created the Bank of France with a monopoly of note issue to help finance his government.[11]

Ireland. In 1824, after poor results with plural note issues by under-sized banks, the British Parliament deliberately switched Ireland from the English set of banking restrictions (the limitation of banks to six or fewer partners) to the Scottish free-banking model (joint-stock banks with an unlimited number shareholders, each with unlimited liability) and thereafter enjoyed results like Scotland's. Howard Bodenhorn (1992, 137) considers it "not surprising" that "free banking in Ireland should rival the success of the Scottish. After 1824, restrictions on banking were repealed, except unlimited liability, and joint-stock banks were formed based on the Scottish mould. Failures were infrequent, losses were minimal ... and the country was allowed to develop a system of nationally branched banks."

The Political Triumph of Central Banking

As Kevin Dowd (1992a, 3–6) fairly summarizes the record of these historical free-banking systems, "most if not all can be considered as reasonably successful, sometimes quite remarkably so." In particular, he notes that they "were *not* prone to inflation," did not show signs of natural monopoly, and boosted economic growth by delivering efficiency in payment practices and in intermediation between savers and borrowers (emphasis in original). Those systems of plural note issue that *were* panic prone, like those of pre-1913 United States and pre-1832 England, were not so because of competition but because of legal restrictions that significantly weakened banks.

Where free banking was given a reasonable trial, for example in Scotland and Canada, it functioned well for the typical user of money and banking services. Why then did every nation adopt central banking? Free banking often ended because the imposition of heavy legal restrictions or creation of a privileged central bank offered revenue advantages to politically influential interests. Economic historian Charles Kindleberger (1994, pp. ix–xii) has referred to a "strong revealed preference in history for a sole issuer." As George Selgin and I have noted elsewhere, the preference that history reveals is that of the fiscal authorities, not of money users (Selgin and White, 1999, 154–65). In some places (e.g., London) free banking never received a trial for the same reason. Central banks primarily arose, directly or indirectly, from legislation that created privileges to promote the fiscal interests of the state or the rent-seeking interests of privileged bankers, not from market forces.

The Bank of England in 1694, in Walter Bagehot's (1877, 92) words, "was founded by a Whig Government because it was in desperate want of money." As a quid pro quo for lending to the government, the bank's charter was made exclusive, and Parliament soon decreed that no other note-issuing bank could have more than six partners. Over time, other legislation secured to the bank a complete monopoly of note issue in England and Wales. Of particular importance was Peel's Bank Charter Act of 1844, which was supported by the currency school's theoretical argument that competitive banking was a source of instability and only a single issuer could properly control the stock of currency.

The fiscal origins of the Bank of France's privileges were especially straightforward. Napoleon Bonaparte was a shareholder in the bank, as was his government. The government quite deliberately gave the bank a complete legal monopoly of note issue in 1803 and then borrowed from it heavily to finance Bonaparte's wars (Nataf 1992, 134). Schuler (1992) finds that Sweden was another case where the impetus for ending competition in note issue was to give seigniorage profit to the government's bank, as were the cases of Italy, Portugal, Spain, Brazil, and China.

In the United States, as in England, restrictions on banks of issue imposed for fiscal reasons led indirectly to central banking. The National Banking Acts passed during and just after the Civil War tied the authorized volume of a bank's note issue to its holdings of federal bonds. The resulting seasonal "inelasticity" of the currency stock created a series of financial panics. The demand for a remedy to the panics, in an environment of progressive thought, produced the Federal Reserve Act.[12]

Until the Federal Reserve Act, passed on the eve of World War I, the classical gold standard operated without central banks in most of the leading economies outside Europe, namely the United States, Canada, Mexico, the nations of Central America and South America (except Uruguay), India, Australia, New Zealand, South Africa, and Rhodesia and other colonial territories of Africa.[13] The war brought the classical gold standard to an end. The governments of Britain, France, Germany, and other combatant nations of Europe suspended the gold standard so their central banks could print money to finance war expenditures. The 1920s and 1930s were not decades of a restored classical gold standard but of international monetary chaos. As Leland Yeager (1966, 290) has put it: "The gold standard of the late 1920s was hardly more than a façade.... Gold standard methods of balance-of-payments equilibrium were largely destroyed and were not replaced by any alternative." National governments that pressed their central banks to violate the norms of the gold standard were not about to consider free banking.

In his lectures published as *Monetary Nationalism and International Stability* of 1937, Hayek was a fairly lonely voice arguing the virtues of an automatically operating international gold standard in which national central banks do not manipulate interest rates or impose quantitative restrictions to impede international gold flows and do not sterilize the effect of flows on domestic money stocks. He pointed out that gold reserve flows between countries do not deserve their reputation for being inherently disruptive. They impose an inflationary boom on the inflow country and a credit crunch in the outflow country only because banking systems end at the border. Banking systems became nationally distinct because international branching of banks was not allowed and because legal restrictions made a central bank the sole holder of each nation's gold reserve. The imposition of restrictions leading to a "one-reserve system" (as Bagehot had called it) was the reason that nationally specific bank lending expanded with gold inflows and contracted with gold outflows. Hayek (1937, 77) concluded:

> The rational choice would seem to lie between either a system of "free banking," which not only gives all banks the right of note issue and at the same time makes it necessary for them to rely on their own reserves, but also leaves them free to choose their field of operation and their correspondents without regard to national boundaries, and on the other hand, an international central bank.[14]

Unfortunately for the reception of Hayek's argument, the debate over free banking versus central banking had almost everywhere ended before 1937.[15] The last industrialized countries without central banks, Canada and New Zealand, had adopted them in 1934. Free banking on a gold standard was inconsistent with activist monetary policy, and the opportunity to conduct activist monetary policy was one of the important arguments made for establishing the Bank of Canada over the commercial bankers' objections. The Keynesian Avalanche after 1936 cemented the victory. Discussions among monetary economists between 1937 and 1962 almost entirely took central banking for granted. A few non-Keynesian economists still favored a role for gold as a long-run constraint on central banks, but the consensus view on "rules versus discretion" was that central banks needed a great deal of discretion for Keynesian policymaking.

Rationales for Central Banking and Deposit Insurance

Charles Goodhart (1988, pp. 1–2) has prominently argued that "the role and functions of central banks have evolved naturally over time." But the development of central banking was "natural" only in the sense of understandable or inevitable (if you give a bank enough privileges, *naturally* it becomes a central bank), not "natural" in the sense of the result of market forces (as in the phrase "natural monopoly"). Central-banking legislation often arose—both the United Kingdom and the United States exhibit this pattern—from attempts to remedy weaknesses caused by earlier legal restrictions on banking by imposing a further layer of intervention. Goodhart (1988, 1–2) himself notes that in the case of the Bank of England its "privileged legal position, as banker to the government and in note issue, then brought about consequently, and, naturally, a degree of centralization of reserves."[16] In general, central banks emerged historically not because they were needed to play a vital role left unfilled in an unregulated banking system but because of privileges and legal restrictions.

Goodhart (1988, 85) offers a theoretical argument for having a government-sponsored central bank as a lender of last resort. He argues that the public has a "need for quality control and supervision" of banks by some third party and that the banks need a lender of last resort. He recognizes that private clearinghouse associations, organized as clubs of member banks, have historically played these roles, but he argues that the club needs an independent arbiter to overcome internal conflicts of interest. He supposes that a government central bank can efficiently play the role of a neutral arbiter acting in the public interest. Both of the stipulated needs are doubtful, however. In the least restricted free-banking systems (Scotland, Canada, Sweden, and New England, for example), quality control was not a chronic problem.[17] Goodhart offers no evidence that conflict-of-interest problems actually did arise in clearinghouse associations, or must do so, but rather cites episodes where certain commercial banks were reluctant to lend to their rivals. Goodhart is largely silent on the possibility of, and the problems raised by, conflicts of interest between a central bank and the public. Perhaps most tellingly, in not a single one of the cases of the historical establishment of central banks, summarized in his own book's appendix, were developments driven by the "conflict of interest" problems identified in Goodhart's theoretical argument. Goodhart's is a purely normative theory of central-bank evolution, where "normative" means "not fitting the facts."[18]

The most influential argument against laissez faire banking in the post-1962 literature is undoubtedly the case for deposit insurance based on the Diamond-Dybvig model of bank runs. In a nutshell, they and the literature building on their model argue that (a) an unregulated banking system is inherently prone to runs and (due to "contagion") panics, (b) runs and panics have net harmful effects, and (c) deposit insurance can reduce runs and panics at a cost less than the benefit of doing so (Diamond and Dybvig 1983; see also Aghion, Bolton, and Dewatripont 2000). It is easy to accept (b) in the case of a run on a solvent bank, though not in the case of a run on a bank that is insolvent before the run occurs. The latter kind of run has important benefits. It pulls the plug on a firm that has wasted its creditors' wealth before any further wealth can be lost. The threat of a run provides salutary incentives to all bank depositors to monitor the bank and to the bank's owners and managers to manage its affairs prudently. The overwhelming majority of bank runs, at least in U.S. history, fit into this second category (Kaufman 1988; Calomiris and Kahn 1991; Gorton 1988).

The Diamond-Dybvig case for propositions (a) and (c) is much weaker than is usually realized, having been subject to a number of devastating criticisms.[19] The historical criticism is that Diamond-Dybvig is not a useful model for explaining historical patterns of bank runs. The theoretical criticisms point to the model's nonrobustness. Small tweaks to the model's assumptions, in the direction of greater realism, undo the results.

In brief, the Diamond-Dybvig bank is run-prone because it is so inherently fragile that a run will always do it in. Any expectation of a run is then self-justifying: if you think others are running, it's rational for you to run as well, to avoid being one of the people at the end of the line who will not be repaid. The result is a "sunspot" model of bank runs: any event can trigger a run if each depositor *thinks* that such an event will make *others* run, because then for each depositor the dominant strategy is to run; and thus the event *will* cause a run and will bring down the bank. Such a self-justifying run can occur randomly or be triggered by an intrinsically irrelevant event. In the Diamond-Dybvig model, deposit insurance—mirabile dictu—can *costlessly* remedy the problem of bank runs. The Diamond-Dybvig bank never fails for any reason other than a run, and deposit insurance prevents runs from ever happening by turning "run the bank" into a nondominant strategy for customers, so the potential deposit insurance remedy will never have to be implemented.

The concepts of "panic" and "contagion" (suggesting that nobody would need to stop lending if nobody else did so), loosely associated with the Diamond-Dybvig model (loosely, because taken literally they model only a single bank, not a system), were often invoked by commenters on the Southeast Asia exchange-rate crises of 1997. They have more recently been heard in discussions of the eurozone sovereign debt crisis.

In historical experience with uninsured banking systems, bank runs did not occur merely randomly, or because of irrelevant events, but followed definite temporal patterns. They typically occurred at the onset of recessions. Furthermore, runs on prerun-solvent banks weren't a problem in all banking systems but characteristically only in weak banking systems, that is, in places where banks often failed, such as the United States outside New England and England outside London in the 19th century. They were not a problem where the banks seldom failed, as in Canada or Scotland under free banking. A theory of bank runs that better matches historical experience, that is, better explains the time-series and cross-country variations, is that runs happened when depositors received bad news indicating that the bank might be *already* (prerun) insolvent. Depositors would run because assets might already be too small to pay all depositors back. Likewise, correlated attacks on central-bank exchange-rate pegs (as in Southeast Asia in 1997) and correlated investor movements against the sovereign bonds of highly indebted countries are better explained by reactions to fundamentals than by sunspots or purely self-feeding concerns about default.

Critics of the Diamond-Dybvig model have pointed to at least four ways in which the Diamond-Dybvig bank is so unlike a real-world bank that the implications of the model are of questionable relevance to real-world banks. First, real-world banks have equity holders who stand in line behind other claimants, whereas the Diamond-Dybvig bank has no junior claimants and so is always insolvent in its second period when running is an option. Second, real-world banks can temporarily suspend redemption of their note and deposit claims, in which event customers are inconvenienced but can still spend the claims. The Diamond-Dybvig bank cannot suspend redemption of its deposits without its customers starving because its deposits are not a means of payment but only claims to the economy's sole consumption good. Third, the deposit insurance that saves the day in the Diamond-Dybvig world relies on the deposit insurer having a technique for undoing the bank's first-come-first-served constraint in meeting withdrawals (namely, the insurer can credibly promise to claw back first-served payouts if necessary to give equal payouts to the last served). But Diamond-Dybvig models inconsistently do not allow the bank to use that technique itself. Consistency would remove either the feasibility (nobody can do it) or the need for third-party deposit insurance (because the bank can make the same promise part of its deposit contract). Fourth, Diamond-Dybvig models speak loosely of "panics" but consider only a one-bank world. A world of multiple banks opens the possibility of interbank loans to relieve illiquidity at any one bank.

New Arguments for Gold and Free Banking

Other theoretical developments have produced new arguments for a commodity standard and free banking. As already noted, Friedman and Schwartz credited the "rational expectations" approach with helping revive recognition that the constitutional features of monetary regimes are vitally important to their success or failure. From rational expectations came the Kydland-Prescott model of the tragedy of well-meaning discretionary monetary policy even where the central bank faces no informational or timing problem. Finn E. Kydland and Edward C. Prescott (1977, 475) provided a simple macroeconomic policy model in which "doing what is best, given the current situation, results in an excessive level of inflation, but unemployment is no lower than it would be if inflation (possibly deflation or price stability) were at the socially optimal rate." They concluded that "policymakers should follow rules rather than have discretion" (p. 489).

The suggestion that a gold standard provides a suitable rule did not appear in the 1977 Kydland-Prescott article, but it did appear in the heavily cited 1983 follow-up article by Robert Barro and David Gordon. Barro and Gordon applied the Kydland-Prescott model historically to explain why inflation rose with the abandonment of the commitment to a gold standard. They then observed:

> The model stresses the importance of monetary institutions, which determine the underlying rules of the game. A purely discretionary environment contrasts with regimes, such as a gold standard or a paper-money constitution, in which monetary growth and inflation are determined via choices among alternative rules. ... Although we would be uncomfortable attempting to forecast a systematic direction of error in future institutional choices, we might be willing to label a particular past choice—such as the movement away from the remnants of the gold standard and fixed exchange rates—as a mistake. (Barro and Gordon 1983, 608)

Kydland went on to coauthor several papers underlining the virtues of the gold standard's rule-boundedness. Michael Bordo and Kydland (1995, 424) observed that "adherence to a specie standard rule enabled many countries to avoid the problems of high inflation and stagflation that troubled the late 20th century."[20]

A second theoretical development favoring strict rules was the "unpleasant monetarist arithmetic" concept of Thomas J. Sargent, Neil Wallace, and Preston Miller. Their concern with government debt monetization was considered far-out when first voiced in 1981, but it now seems prescient in light of the eurozone sovereign debt crisis. As if anticipating the events in Greece and Ireland 20-some years later, they warned that chronically excessive government budget deficits can push an economy into such a high debt-to-GDP ratio that real government bond yields rise above the economy's growth rate. Ever-rising debt service will then make the debt-to-GDP ratio grow without limit even if the primary budget (excluding debt service) returns to balance (Sargent and Wallace 1981; Miller and Sargent 1984; Sargent 1984, 1986). In this scenario, the ability to continue financing spending with additional borrowing eventually hits a ceiling for Laffer curve–type reasons. That is, at some point additional bond sales into a saturated market will raise the real interest rate the government has to pay and thus its debt service to such an extent that the net proceeds of bond sales are zero. Money printing then becomes the only method left for covering ongoing budget deficits. The resulting price inflation cannot be stopped, because money creation cannot be stopped, unless there is a fiscal reform. One means of fiscal reform is to tie the hands of the monetary authority, creating a credible precommitment not to monetize debt that limits the feasible path of deficits.

A more fundamental remedy, by contrast to merely having the monetary authority announce its plans ahead of the fiscal authority, is to switch from a fiat-money regime to a commodity-money regime to effectively restrict the path of money creation. In a 2010 interview, Sargent commented favorably on the gold standard:

> Remember that under the gold standard, there was no law that restricted your debt-GDP ratio or deficit-GDP ratio. Feasibility and credit markets did the job. If a country wanted to be on the gold standard, it had to balance its budget in a present-value sense. If you didn't run a balanced budget in the present-value sense, you were going to have a run on your currency sooner or later, and probably sooner. So, what induced one major Western country after another to run a more-or-less balanced budget in the 19th century and early 20th century before World War I was their decision to adhere to the gold standard. (Rolnick 2010, 36)

Sargent here seemed to assume that a government central bank issues the country's gold-redeemable currency and bears the brunt of a speculative attack. Of course, as we have noted, many countries under the classical gold standard before World War I, such as the United States, Canada, and Australia, had in fact no central bank but instead decentralized private note issue. A more general statement of the disciplinary mechanism to cover such regimes would be if a country didn't run a balanced budget in the present-value sense (spending balanced by present taxes or a credible commitment to present-value-equivalent future taxes), the international bond market would put a high default premium on its bonds, eventually making further net bond finance impossible.

In the same interview, Sargent appealed to "unpleasant arithmetic" to explain the Greek and other European sovereign debt crises. Despite the European Central Bank's rules against any member country's running a large deficit or accumulating a high debt-to-GDP ratio,

> a number of countries at the European Union economic periphery—Greece, in particular—violated the rules convincingly enough to unleash the threat of unpleasant arithmetic in those countries. The telltale signs were persistently rising debt-GDP ratios in those countries. Of course, the unpleasant arithmetic allows them to go up for a while, but if that goes on too long, eventually you're going to get a sovereign debt crisis. (Rolnick 2010, 36)

This diagnosis bolsters the case for the ultra-strict precommitments implied by a gold standard with free banking.[21]

Notes

1. I take the phrase from McCormick (1992).
2. The first half of this section draws heavily from White (2012, ch. 11).
3. For details see White (1995).
4. Robbins's discussion was noted by Rothbard in Yeager (1962, 131).
5. See the N-gram at http://books.google.com/ngrams/graph?content =free+banking&year_start=1960&year_end=2008&corpus=0&smoothing=3.
6. That is, as progressivism and social democracy triumphed politically over classical liberalism. See also Selgin and White (1999).
7. On the Bank of Canada Act, see Bordo and Redish (1987). On banking stability in the Great Depression, see Grossman (1994).
8. For a harsher assessment of Swiss free banking, see Neldner (1998). In reply to Neldner, see Fink (2011).
9. New work on Chile's free-banking experience is under way.
10. For a different view, see Turner and Hickson (2002).

11. See Nataf (1992). The quotes from Courcelle-Seneuil are as provided and translated by Nataf.

12. See V. Smith ([1936] 1990, ch. 11). In his summary table, Kurt Schuler (1992, Table 2.1) attributes the end of free banking in various countries to "seigniorage," to "crisis," or to "theory." He puts down "theory" for both England and the United States, but in both cases all three reasons operated.

13. See Schuler (1992, Table 2.1, pp. 40–45). China was on a silver standard without a central bank. Putting it the other way around, the list of central banks before 1900 was limited to 15 European nations plus Japan, Indonesia, Uruguay, and the Netherlands Antilles. See Goodhart, Capie, and Schnadt (1994, p. 6).

14. For elaboration and embroidery on Hayek's argument, see White (1998, 377–401).

15. An exception was Venezuela, which had a system of competitive note issue without a central bank and intellectual defenders of the system, until the government established a central bank in 1940. See Crazut (1990, pp. 33–61).

16. See my review of Goodhart's (1988) book (White 1990). See also Goodhart (1987, 1994).

17. Goodhart cites Friedman's (1960) *Program for Monetary Stability*, making the claim that free-banking systems were rife with fraud, but Friedman and Schwartz (1986) later acknowledged that the historical evidence contradicted his claim.

18. See Goodhart (1988, p. 45). Here again I draw on my book review (White 1990). See also Richard H. Timberlake's (1990) review of Goodhart and George Selgin's (1993) essay-review.

19. For reviews of the critical literature, see Dowd (1992c) and White (1999, ch. 5). In the rest of this section, I mostly summarize the discussion in the latter.

20. See also Bordo and Kydland (1996, pp. 55–100) and Kydland and Wynne (2002).

21. In a recent working paper, Sargent (2010, pp. 5, 14) addresses "unfettered financial intermediation, also known as free banking," but unfortunately identifies it with what he calls "a real bills policy."

References

Aghion, Philippe, Patrick Bolton, and Mathias Dewatripont. 2000. "Contagious Bank Failures in a Free Banking System." *European Economic Review* 44 (4): 713–18.

Bagehot, Walter. 1877. *Lombard Street*. London: Henry S. King.

Barro, Robert J., and David B. Gordon. 1983. "A Positive Theory of Monetary Policy in a Natural Rate Model." *Journal of Political Economy* 91 (4): 589–610.

Becker, Gary S. (1956) 1993. "A Proposal for *Free Banking*." In *Free Banking*, vol. 3, edited by Lawrence H. White, pp. 20–25. Aldershot, UK: Edward Elgar.

Black, Fisher. 1970. "Banking and Interest Rates in a World without Money: The Effects of Uncontrolled Banking." *Journal of Bank Research* 1 (3): 9–20.

Bodenhorn, Howard. 1992. "Free Banking in Ireland." In *The Experience of Free Banking*, edited by Kevin Dowd, pp. 137–56. London: Routledge.

Bordo, Michael D., and Finn E. Kydland. 1995. "The Gold Standard as a Rule: An Essay in Exploration." *Explorations in Economic History* 32 (4): 423–64.

———. 1996. "The Gold Standard as a Commitment Mechanism." In *Modern Perspectives on the Gold Standard*, edited by Tamim Bayoumi, Barry Eichengreen, and Mark P. Taylor, pp. 55–100. Cambridge, UK: Cambridge University Press.

Bordo, Michael D., and Angela Redish. 1987. "Why Did the Bank of Canada Emerge in 1935?" *Journal of Economic History* 47 (2): 405–17.

Briones, Ignacio, and Hugh Rockoff. 2005. "Do Economists Reach a Conclusion on Free-Banking Episodes?" *Econ Journal Watch* 2 (2): 279–324.

Calomiris, Charles W., and Charles M. Kahn. 1991. "The Role of Demandable Debt in Structuring Optimal Banking Arrangements." *American Economic Review* 81 (3): 497–513.

Cameron, Rondo E. 1967. "Scotland, 1750–1845." In *Banking in the Early Stages of Industrialization*, edited by Rondo E. Cameron, Olga Crisp, Hugh T. Patrick, and Richard Tilly, pp. 60–99. New York: Oxford University Press.

———, ed. 1972. *Banking and Economic Development: Some Lessons of History.* New York: Oxford.

Crazut, Rafael J. 1990. *El Banco Central de Venezuela: Notas sobre su Historia y Evolución 1940–1990.* Caracas: Banco Central de Venezuela.

Diamond, Douglas, and Philip Dybvig. 1983. "Bank Runs, Deposit Insurance, and Liquidity." *Journal of Political Economy* 91 (3): 401–19.

Dowd, Kevin. 1992a. "Introduction." In *The Experience of Free Banking*, edited by Kevin Dowd, pp. 1–6. London: Routledge.

———. 1992b. "Free Banking in Australia." In *The Experience of Free Banking*, edited by Kevin Dowd, pp. 48–78. London: Routledge.

———. 1992c. "Models of Banking Instability." *Journal of Economic Surveys* 6 (2): 107–32.

———. 1992d. "The Monetary Economics of Henry Meulen," *Journal of Money, Credit and Banking* 24 (2): 173–83.

Fink, Alexander. 2011. "Free Banking as an Evolving System: The Case of Switzerland Reconsidered." Working paper, University of Leipzig, 2011.

Friedman, Milton. 1960. *A Program for Monetary Stability.* New York: Fordham University Press.

Friedman, Milton, and Anna J. Schwartz. 1986. "Has Government Any Role in Money?" *Journal of Monetary Economics* 17 (1): 37–62.

Goodhart, Charles. 1987. "Why Do Banks Need a Central Bank?" *Oxford Economic Papers* 39 (1): 75–89.

———. 1988. *The Evolution of Central Banks.* Cambridge, MA: MIT Press.

———. 1994. "The Free Banking Challenge to Central Banks." *Critical Review* 8 (3): 411–25.

Goodhart, Charles, Forrest Capie, and Norbert Schnadt. 1994. "The Development of Central Banking." In *The Future of Central Banking*, edited by Forrest Capie, Charles Goodhart, Stanley Fischer, and Norbert Schnadt, 1–261. Cambridge, UK: Cambridge University Press.

Gorton, Gary. 1988. "Banking Panics and Business Cycles." *Oxford Economic Papers* 40 (4): 751–81.

Grossman, Richard S. 1994. "The Shoe That Didn't Drop: Explaining Banking Stability During the Great Depression." *Journal of Economic History* 54 (3): 654–82.

Hayek, F. A. 1937. *Monetary Nationalism and International Stability.* London: Longmans.

Kaufman, George G. 1988. "Bank Runs: Causes, Benefits, and Costs." *Cato Journal* 7 (3): 559–94.

Kindleberger, Charles P. 1994. "Forward" to Marie-Therese Boyer-Xambeu, Ghislain Deleplace, and Lucien Gillard, *Private Money and Public Currencies: the 16th Century Challenge.* Armonk, New York: M. E. Sharpe.

Kydland, Finn E., and Edward C. Prescott. 1977. "Rules Rather Than Discretion: The Inconsistency of Optimal Plans." *Journal of Political Economy* 85 (3): 473–92.

Kydland, Finn E., and Mark A.Wynne. 2002. "Alternative Monetary Constitutions and the Quest for Price Stability." *Federal Reserve Bank of Dallas Economic and Financial Policy Review* 1 (1): 1–19. http://dallasfed.org/assets/documents/research/efpr/v01_n01_a01.pdf.

McCormick, Brian. 1992. *Hayek and the Keynesian Avalanche*. New York: St. Martin's Press.

Meisel, Adolfo. 1992. "Free Banking in Colombia." In *The Experience of Free Banking*, edited by Kevin Dowd, pp. 93–102. London: Routledge.

Miller, Preston J., and Thomas J. Sargent. 1984. "Reply to Darby." *Federal Reserve Bank of Minneapolis Quarterly Review* 8 (2): 21–26.

Mises, Ludwig von. (1924) 1990. *The Theory of Money and Credit*. Indianapolis: Liberty Fund.

Nataf, Phillipe. 1992. "Free Banking in France (1796–1803)." In *The Experience of Free Banking*, edited by Kevin Dowd, pp. 123–36. London: Routledge.

Neldner, Manfred. 1998. "Lessons from the Free Banking Era in Switzerland: The Law of Adverse Clearings and the Role of Non-issuing Credit Banks." *European Review of Economic History* 2 (3): 289–308.

Price, Bonamy. (1869) 2000. *The Principles of Currency: Six Lectures Delivered at Oxford.* Reprinted in *The History of Gold and Silver*, vol. 3, edited by Lawrence H. White. London: Pickering & Chatto.

Robbins, Lionel. 1937. *Economic Planning and International Order.*

Rolnick, Thomas. 2010. "Interview with Thomas Sargent." *The Region*, Federal Reserve Bank of Minneapolis, September 2010.

Sargent, Thomas J. 1984. "Reply to Darby." *Federal Reserve Bank of Minneapolis Quarterly Review* 8 (2): 21–26.

———. 1986. *Rational Expectations and Inflation*. New York: Harper and Row.

———. 2010. "Where to Draw Lines: Stability versus Efficiency." New York University, September 6. https://files.nyu.edu/ts43/public/research/phillips_ver_9.pdf.

Sargent, Thomas, and Neil Wallace. 1981. "Some Unpleasant Monetarist Arithmetic." *Federal Reserve Bank of Minneapolis Quarterly Review* 5 (3): 1–17.

Schuler, Kurt. 1992. "The World History of Free Banking." In *The Experience of Free Banking*, edited by Kevin Dowd, pp. 7–47. London: Routledge.

Schumpeter, Joseph. 1954. *The History of Economic Analysis*. New York: Oxford University Press.

Selgin, George. 1988. *The Theory of Free Banking*. Totowa, NJ: Rowman and Littlefield.

———. 1992a. "Bank Lending 'Manias' in Theory and History." *Journal of Financial Services Research* 6 (2): 169–86.

———. 1992b. "Free Banking in Foochow." In *The Experience of Free Banking*, edited by Kevin Dowd, pp. 103–22. London: Routledge.

———. 1993. "The Rationalization of Central Banks." *Critical Review* 7 (2–3): 335–54.

Selgin, George, and Lawrence H. White. 1990. "Laissez-Faire Monetary Theorists in Late Nineteenth Century America." *Southern Economic Journal* 56 (3): 74–87.

———. 1999. "A Fiscal Theory of Government's Role in Money." *Economic Inquiry* 37 (1): 154–65.

Smith, Adam. (1776) 1981. *An Inquiry into the Nature and Causes of the Wealth of Nations*, edited by R. H. Campbell, A. S. Skinner, and W. B. Todd. Indianapolis: LibertyClassics.

———. 1982. *Lectures on Jurisprudence*, edited by R. L. Meek, D. D. Raphael, and P. G. Stein. Indianapolis: Liberty Fund.

Smith, Vera. (1936) 1990. *The Rationale of Central Banking*. Indianapolis: Liberty Fund.

Thornton, Henry. (1802) 1939. *An Enquiry into the Nature and Effects of the Paper Credit of Great Britain*, ed. F.A. Hayek. London: George Allen and Unwin.

Timberlake, Richard H. 1990. "The Evolution of Central Banks: Charles Goodhart." *Journal of Banking and Finance* 14 (4): 821–25.

Turner, John, and Charles Hickson. 2002. "Free Banking Gone Awry: The Australian Banking Crisis of 1893." *Financial History Review* 9 (2): 147–67.

White, Lawrence H. 1990. "The Evolution of Central Banks, by Charles Goodhart." *Economica* 57 (225): 135–37.

———. 1995. *Free Banking in Britain*. 2nd ed. London: Institute of Economic Affairs. http://www.iea.org.uk/record.jsp?ID=115&type=book.

———. 1998. "Monetary Nationalism Reconsidered." In *Money and the Nation-State*, edited by Kevin Dowd and Richard H. Timberlake, pp. 377–401. New York: Transaction Publishers.

———. 1999. *The Theory of Monetary Institutions*. Oxford: Blackwell.

———. 2012. *The Clash of Economic Ideas*. New York: Cambridge University Press.

Yeager, Leland B., ed. 1962. *In Search of a Monetary Constitution*. Cambridge, MA: Harvard University Press.

———. 1966. *International Monetary Relations: Theory, History, and Policy*. New York: Harper and Row.

10. Contemporary Private Monetary Systems

Kevin Dowd

This chapter examines contemporary private or nongovernmental monetary systems. At one level, mention of a private monetary system has still not lost its capacity to shock: it suggests individuals printing their own banknotes and putting them into circulation or even minting their own coins. Yet at another level, privately issued money is familiar and commonplace, and all kinds of private moneys already circulate widely. Examples include gift certificates, grocery store vouchers, and Chuck E. Cheese tokens. Bank deposits are another example. In fact, most of the outstanding money in circulation today consists of privately issued bank deposits. However, my focus of interest is not with these familiar, regulated, and frankly boring forms of private money but rather with unregulated or loosely regulated varieties of private money that emerge spontaneously through market forces and operate outside government control: individuals printing their own currency or minting their own coins are perfect examples.

Most private monetary systems operating outside standard banking regulations consist of local paper currency or credit systems such as local economic trading systems, community mutual credit systems, time banks, local paper currency, and company scrip,

This chapter is a much revised version of an earlier draft prepared for the Liberty Fund Conference, "In Search of a Monetary Constitution Revisited," April 19–22, 2012, in Freiburg, Germany. I thank Viktor Vanberg and Lawrence H. White for the invitation to participate in this conference, and I thank Steve Baker MP, Philip Booth, Dave Campbell, Doug Jackson, Gordon Kerr, Duncan Kitchin, Martin Hutchinson, Bernard von NotHaus, and Basil Zafiriou for many very helpful inputs that have much improved the paper. The usual caveat applies. A longer version will also appear in an Institute of Economic Affairs monograph.

which was often issued as a means of payment when regular currency was unavailable, such as in remote mining towns or on long voyages.[1] They also include some forms of local private bank currency, such as the Clearinghouse Loan Certificates and other forms of privately issued emergency currency issued by U.S. banks in the period before the founding of the Federal Reserve.[2] Well-known contemporary examples in the United States include Potomacs, Ithaca Hours, and BerkShares. Innumerable instances of these systems have been recorded over the years, and one would imagine that many thousands of them must be operating in the United States today. In fact, so many examples exist across the world that a research journal is even devoted to them, the *International Journal of Community Currency Research*.[3] A second form of private money is private coinage, which also has a long and successful—not to mention colorful—history.[4]

A persistent and complex theme of historical private money systems is their often uneasy relationship with the state. The state has typically had a dual role toward them, in most cases as destroyer but in other cases as a creator of sorts or at least unwitting midwife. On the one hand, its typical response has been to stamp them out. The usual motive was the obvious one: private monetary systems were often seen as a threat to the ability of the state to raise seigniorage and an affront to the prerogatives of the state itself. On the other hand, though it never set out to do so, the state itself often enabled these systems by creating the circumstances that led them to emerge in the first place. The system of Clearinghouse Loan Certificates mentioned earlier is a good example: this was a direct consequence of the note issue restrictions of the National Banking System legislation. Another example is the bills-of-exchange system in early 19th-century Lancashire in England (see, e.g., Baxendale 2011): this arose to fill a gap created by the refusal of the Bank of England to service the area, combined with the legal inability of other banks to do so. In these and many other cases, private money emerged to fill a market niche that the state itself had created.

This chapter focuses on three contemporary (and predominantly U.S.) cases of private monetary systems that have received a lot of recent publicity:

- The Liberty Dollar: this is a dollar-denominated, gold- and silver-based monetary system that can function in an environment where the values of the precious metals have fluctuated greatly against the greenback.

- Digital gold currency (DGC) with the focus on the best-known such system, e-gold: these are gold-based payments systems that proved to be particularly useful for international payments.

- Bitcoin: this is the first successful example of the most recent form of private currency, cryptocurrency, and is pathbreaking in a number of ways: it is a radical new type of currency based on the principles of strong cryptography; it has a novel production process—a form of digital "mining" for want of a better description—that we have never seen before; it offers users the potential for anonymous and untraceable transactions; it runs itself and is the first-ever private monetary system that is completely decentralized; it is not so much unregulated as unregulatable; and it apparently cannot be shut down. Bitcoin is truly revolutionary.

Each of these is or was highly successful, and each has all the attributes of a self-standing monetary system, including its own medium or unit of account, medium of exchange, and store of value. Such systems can therefore function independently of any government monetary systems and, conceivably, replace them.

As with their historical predecessors, all three cases illustrate that the U.S. government remains hostile to private money. Though both the Liberty Dollar and e-gold prove that strong public demand exists for silver- or gold-based private money and were successful in providing it, they were attacked by the government, and after highly questionable legal processes, their founders were convicted of criminal activities and their operations closed down. One can safely infer that the government would even more readily go after Bitcoin if it could but currently lacks the means to do so: whereas the Liberty Dollar and e-gold were produced by identifiable individuals that the government could take down, Bitcoin is an altogether different proposition: it is an apparently unbreakable cryptocurrency issued by an anonymous user network, widely used on anonymous hidden exchanges that the government can't locate, and was promoted and designed by cyber (or, should I say, cypher) anarchists who openly aspire to shut down the government itself. The issues raised by contemporary private monetary systems are, thus, far-reaching indeed.

215

This chapter is organized as follows. The next section examines the case of the Liberty Dollar, and the following one examines digital currency, with the emphasis on DGC systems and the case of e-gold. The next section examines Bitcoin and other cryptocurrencies. The following section discusses one of the most remarkable features of cryptocurrencies, their ability to protect individuals' financial privacy and the profound implications following from that, including people being able to operate beyond government control and the ensuing issues raised by a newly emerging anarchic social order. The final section concludes.

The Liberty Dollar

Launched in October 1998, the Liberty Dollar was designed by Bernard von NotHaus, the founder of the National Organization for the Repeal of the Federal Reserve and the Internal Revenue Code. At its inception, von NotHaus announced that his objective was to "be to the Federal Reserve System what Federal Express was to the Post Office" by providing a private voluntary barter currency as an alternative to Federal Reserve currency. The new Liberty Dollar was to be based primarily on gold and silver coinage—strictly speaking, I should say "medallions"[5] —and its precious metallic basis was to provide protection against the inflation to which the inconvertible greenback is prone, thanks to the Federal Reserve's predilection for expansionist monetary policies.

The Liberty Dollar consists primarily of medallions in gold and silver; a second component consisted of certificates redeemable on demand in specie stored securely in a warehouse in Idaho; and a third component, the "eLibertyDollar," consisted of digital warehouse receipts.[6] Thus, the Liberty Dollar existed in specie, paper, and digital form, and all forms of the Liberty Dollar were denominated in dollars, that is, the unit of account was the dollar.

However, the designers of the Liberty Dollar faced a major technical problem: how could the Liberty Dollar trade at par against the greenback dollar, when the value of the Liberty Dollar is based on the values of the precious metals, but the value of the U.S. dollar depends on Federal Reserve policy? Put simply, how can the gold- and silver-based Liberty Dollar circulate at par against the depreciating greenback?

216

The way in which the Liberty Dollar handled this problem is very interesting.[7] Consider that a silver Liberty Dollar medallion with a face value of 10 dollars minted in 1998 would be minted using an ounce of silver at a time when the market price of silver was about US$5 an ounce. The difference between the 10 dollar face value and the US$5 cost of the silver input covers costs of production and any minter's profit, and the medallion itself would be sold for US$10. Other things being equal, if the market price of silver then remained about US$5, the organization could continue to mint such medallions indefinitely—and it would keep selling them for US$10, which means that the Liberty Dollar and the U.S. dollar would trade at par, one dollar for the other.

However, as the U.S. dollar price of silver rises—caused in the long run by the ongoing expansionary monetary policy of the Federal Reserve—the profit from minting falls. Eventually a point is reached—at around a silver price of US$7.50—beyond which continuation of minting is no longer economic: so if the Liberty Dollar organization continued to mint such medallions, it would eventually be bankrupted. If the price of silver were then to rise beyond US$10, the Liberty Dollar medallions with a face value of 10 dollars would have a silver content worth more than US$10 and their price against the greenback would rise, that is, the Liberty Dollar medallion with a face value of 10 dollars would trade for more than US$10.

To forestall these problems, once the price of silver hit US$7.50, the standard one-ounce silver Liberty Dollar was rebased upward to have a face value of 20 dollars. This entailed the following:

- The Liberty Dollar organization would now issue one-ounce silver medallions with a face value of 20 dollars rather than a face value of 10 dollars as before, and these would be sold for US$20.

- Note that this change means that the new 20-dollar Liberty Dollar medallions would have the same metallic content as the old 10-dollar Liberty medallions.

- Any holders of the earlier one-ounce silver medallions with a face value of 10 dollars would be entitled to exchange them for the new one-ounce silver medallions with a face value of 20 dollars: because the two have the same content, we can think of this as the Liberty Dollar organization simply "restamping" the earlier 10-dollar medallions as 20-dollar ones.

The net result is that the Liberty Dollar would remain trading at par[8] against the U.S. dollar, and in the process, people holding Liberty Dollars would have doubled the value of their holdings against the greenback. As von NotHaus explained:

> The first move up (rebasement) was a big WOW for the Liberty Dollar as the currency actually moved up [against the greenback] as the model called for. And when it did, DOUBLE WOW ... people rushed to exchange their $10 Silver Libertys for new $20 Silver Libertys and double their money ... it was smashing success.[9]

For their part, the paper certificates had a dollar face value and an entitlement to a specific amount of silver. For example, early certificates contemporary with the 10-dollar one-ounce silver Liberty medallion would have a face value of 10 dollars and entitle the holder to demand one ounce of silver of 0.999 fineness from the organization's warehouse. These certificates were not notes akin to those of a silver- or gold-standard bank operating on a fractional reserve but were actually warehouse receipts backed by a 100 percent reserve. However, when the coins themselves were rebased, certificate holders would be invited to swap them for new certificates with the new face value: for example, when the one-ounce silver 10-dollar Liberty was rebased to a one-ounce silver 20-dollar Liberty, holders of one-ounce silver certificates with a face value of 10 dollars were invited to redeem them for one-ounce silver certificates with a face value of 20 dollars. Holders of eLibertyDollar, the digital equivalent, could have their holdings rebased in the same way. These arrangements protected holders' silver and gold content entitlements and meant that the face values of their certificates or digital holdings kept in sync with the values of the precious metals.

Although intended to compete against the U.S. dollar, the Liberty Dollar was not marketed or represented as official U.S. currency. Indeed, its whole marketing campaign was based precisely on the fact that it was *not* U.S. official currency but, rather, superior to it.[10]

The Liberty Dollar was backed up by a persuasive marketing pitch. To quote from one of its brochures:

> Now you have a clear choice of money. Are you ready to grow and protect your money or will you continue to lose

your purchasing power as the U.S. dollar depreciates?

Just as FedEx brought choice to U.S. Post Office, the Liberty Dollar brings choice to the U.S. dollar and protection for your purchasing power.

The Liberty Dollar is 100% inflation proof. It is real gold and silver that you can use just like cash where it is accepted voluntarily for everyday purchases at your grocery store, dentist or gas station....

When you are paying, ask the cashier, "Would you like plastic, paper or Silver?" Then reach out and drop the Liberty Dollar in the cashier's hand. Join the fun by simply offering the Liberty Dollar for all your goods and services.

The Liberty Dollar was highly successful and became the second-most popular currency in the United States. From 1998 to 2007, Liberty Dollar issues totaled approximately US$65 million to US$85 million in value when (re)valued against silver and gold prices of US$50 and US$2,500, respectively. Over this same period, the Liberty Dollar issued more than 350 different specimens in paper or gold, silver, platinum, or copper specie and was distributed to perhaps 250,000 customers.

Because the Liberty Dollar was periodically rebased to keep in sync with the precious metals, its value rose substantially over time against the depreciating greenback. Someone who bought a one-ounce silver Liberty medallion with a face value of 10 dollars in 1998 and held it until 2013 would have had an investment that more than kept up with inflation, whereas someone who held onto a US$10 greenback would have seen their investment lose about half its value over the period since. Moreover, investors who bought gold Libertys rather than silver ones would have benefited considerably more.

The attitude of the government toward the Liberty Dollar was initially one of tolerance but then hardened: in 2006, the U.S. Mint issued a press release stating that use of the Liberty Dollar was a federal crime (U.S. Mint 2006). In March 2007, von NotHaus filed suit against the Mint seeking a declaratory judgment that these allegations were untrue. The government responded with a raid by the FBI and the Secret Service on the Liberty Dollar offices in Evanston, Illinois, on November 14, 2007, in which they seized virtually everything they could, including coins, paper certificates, and computers. The feds also raided the warehouse in Idaho where the reserves were kept for the Liberty Dollar paper and digital receipts. There they seized approximately nine tons of the gold and silver that backed these receipts—this was not even the property of the Liberty Dollar company anyway, but that of its clients—and so made their redemption by the company impossible.

A federal indictment was then brought against von NotHaus and three others in the U.S. District Court in Statesville, North Carolina, in May 2009, and von NotHaus himself was arrested on June 4. He was charged with, in essence, counterfeiting,[11] conspiracy against the United States, fraud, and sundry other offenses.

The first charge can only be described as risible, for two reasons. The first reason is that counterfeiting requires some attempt to make the "fake" currency look like the "real" one, yet the Liberty Dollar currency was quite different in appearance from official currency. The medallions themselves were easily distinguishable, even if they shared some similarities, such as the dollar sign ($), the words "dollar" and "Liberty," and the year of minting. They differed in obvious ways: they included "USA" (instead of "United States of America") and "Trust in God" (instead of "In God We Trust"); they did not feature the Statue of Liberty or the phrase "legal tender"; and they had other features not found on U.S. coinage, such as an image of Ron Paul, an 0800 phone number, and even a URL. They also differed from official U.S. coinage in being made from precious metals instead of base ones. If these medallions were ever meant to be counterfeit, they were certainly poor ones. The Liberty Dollar certificates were also very different from greenbacks—in fact, none were even green—and had the words "Negotiable American Liberty Currency Silver [or where appropriate, Gold] Certificate" boldly emblazoned on one side and "Warehouse Receipt" on the other, and so could hardly be mistaken for greenbacks. They also bear von NotHaus's own signature, whereas it is traditional for counterfeiters to keep their handiwork anonymous. They were even a different shape from greenbacks and made of different paper.

The second reason is that any charge of counterfeit implies fraud and intent to deceive, yet there was never any evidence of fraud or misrepresentation.

If the Liberty Dollar is sufficiently similar to official currency to constitute a federal offense, then the government should by rights go after anyone who issues anything that could be construed as similar to the official currency. After all, many other private organizations issue alternative-dollar currencies even within the United States. These include issuers of travelers' checks, such as American Express; Parker Brothers, who make the board game Monopoly; and Disney Corporation, whose Disney Dollars are obvious counterfeits signed by Scrooge McDuck.

The von NotHaus defense was that he did not steal, defraud, misrepresent, or force anyone to hold Liberty Dollars or do anything else illegal, and that his customers were satisfied, not least because the value of the Liberty Dollar had risen considerably over time whilst the U.S. dollar depreciated. This defense was, however, rejected, and von NotHaus was convicted of most charges on March 18, 2011. He was acquitted of the fraud charge but convicted of making coins resembling and similar to U.S. coins, of "uttering" and passing unauthorized coins for use as current money, and of conspiracy against the United States. He is currently free on an appearance bond awaiting a potential sentence of up to 22 years in federal prison and a substantial fine.

The suspicion that von NotHaus was singled out because he was seen as subversive would appear to be borne out by a press release issued by the U.S. Attorney's Office after the conviction. In U.S. Attorney Anne Tompkins made a series of assertions so absurd that they have already become legendary. In particular, she asserted that: "Attempts to undermine the legitimate currency of this country are simply a unique form of domestic terrorism" (U.S. Attorney's Office 2011).

In response I would argue:

- There is nothing illegitimate about the Liberty Dollar, which was intended to improve American currency, both by providing a superior alternative to Federal Reserve currency and by providing an incentive for the Fed to improve its currency.

- The Liberty Dollar was succeeding until the government closed it down. Thus, the government is guilty of the very offense it condemns, that is, of undermining legitimate currency.

- Since the Federal Reserve took over responsibility for the currency in 1914, the purchasing power of the currency has fallen by over 95 percent even according to the government's own biased consumer price index statistics. If *this* isn't undermining the currency, one would sure like to know what is. So why has the government not gone against the Fed?

- Since when is competing against an inefficient governmental organization such as the Federal Reserve an act of *terrorism*? By the same logic, Federal Express must be guilty of terrorism because it competes with the U.S. Post Office. How can we have terrorism without either terror or coercion? The Liberty Dollar was about as terroristic as Donut King.

The press release cited Article 1, section 8, clause 5, of the Constitution, which delegated to Congress the power to coin money and to regulate the value thereof. However, this same clause also indicates that the only constitutional money is coined money, and this can be understood as only gold and silver coinage: thus, inconvertible paper money is itself unconstitutional. Furthermore, the Constitution did not give Congress the authority to establish a money monopoly or a central bank—or indeed any bank at all. Consequently, the Federal Reserve and the money it issues are both unconstitutional. The government is therefore not just misrepresenting the Constitution but also drawing selectively from it to suit itself. Legal expert Bill Rounds (2011) goes further and suggests that U.S. Attorney Tompkins recklessly and negligently made false statements of the law regarding the Liberty Dollar case, violated ethics rules, and defamed von NotHaus in the process.

Ms. Tompkins made a second memorable assertion that also makes no sense: "While these forms of anti-government activities do not involve violence, they are every bit as insidious and represent a clear and present danger to the economic stability of this country." So, Ms. Tompkins, can you please explain how the Liberty Dollar's helping to protect the value of the currency that people use presents *any* danger at all to the country's economic stability? One glosses over here the "clear and present danger" posed by the policies of the Federal Reserve—which have brought both the U.S. financial system and the currency to the brink of collapse—but naturally those don't count because the Fed is part of the government.

Leaving aside the absence of logic, the U.S. attorney's comments betray an elementary misunderstanding of the competitive process: in the provision of currency as with anything else, having a single monopoly provider leads to poor quality, and you get good quality only if you open the field up to competition. We saw this when the postal service was opened to competition. And it was *exactly* this public service that the Liberty Dollar was providing when it started to compete against the currency provided by the Federal Reserve, which by any reasonable standard was certainly of low quality, because it is depreciating all the time—whereas the Liberty Dollar was appreciating in value. The root fallacy here is the old idea that "money" is something best provided by an inefficient government monopoly that needs to be protected from competition: it is not.[12]

As for the Liberty Dollar, the company actually had its best year in 2008, after the FBI raid—all that free publicity must have been good for business!—but the company was forced to cease operations after von NotHaus was arrested.

However, new mints are opening up and appear to be doing good business based on the Liberty Dollar model that von NotHaus pioneered. These include the Aspen Dollar; the New Liberty Dollar, which is similar to the old Liberty Dollar but has some extra stay-out-of-jail features;[13] and (my favorite!) the Second Amendment Dollar that is run out of Bud's Gun Shop in Lexington, Kentucky.

Returning to von NotHaus, 27 months and counting, he is still awaiting sentencing, and the case has become a cause célèbre not just in the United States but worldwide.[14] A motion for acquittal or retrial was filed in March 2013 and is a model of eloquence:

> Mr. von NotHaus stands convicted of various statutorily-defined forms of counterfeiting. The irony of this is that if anything is clear from the evidence presented at trial, it is that the last thing Mr. von NotHaus wanted was for Liberty Dollars to be confused with coins issued by the United States government. That would, as witness Vernon Robinson testified, have defeated the whole purpose—to demonstrate to citizens and communities that there is a way to engage in commerce and not use the Federal Reserve system. [note omitted] Whether writing scholarly papers on value-based currency, attracting media attention, or selling t-shirts saying "The Fed can bite me," Mr. von NotHaus has always operated out in the open. His intention—to protest the Federal Reserve system—has always been plain. The jury's verdict

conflates a program created to function as an alternative to the Federal Reserve system with one designed to deceive people into believing it was the very thing Mr. von NotHaus was protesting in the first place. Whatever one's opinion about the merit of value-based currency, the fact remains that the Liberty Dollar was not a counterfeit and was not intended to function as such. The verdict is a perversion of the counterfeiting statutes and should be set aside.[15]

Digital Currency

Digital currency takes many different forms, and there are thousands of different schemes. What they all have in common is electronic stored-value systems—networks of exchange and value accounts that store financial value to be used to pay for goods and services. The most conventional are debit card, credit card, and comparable systems (e.g., PayPal) that allow payments in the existing official unit of account. However, many others use their own unit of account. These include those operated by many large corporations that run loyalty reward systems denominated in "points" or "miles"—one thinks of the frequent-flyer systems operated by airlines, innumerable grocery store reward systems, and so on—many of which are morphing into digital monetary systems.

They also include many Internet-based currency systems that have come and gone over the years. High-profile casualties included Flooz and Beenz, which were casualties of the dot-com crash (and, in the former case, of Whoopi Goldberg's advertising as well): these blossomed briefly but never really caught on, and both firms failed in August 2001. More recent examples are Facebook credits, which allow users to purchase virtual goods on Facebook applications, and Microsoft points, which is the digital currency used by the Xbox Live Marketplace and the Zune store. Both, however, are now being phased out by their sponsoring organizations. Two other well-publicized recent examples of digital currency are Ven[16] and Liberty Reserve;[17] these examples also illustrate how diverse digital currencies can be.

An important class of digital currencies is digital gold currency: digital payment systems in which the unit of account is gold and in which user accounts are backed by gold reserves. Examples include e-gold, e-Bullion, GoldMoney, and Pecunix. A user would buy DGC units using conventional payment methods (e.g., a wire transfer) and then transfer units to another account holder, who could then cash out his holding. Such systems provide an attractive way to effect international payments transactions because they make such transactions inexpensive and (at least in the early days) to some extent anonymous. Initially, at least, they were also beyond the reach of bank regulations (because providers are not banks) and regulations governing money transfer (because the transfers were not of legal money per se but of claims to units of gold). Since they emerged, however, governments have fought hard—with success—to bring such systems under their control.

One feature of these systems is that of irreversibility: reversing transactions is difficult, if not impossible, even in the case of error, unauthorized use, or failure of a vendor to provide goods. This feature makes DGC transactions akin to cash transactions. Irreversibility makes for lower operating costs, instant clearing, and ready access to transferred "funds." In this, DGC transactions differ from many conventional systems (such as credit or debit card systems) that allow customers to dispute or reverse transfers but that are more costly and typically slower.

Perhaps the best-known DGC system is e-gold (though we should not forget, of course, that the Liberty Dollar—or rather, its digital version—was another form of DCG [see above]).[18] This was founded in 1996 by Doug Jackson, a libertarian oncologist with a passion for Austrian economics. Envisaged as a private international gold currency, e-gold was based in Melbourne, Florida, but registered in Nevis in the Caribbean: Jackson argued that it was exempt from regulation not just because of its "offshore" status, but also because it was a payment system rather than a *money* transmitter or bank.

E-gold was very user-friendly. Accounts could be set up in minutes, and for most of its history there was no checking of names or IDs and little monitoring of customer accounts.[19] Customers could purchase units of e-gold using a credit card or a wire transfer, e-gold units were easily and quickly transferred to other e-gold account holders, and cashing out was straightforward. Fees were very low.

By 2005, e-gold had grown to become second only to PayPal in the online payments industry: it had 1.2 million accounts, and transactions that year totaled $1.5 billion. It had become a worldwide enterprise, convenient for international transactions. At its peak, the currency was backed by 3.8 metric tons of physical gold held in London and Dubai, valued at more than $85 million.

The popularity of e-gold came with a downside, however: it became very popular with online criminals too, who saw it as an anonymous way of moving money around.[20] These criminals included the mob, drug dealers, and con artists peddling Ponzi schemes and credit card scams. They also included an outfit called Shadow Crew, an international cybercrime syndicate with 4,000 members worldwide, which was engaged in massive ID theft and credit card fraud and used e-gold as a vehicle to launder the proceeds of its crimes. One of its members, Omar Dhanani, boasted on a chat room in 2004 that he moved between $40,000 and $100,000 a week through e-gold. Another case involved a criminal who went by the pseudonym "segvec" and who was involved in a huge credit card fraud. He was not even on law enforcement's radar until Jackson discovered his suspicious activities; they then got involved after he informed them, and they persuaded themselves that he was Ukrainian. Meanwhile, Jackson tracked him down to Florida, and he turned out to be Albert Gonzalez, a criminal informant working at the time for the Secret Service, operating out of their offices, on their stipend.

Law enforcement then turned on e-gold and indicted its principals in April 2007. The charges boiled down to e-gold's being an unlicensed money-transmitting entity and a de facto means of moving the proceeds of illegal activities; it was also alleged that the principals had tacit knowledge of this activity but had done nothing about it.[21] The charges were never proven, but facing a possible 20 years in jail and a $500,000 fine, in July 2008 Jackson agreed to a plea bargain and in November was sentenced to six months of home detention, three years' supervision, 300 hours of community service, and a small fine. As Jackson explained afterward in an e-mail:

> Our case was lost when the judge made a ruling in response to our motion to dismiss that was so prejudicial that, in conjunction with what we were then told regarding the horrifying perversion of the doctrine of "relevant conduct" [used in federal sentencing guidelines[22]], would have made it insanely reckless to risk an even worse miscarriage.

Even the judge acknowledged that Jackson had not committed any fraud or intended to break the law and confirmed the veracity of the company's gold reserve audit. E-gold was thereafter wound down.

And so another worthwhile American private-money experiment ended in a miscarriage of justice.

Another DGC company was GoldMoney, founded in 2001 and run by James Turk from Jersey in the Channel Islands. GoldMoney provided both gold bailment and DGC services. This firm was widely regarded as the market leader in the gold currency sector and had over $2 billion of assets in storage by 2011. However, in January 2012 it withdrew from the DGC business, citing the impact of new regulations that made the business unprofitable. GoldMoney was, therefore, yet another casualty of the government—in this case the U.K. government.

Cryptocurrency: Bitcoin

A more radical and indeed revolutionary private currency is Bitcoin:[23] the most successful, though not the first,[24] of a new type of currency known as cryptocurrency. This is a form of highly anonymized computer currency based on the use of cryptography to control the creation and transfer of money. The designers of cryptocurrency sought to create not just a new currency but also a new anarchist social order. To quote one of the pioneers in this area, Wei Dai, in 1998, the objective is to achieve a cryptoanarchy[25] in which "the government is not temporarily destroyed but permanently forbidden and permanently unnecessary. It's a community where the threat of violence is impotent because violence is impossible, and violence is impossible because its participants cannot be linked to their true names or physical locations."[26]

Bitcoin was invented in 2009 by an anonymous programmer using the nom de plume Satoshi Nakamoto (2009a).[27] Its key innovation relative to earlier forms of digital currency is that it is completely decentralized and has no central authority or organizer whatever.

Bitcoin is a type of e-cash system in which no central body exists to authorize or track transactions; instead, these tasks are carried out collectively by the network itself. Transactions are carried out using a digital "coin" that utilizes public-key cryptography: when a coin is transferred from *A* to *B*, *A* adds *B*'s public key to the coin and digitally signs the coin using a private key. *B* then owns the coin and can transfer it further. The network collectively maintains a public list of all previous transactions, and before any coin is processed, it is checked by the network to ensure that the user hasn't already spent it: this prevents a user from illicitly spending the same coin over and over again.

Nakamoto (2009b) himself gave a clear explanation of the thinking behind Bitcoin in an e-mail announcing its launch on February 11, 2009:

> The root problem with conventional currency is all the trust that is required to make it work. The central bank must be trusted not to debase the currency, but the history of fiat currencies is full of breaches of that trust....
>
> A generation ago, multi-user time-sharing computer systems had a similar problem. Before strong encryption, users had to rely on password protection to secure their files, placing trust in the system administrator to keep their information private. Privacy could always be overridden by the admin based on his judgment call weighing the principle of privacy against other concerns, or at the bequest of his superiors. Then strong encryption became available to the masses, and trust was no longer required. Data could be secured in a way that was physically impossible to access, no matter for what reason, no matter how good the excuse, no matter what.
>
> It's time we had the same thing for money. With e-currency based on cryptographic proof, without the need to trust a third party middleman, money can be secure and transactions complete.
>
> One of the fundamental building blocks for such a system is digital signatures. A digital coin contains the public key of its owner. To transfer it, the owner signs the coin together with the public key of the next owner. Anyone can check the signatures to verify the chain of ownership. [This] works well to secure ownership, but leaves one big problem unsolved: double-spending. Any owner could try to re-spend an already spent coin by signing it again to another owner. The usual solution is for a trusted company with a central database to check for double-spending, but that just gets back to the trust model....
>
> Bitcoin's solution is to use a peer-to-peer network to check for double-spending ... the result is a distributed system with no single point of failure.

The Supply of Bitcoin

Bitcoins are created in a process known as "mining." This process uses computer power to search for solutions to pseudo-random number computational problems in a way analogous to a gold miner looking for gold. Finding solutions is not easy, but when a Bitcoin miner hits upon a solution, he is rewarded with Bitcoin that he can spend. The solution is then verified by the network: unlike finding a solution, verifying one is easy. The process is designed in a way that ensures that the amounts produced are almost exactly known in advance. Anyone can mine for Bitcoin, but the network adjusts the difficulty of finding Bitcoin to the number of active miners and the computer power used in a way that was initially set to generate a production rate of 50 BTC every 10 minutes, but this rate halved in late November 2012 and will keep halving thereafter every 4 years, and the rules are constructed so that the total amount mined can never exceed 21 million.

The projected supply of Bitcoin is therefore highly predictable and is shown by the black line in Figure 10.1: the supply rises at a periodically decreasing rate to approach a limiting value of 21 million as production of new Bitcoin gradually fizzles out. However, as with other forms of currency, when considering supply we also have to take account of attrition—Bitcoin's disappearing because people lose data wallets containing their Bitcoin codes, lose their encryption codes, or experience hard drive failures with no backup. Accordingly, the second (dashed-red) line gives the projected supply of Bitcoin assuming an illustrative attrition rate of 0.5 percent a year. In this case, we see that the projected stock of Bitcoin taking account of attrition rises to a peak of about 18.4 million in 2029 and thereafter falls.

As a consequence, leaving aside the possibility of some internal flaw or disaster that destroys the system, the only real uncertainty about the future supply of Bitcoin relates to the attrition rate.[28]

The Demand for Bitcoin

Turning to the demand side, the first question is why would anyone demand Bitcoin, that is, be willing to trade something valuable for it? One argument is that people would demand Bitcoin for use as a medium of exchange *if* they believe that other people would accept it in payments, but then why would they believe that? The

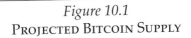

Figure 10.1
PROJECTED BITCOIN SUPPLY

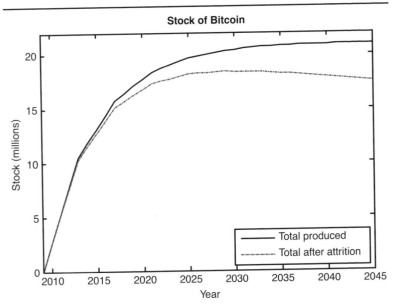

traditional answer in monetary theory is that starting de novo, people would be prepared to trade for X—whether X be paper, Bitcoin, gold, or anything else—in the belief that someone else would accept X in payment *only if* it had some alternative nonmonetary use. If it has no alternative use—if it is intrinsically useless—then there is a first-mover problem: no one would be the first to trade for X, and X would never get off the ground as money. Consequently, although it is *possible* to conceive of an equilibrium in which each accepts X as money because others do so, we would *never get there* because X would *never get started* as money: the potential new currency X would be permanently stuck at its launch pad. The implication is that Bitcoin could never get started as a new currency.

Yet it managed to do so; the plain fact is that Bitcoin *has* already achieved a positive price in the market and *has* taken off as a medium of exchange, so arguing that it *could not* is akin to haggling over the possibility of manned flight after just watching the Wright brothers.[29]

230

A possible explanation for its successful takeoff might simply be that early trades were among a small group of enthusiasts who shared a similar mindset and commitment to the Bitcoin enterprise;[30] they managed to get it up and running on a small scale,[31] and other people gradually joined it as became clear that the Bitcoin system was working—and especially when it became apparent that the anonymity of Bitcoin made it ideally suited for anonymous illegal trades.

This suggests that a key factor driving the demand for Bitcoin is the transactions demand for contraband purposes. The anonymity of Bitcoin also suggests a demand for Bitcoin for tax evasion, money laundering, and similar purposes and a store of value demand in which people use Bitcoin to escape financial repression by their own governments. However, we should not overlook the potential of Bitcoin for mundane legal transactions as well. After all, transactions are straightforward, inexpensive, fast, and irreversible; they are also highly secure and potentially untraceable.

History of the Bitcoin Market

Examining how Bitcoin market prices and the quantities traded have behaved to date is interesting.[32] These are shown in Figure 10.2.[33] The first trade occurred on April 25, 2010, and the first Bitcoin price was 3 cents. Early prices and quantities were low, and almost three months passed before the first end-of-day price reached 10 cents. However, once it got going, the market price rose strongly, peaked at nearly US$30 in June 2011, and fell back sharply; it then gradually recovered and in March and (especially) April 2013 rose strongly again to peak at almost US$215 on April 8; it then fell back to just over US$63 eight days later, rallied again, and is currently (July 13, 2013) US$121.90. These highlights mask a considerable amount of day-to-day and intraday volatility. In short, the price has risen enormously[34] since the market started but also been very volatile, and the market survived several major crashes that some thought would have destroyed it.

The current stock of Bitcoin is about 10.5 million, and hence the total monetary value of the existing Bitcoin stock is currently about US$1.260 billion, up from the princely total of 99 cents on the first day of public trading.

The quantities traded are shown in the lower panel and are also very volatile: they show pronounced peaks, most notably an early peak of almost 200,000 in October 2010, a peak of nearly twice that size in late 2011, and a peak of almost 600,000 in April 2013. Since the supply of Bitcoin has been stable, this price and volume volatility can only be ascribed to a volatile demand.

Figure 10.2
BITCOIN TRADING

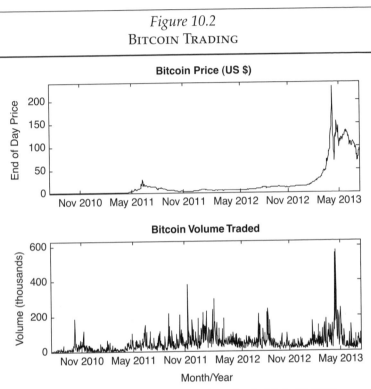

SOURCE: http://www.bitcoincharts.com; downloaded July 13, 2013.

This volatility can be partly explained by occasional attacks and associated attempts at market manipulation and by occasional bursts of publicity. An example of the former occurred in June 2011 when a hacker got into the Mt. Gox website and stimulated a massive sell-off, after which the price of Bitcoin plummeted. Examples of the latter were the very rapid surges in Bitcoin prices that followed highly publicized articles on Bitcoin in *Forbes* on April 20, 2011 and in *Gawker* on June 1 2011, which served to introduce the currency to new users; prices on the exchange also fell frequently in response to bad publicity, which was a common occurrence too.

Current State of the Bitcoin Market

Once Bitcoin took off, it soon became apparent that a major source of demand came from those trading on an anonymous exchange called Silk Road that was founded in February 2011 and specialized in trading illegal drugs. The size of this market is hard to determine, and estimates of its size and rate of growth vary widely. Estimates on the Silk Road forum in mid-2012 put the number of customers between 30,000 and 150,000. However, a study of Silk Road by Nicolas Christin (2012) suggested that the size of the market was smaller than this range would suggest: studying the market over eight months up to mid-2012, he estimated that the market had a total revenue of about US$1.9 million per month by this point, with the numbers of sellers increasing, and generated a monthly commission to the exchange of about US$143,000. He also identified a tight coupling between Silk Road and the Mt. Gox exchange, and he estimated that daily sales on Silk Road corresponded to about 20 percent of the Mt. Gox activity. More recently, Christin has been quoted as saying that the volume of trading on Silk Road nearly doubled during the period over which he studied it (Franklin 2013) and by March 2013 was already far bigger than it was when his fieldwork ended (Ball 2013).

Bitcoin is being used for run-of-the-mill legal transactions as well. A recent article in the *Guardian* newspaper reported that Bitcoin was rising in popularity for day-to-day transactions in the Kreuzberg area of Berlin, for instance (Connolly and Grandjean 2013). Bitcoin was also reportedly accepted by pizza delivery chains in the United States, by New York City bars and British pubs, and by a bed and breakfast in Ireland. People have reputedly put their properties up for sale against Bitcoin. Reasons cited for using Bitcoin included its having lower transactions costs and being cheaper for retailers than credit cards: such reasons suggest the potential for considerable future growth in the "legitimate" use of Bitcoin.[35] There were also reports of Bitcoin ATMs, which would exchange dollars for Bitcoin, and of companies starting to pay their employees in Bitcoin: for example, in March 2013, Expensify started to offer to pay its non-U.S. employees in Bitcoin to avoid the high charges of PayPal.

Bitcoin also takes various physical forms: in essence physical tokens convertible into real (that is to say, electronic) Bitcoin, which can be used in hand-to-hand exchange. These include physical Bitcoin coins (known as Casascius Bitcoin) and Bitbills (plastic cards or Bitcoin notes). Both have hologram-protected sealed components containing the keys to access a Bitcoin. These can circulate as hand-to-hand currency, their value assured by their convertibility into digital Bitcoin. At any time, the seal can be broken and the key recovered to allow the digital Bitcoin to be spent, but once the seal is broken it becomes obvious that the coin has been spent; it is then essentially worthless. Similar digital-to-physical Bitcoin innovations include PrintCoin, which is similar to checks or debit cards drawn on Bitcoin accounts, and (just launched) Firmcoin, which is essentially a reloadable Bitbill. Thus, a mere two years after its beginning, Bitcoin achieved the remarkable distinction of being the first currency in history to go from digital to physical rather than the other way round.[36]

Threats to Bitcoin

Bitcoin is vulnerable to threats. One source of threats is cryptographic. Modern cryptographic systems depend on the assumption that an attacker would need a very long time—decades, in fact—to decrypt a message, and it has been argued that this could change in the face of future advances in technology (e.g., the development of quantum computers) or in mathematics (e.g., new algorithms). Major improvement in advances in computing technology must surely be inevitable, but Bitcoin automatically corrects for improvements in cryptographic technology or computational power by increasing the difficulty parameter[37] in the Bitcoin mining technology; routine (or even not so routine) improvements in computational power should therefore pose no problem.

This said, one can never rule out the possibility of a development that completely breaks the cryptography: "undecipherable" codes have been broken before. The nightmare scenario, in this context, is where a virus or a huge leap in raw computer power leads the public key feature of Bitcoin to be broken open to reveal the identities behind all the Bitcoin trades that have ever taken place.

Another threat is from botnets—large robotic networks of home PCs that are taken over by a virus and then controlled remotely.[38] These networks can be used for various nefarious purposes, but two in particular are relevant to Bitcoin.

234

The first is to mount distributed denial-of-service (DDoS) attacks against Bitcoin exchanges: essentially, the target site is overwhelmed with too much traffic in an attempt to disrupt its activities. This has happened on a number of occasions, and the most notable target is Mt. Gox. The motives for such attacks would appear to be to destabilize Bitcoin by undermining confidence in the exchange or to manipulate the market for profit or both: attackers sell in an attempt to trigger a panic and then buy up Bitcoin afterward at much lower prices. These attacks have been damaging—a DDoS attack on Mt. Gox on April 3, 2013, led to major disruption, a sharp fall in Bitcoin prices, and a lot of bad publicity—but Bitcoin exchanges have weathered these and other attacks and are becoming more experienced at handling them.[39]

A second use of botnets is to mine for Bitcoin. Botnets are a major problem for honest Bitcoin miners who lose revenue to them, and conceivably botnets might be able to drive honest miners out of business because of their lower costs. The cost of operating a botnet boils down to the cost of infecting them, since the computer rental and electricity consumed are stolen, whereas an honest miner has to pay the full operating cost.[40] Were this to happen, the entire Bitcoin industry would become criminalized, and the integrity of the market itself potentially undermined as honest players leave and the market increasingly attracts unwelcome attention from law enforcement (Güring and Grigg 2011).

Fortunately, this problem of botnet mining seems to be correcting itself: professional miners are increasingly turning to custom-made chips known as Asics (application-specific integrated circuits) for mining purposes, and these are much faster than conventional desktop PCs. Asic mining will then make botnet mining uncompetitive, and the problem should disappear.

Another threat is that from collusive behavior. This threat was explicitly considered in the original design of the Bitcoin system: if a rogue node in the system were to give itself a larger reward than the protocol allows, other nodes are supposed to reject the attempt, and the difficulties of "gaming" the system through collusion should increase as the network gets bigger and ultimately make collusion impossible. However, Lee (2011) argues that collusion might be possible because a handful of clients are likely to account for the overwhelming majority of nodes at any one time. He suggests that a group of big players could then collude by changing the rules (e.g., by awarding themselves 100 Bitcoins instead of 50 for winning a round).

This is a reasonable argument, but were it correct, rogue nodes should *already* have created so much new Bitcoin that the currency would have hyperinflated by now, and this hasn't happened. I am therefore inclined to think that the Bitcoin network is now past the point where such threats could bring Bitcoin down.

Other threats of collusive behavior have been suggested. Lee (2011) suggests that key players might be able to cartelize the Bitcoin market, creating controlling institutions with central-bank-like powers. Similarly, Grinberg (2012) suggests that Bitcoin's five-member development team—which is responsible for maintaining, debugging, and improving the software—might take over the system and function like a Bitcoin central bank. Such arguments mirror earlier arguments (such as that of Goodhart [1988]) that market forces would lead free banking to eventually give way to central banking. The response is twofold. First, although market structure and forms of self-regulation are already emerging in the Bitcoin market, the powers of large players are themselves limited by the market, by the threat of free entry, and by the absence of legal compulsion. Thus, any market-based rules would be akin to club rules and would be very different from the regulations imposed by modern central banks, which are of an altogether more sweeping nature and made possible only by state intervention and the underlying threats of state coercion. Second, the historical record indicates that modern central banking did not in fact evolve naturally through market forces but through a long series of state interventions (see Dowd 1990). As for the Bitcoin market, no evidence indicates that the development team has made any effort to take control of the Bitcoin system; on the contrary, its role has been limited to software improvement and firefighting.

The Future of Bitcoin

Speculating on how future Bitcoin prices might behave is interesting. Let's begin by considering a simplified textbook demand-for-money function that ignores the impact of the interest rate on money demand:

(10.1) $\quad \dfrac{M}{P} = \alpha Y^{\beta}$

where M is the nominal demand for money; P is the price level; Y is real income as a proxy for the level of transactions; β is the income elasticity of demand, which empirical demand for money studies suggest might be in the region of about 0.5; and α is a normalizing constant.

This suggests a corresponding Bitcoin demand function of the form:

(10.2) $\quad P^{B}M^{B} = \alpha Y^{\beta}\,\theta$

where M^{B} is the demand for Bitcoin, P^{B} is the relative price of Bitcoin against goods and services (or the inverse of the price level measured in Bitcoin), and $0 \le \theta \le 1$ is the Bitcoin market share.

Using lowercase letters under dots to represent their growth rates, and setting $\beta \approx 0.5$, we then get:

(10.3) $\quad \dot{p}^{B} + \dot{m}^{B} = \beta\,\dot{y} + \dot{\theta} \approx 0.5 \times 0.02 + \dot{\theta} = 0.01 + \dot{\theta}$

if we assume an illustrative real economic growth rate of 2 percent.

The simplest case is that of the very long run, assuming that no more Bitcoin is being produced and that the demand for Bitcoin has stabilized relative to competitors, that is, θ is constant, which among other possibilities, would cover the $\theta = 1$ case where Bitcoin had taken over the market and driven out competitors. Allowing for the stock of Bitcoin to fall at an attrition rate of 0.5 percent for illustrative purposes, equation (10.3) becomes:

(10.4) $\quad \dot{p}^{B} - 0.005 \approx 0.01$

$\quad\quad \Rightarrow \dot{p}^{B} \approx 0.015$

The price of Bitcoin would therefore rise at about 1.5 percent a year, which implies that if prices were measured in Bitcoin, we would have a long-run Bitcoin deflation rate of (about) 1.5 percent. In sum, in this very long run—assuming Bitcoin ever got to it—goods prices in Bitcoin would be prone to deflation arising from the combination of economic growth and the Bitcoin attrition rate.[41]

The shorter-term cases are more complicated because we also have to consider a possibly changing Bitcoin market share and the impact of the rising supply of Bitcoin. In these cases, assuming the same parameters as above and rearranging, (10.3) becomes:

$$(10.5) \quad \dot{p}^B \approx 0.01 + \dot{\theta} - \dot{m}^B$$

This tells us that in the short run the growth rate of the price of Bitcoin $\dot{p}^B$ depends on the future growth rate of market share $\dot{\theta}$ and the future growth rate of the supply of Bitcoin $\dot{m}^B$: higher $\dot{\theta}$ pushes it up, higher $\dot{m}^B$ pushes it down. Analysis is complicated further if we make $\dot{\theta}$ an endogenous variable depending on $\dot{p}^B$, but we also know that $\dot{m}^B$ (though currently still high, about 7 percent over 2013) is rapidly falling and will soon fade out. We can then envisage three main possibilities:

- The future growth rate of market share $\dot{\theta}$ might be low, in which case the driving factor would be $\dot{m}^B$. We might then expect the price of Bitcoin to fall, but at a decreasing rate as $\dot{m}^B$ slows down. In this case, the market would soon approach its longer-term equilibrium, but Bitcoin would have a very small market share.

- The future growth rate of market share $\dot{\theta}$ might be high enough to make it the driving factor, in which case we might expect the price of Bitcoin to continue to trend upward. Moreover, if the growth rate of market share is high enough, we could get a situation where $\dot{p}^B$ was sufficiently high for sufficiently long as to make Bitcoin the object of a speculative bubble or bubble-bust cycle: people rush into Bitcoin as an investment and the market later tanks, possibly to recover and repeat the experience again and again. Indeed, such a scenario would appear to be a good description of the history of the Bitcoin market to date.

- Something might happen to destroy the demand for Bitcoin altogether. This might happen in response to a particularly severe market bust or (more likely) if something were to happen to compromise the integrity of the Bitcoin market or if the government or some competitor currency were eventually able to stamp or drive Bitcoin out.

The fact that none of these possibilities can easily be ruled out tells us that the future Bitcoin market is highly unpredictable.

The takeaway message is that although the Bitcoin system produces a highly predictable *supply* of money, the *demand* is very unpredictable—and the Bitcoin system possesses no stabilizing factors.

From the point of view of Bitcoin price stability, the root problem is a fundamental and inescapable tension between (a) the inelastic Bitcoin supply schedule, (b) achieving significant take-up relative to existing currencies, and (c) avoiding a rate of price increase that would likely trigger a bubble or bubble-bust cycle. Given (a), one can have either (b) or (c) but probably not both. Put differently, given the way Bitcoin is designed, a major increase in demand is impossible without a corresponding increase in the Bitcoin price.

A related problem exists. A sharp rise in the price of Bitcoin means a sharp fall in the price of anything denominated in Bitcoin, that is, hyperdeflation. In this case, many people would be reluctant to buy anything with Bitcoin: the temptation would be to hoard Bitcoin instead. Conversely, if Bitcoin prices fall, people would be reluctant to acquire Bitcoin for fear that the currency might soon become worthless. To quote Willard Foxton (2013) in the *Daily Telegraph*:

> As an economy where Bitcoin was the main currency, Silk Road recently went through a hyper-deflation almost unprecedented in economics. Following the recent surges in the value of Bitcoin, people have been selling less and less, initially because the value of the Bitcoins was going up so fast people were unwilling to part with them; then, once the Bitcoin price started crashing, dealers were unwilling to part with valuable drugs for Bitcoins worth who-knows-what.

This illustrates how major volatility in the price of Bitcoin can seriously affect its ability to perform its most basic function as currency—but even so, the market continued to operate.

Returning to the issue of the future of Bitcoin, my best-guess scenario is that in the short to medium term—barring a major upset—the most likely scenario for the Bitcoin market is more of the same but with the market lurching toward maturity. The Bitcoin market will continue to grow, but in a fitful manner with one boom-bust cycle after another before settling down as the growing size of the market makes manipulative attacks more difficult and the exchange's risk management continues to improve.

Will Bitcoin grow to displace conventional currency? Probably not. However, to focus on the size of the Bitcoin market relative to conventional currency is to miss the main point—that the significance of Bitcoin lies not in its size but in its nature and, in particular, its novelty and the fact that it is ideally suited to a niche market driven by legal restrictions—that is, that a key reason people demand Bitcoin is to do things they are not legally permitted to do, whether that is to buy illicit goods, launder money, evade exchange controls or taxes, or hide their wealth. Because the underground economy is likely to continue to grow, so, too, is the demand for Bitcoin and other currencies that service that economy.

This creates a delightful irony: the more the state restricts or prohibits forms of commerce, the more the Bitcoin market will thrive as individuals use it to evade state control. Thus, the state itself is the main driving factor behind the growth of the Bitcoin market. An obvious corollary follows: if the state *really* wants to get rid of Bitcoin, it should eliminate the state controls that feed it. It could end the war on drugs, end restrictions on money transmitters, reduce or eliminate income taxes and the agencies that enforce them, end policies of financial repression, and reestablish the privacy of individuals' personal financial information.

Nonetheless, in the longer run, Bitcoin is almost certain to fail—and this is no bad thing. The pioneers in any industry are rarely the ones who last longer term: Who remembers Betamax from the early days of the video industry? Bitcoin might have been the first successful cryptocurrency, but whether being the first mover in this area is an advantage in the longer term is not yet clear. Any major design flaws in the Bitcoin model are set in concrete, and competitors can learn from them. The cryptocurrency market is also an open one, and competition can only be a good thing—and, indeed, a considerable number of new competitors have already entered the field. These include, among others, Litecoin, Namecoin, PPCoin, Freicoin, Ripple, Primecoin, and Feathercoin.[42] Most of these will probably soon fail, but as competition in the market develops, no one can predict which cryptocurrencies will be best suited to the market and achieve long-run success. For what it is worth, my guess is that Bitcoin will eventually be displaced by other cryptocurrencies with superior features.

The ideal—one is tempted to say, the gold standard in this area—would be one or more cryptocurrencies that were able to achieve stable purchasing power through elastic but fully automatic and hence nondiscretionary supply schedules and that also have the ability to maintain state-of-the-art security. Going further, we might even hope that cryptocurrencies eventually become so widely accepted that they drive government currencies out of circulation and expel the government from the monetary system once and for all.

Broader Implications of Cryptocurrency

The broader implications of cryptocurrency are extremely profound. The key issues here are well worth dwelling on and relate to the freedom of the individual to trade, accumulate, move, and protect his or her financial wealth—in other words, the right to financial freedom. Intertwined with these are deep moral questions and, needless to say, the government response. The root issue is, of course, the individual versus the state.

The implications of Bitcoin and associated innovations go much further than merely facilitating the purchase of illegal commodities. A good starting point is to note that the system has no regard for international borders and can be used by anyone with access to the Internet. As one blogger then put it, "As long as my encrypted [Bitcoin] wallet exists somewhere in the world, such as on an e-mail account, I can walk across national borders with nothing on me and retrieve my wealth from anywhere in the world with an internet connection" (Schlichter 2011).

This gives Bitcoin great potential as an internationally mobile store of value that offers a high degree of security against predatory governments and unsafe banks, thus fulfilling but also extending the role that Swiss bank accounts used to fill before Swiss banks were intimidated into "cooperation" with, especially, U.S. law enforcement chasing secret bank accounts. The possible uses for such an internationally mobile medium include squirreling away one's wealth safely abroad, circumventing exchange and capital controls, anonymously transferring money (including money laundering), and evading taxes. Consider three diverse examples.

First, the Unlawful Internet Gambling Enforcement Act of 2006 currently requires payments systems to block U.S. residents from placing bets at online gambling and betting sites. However, U.S. residents minded to do so can place bets on any site that accepts Bitcoin. A good example is the Bitcoin gambling site Satoshdice: this was an Internet sensation and within weeks of its launch in April 2012 was said to be accounting for more Bitcoin transactions than all other uses combined.[43]

A second is the right to make payments to whomsoever one wishes—and in particular, to outfits of which the government disapproves. The outstanding example is WikiLeaks. Following a massive release of secret U.S. diplomatic cables by WikiLeaks in November 2010, the U.S. government orchestrated an illegal financial blockade by pressuring major payments providers such as VISA, MasterCard, Bank of America, and PayPal to block payments to WikiLeaks or freeze the group's accounts so it could not access funds already collected. WikiLeaks was, however, able to circumvent this blockade by accepting payments in Bitcoin.[44] To quote Jon Matonis (2012):

> Freedom of payments is an extension of financial privacy and digital cash-like transactions without financial intermediaries become a critical piece of that foundation. It should be offensive to most free-minded people that **you** are not the final arbiter of how and where you spend your money. Bitcoin restores the balance. (emphasis in original)

One could also imagine Bitcoin being used to make payments to proven criminal groups. But is it the government's place to restrain us before the fact from sending money to parties it disfavors but whom it has not convicted of any crime?[45]

A third is to make investments free of government control, for example, to evade taxes on investment returns or capital gains. As things currently stand, individuals who are careful about security can invest their wealth in Bitcoin and in so doing evade taxes for which they would normally be liable. However, they then face the problem of being exposed to Bitcoin price risk. The natural solution is to hedge their Bitcoin wealth: a U.S.-domiciled investor might want to hedge against the risk that Bitcoin could fall against the U.S. dollar, and the problem is that the hedge position might not be anonymous, since a typical U.S. dollar hedge would be with a regular broker or exchange. So what is needed here is to be able to anonymously acquire, for example, Bitcoin derivatives whose values will fluctuate with the U.S. dollar/Bitcoin exchange rate. One can imagine these soon becoming available, and already a new service, Open Transactions,[46] offers users the opportunity to use Bitcoin to acquire anonymous positions denominated in other currencies. Such services should enable Bitcoin investors to hedge their Bitcoin positions anonymously. One can then imagine that widespread tax evasion of this sort would put pressure on governments worldwide to reduce tax rates and, in doing so, reduce the incentive to evade tax in the first place.

Implicit in the preceding is simply the ability of Bitcoin to enable individuals to protect their wealth. This, in turn, is intimately related to the financial privacy that was once provided by bank secrecy laws. As Martin Hutchinson (2013) recently wrote, bank secrecy is no less than a key civil liberty. Bitcoin helps fill the role once provided by bank secrecy laws.[47]

Government has no easy way to prevent these and similar uses of Bitcoin to evade government control. The combination of anonymity and independence means that governments cannot bring down Bitcoin by conventional methods, although they may occasionally catch individuals and organizations that get careless. They can't bring Bitcoin down by taking down particular individuals or organizations because the system isn't dependent on any individual or organization—there is no single point of failure. They could shut down the Bitcoin website Bitcoin.org or harass exchanges such as Mt. Gox, but this wouldn't make much difference, and the Bitcoin community would carry on regardless.[48] Governments would instead have to take out the whole Bitcoin community, and they can't do that because they can't identify who the Bitcoin community might be—and they can't (yet) spy on everyone, although recent revelations about PRISM suggest they are making major efforts to do exactly that.[49]

We should also put governmental responses into context. For a long time now, it has been clear that these are not so much responses to breaches of this or that law but a sustained attack on freedom itself. Rights to freedom were subject to more and more exceptions: there were exceptions to counter money laundering, terrorism, offshore financial centers that offered less onerous legal regimes (such as lower tax rates), payments to whistleblowers and organizations on government blacklists, and so forth. In the Land of the Free, people used to be free to do almost anything; now they are free to do anything except what is on a long and growing government list of what they can't do.[50] We have gone from a situation where privacy—including financial privacy—was respected to one where it is now openly repudiated, not just in the name of some allegedly greater good (war against terror or whatever), but openly repudiated: there is no longer any right to privacy, period.

But the good news is that thanks to strong cryptography, the balance of power is swinging back to the individual, and Big Brother can't do much to stop it. Censorship, prohibition, oppressive taxes, financial repression, and repression generally will all be undermined as people increasingly escape into the cyphersphere where they can operate freely away from government harassment.[51]

Conclusions

These case studies of contemporary private monetary systems indicate beyond any doubt that the demand for private money is very much alive and well, and private monetary systems are successful because the money they provide is superior to that provided by the state. They also show that the issuers of private money are able to win the trust of their customers—and at a time when trust in government money must be close to an all-time low.

The Liberty Dollar demonstrates that public demand exists for precious-metal coinage and that modern private mints can be profitable enterprises. The biggest problem faced by private minters is that of attack by the state. Throughout history states have regarded the issue of coinage as their own prerogative and for the most part have regarded private minting outside their control as an attack on the sovereign itself; they have traditionally treated it as such, often with great brutality. The Liberty Dollar case shows that this medieval mindset is still going strong even in the modern United States.

For their part, the experiences of DGC systems show that these can provide an efficient international private monetary system—and a form of private gold standard with all the features (own unit of account, medium of exchange, store of value, etc.) of a full monetary system. As with other online systems, security issues always exist, but these are manageable. But as with private minters, the big problem they face is their vulnerability to attack by the state. Because the operators of these systems are identifiable, they have in practice no choice but to comply with government demands, and the experience of e-gold shows that they are not necessarily safe from the government even then.

In different ways, both the Liberty Dollar and DGC systems point to the continuing allure of gold. Advocates of fiat money might sneer—"barbarous relic" and all that—but the attraction of gold should hardly be a surprise given the appalling record of fiat money since the link to gold was cut in 1971. Since 1971 the U.S. dollar has lost almost 85 percent of its value even by official government statistics, whereas the value of gold in real purchasing-power terms has increased by over 500 percent. With a record like that, why *wouldn't* people prefer gold to paper money?

People also have the choice of cryptocurrency, which is a very different proposition. At the broadest level, and whatever its limitations and eventual fate, Bitcoin reminds us yet again of the ability of the private sector to produce astonishing innovations that are almost impossible to anticipate. To start with, the very existence of Bitcoin proves that anyone can create money that other people will accept using a computer that takes as its only inputs an algorithm and processing power. This new currency is similar to a commodity money such as gold under a gold standard insofar as it is costly to produce and inelastic in supply. Bitcoin is, however, truly radical in a number of other respects. Breakthrough number one is that it is the first currency ever to achieve takeoff despite having no intrinsic value. In this it differs from modern fiat currencies that also have no intrinsic value—I ignore here alternative uses for paper money such as wallpaper and sanitary uses—which started off as convertible currencies only to have the commodity link later severed. Bitcoin also differs from conventional note and deposit money in that it can in no way be construed as debt. Breakthrough number two is that Bitcoin provides a novel solution to the trust problem: instead of relying on any individual or organization, it achieves trust using a peer-to-peer network. Relatedly, Bitcoin and other cryptocurrencies are completely nongovernmental. Breakthrough number three is that once it got up and running, Bitcoin became independent of any individuals or organizations and can therefore continue without them—and this makes it very hard to shut down. Finally, breakthrough number four is that Bitcoin has the potential to achieve a very high degree of anonymity. This characteristic opens up almost unimaginable possibilities for private parties to free themselves from state control—to buy illegal drugs, protect their wealth from the government, or whatever. This, in turn, raises profound issues of an emerging spontaneous social order and, in particular, the prospect of a cryptoanarchic society in which there is no longer any government role in the monetary system and, indeed, no government at all.

Notes

1. Timberlake (1987) provides a classic study on private scrip money.
2. Again, Timberlake provides the definitive study: Timberlake (1984).
3. See http://ijccr.net/.
4. There are many studies of private coinage. Examples include Brough (1898), Barnard (1917), and more recently, Selgin (2008).
5. In private correspondence, von NotHaus informs me that the Liberty Dollar organization was always extremely careful never to refer to any of its specie pieces as a coin. Use of the term "coin" by the Liberty Dollar organization would have been in violation of 18 U.S.C. § 486, which states:

> Whoever, except as authorized by law, makes or utters or passes, or attempts to utter or pass, any coins of gold or silver or other metal, or alloys of metals, intended for use as current money, whether in the resemblance of coins of the United States or of foreign countries, or of original design, shall be fined under this title or imprisoned not more than five years, or both.

I shall therefore use his terminology for reasons of legal precision, but readers are free to interpret the terms "coin" and "medallion" interchangeably if they wish.
6. The digital version of the Liberty Dollar was launched in November 2002, and users could e-mail digital Liberty Dollars to each other or use them in online trade. The system was highly secure and audited monthly, and charges were very low (zero for transactions under $10 and 37 cents for other transactions) and much lower than was being charged, for example, by VISA or MasterCard. This was highly successful and, indeed, a large amount of the Liberty Dollar gold and silver that was eventually confiscated by the government in 2009 backed the digital warehouse receipts.
7. For more details of the facts and mechanics of the Liberty Dollar, see, for example, NotHaus (2003) or Pratt (2011).
8. Strictly speaking, it would be more accurate to say that "in print" or newly minted 20-dollar one-ounce silver Libertys would now be trading for US$20. However, the older "out of print" 10-dollar one-ounce silver Libertys would now trade at a new price—approximately US$20—reflecting the rights of their owners to trade them in for the new 20-dollar silver Libertys that are now selling at US$20. Of course, and speaking more generally, because they are also collectibles, the prices of out-of-print issues are affected by how many of any particular issue are available, and the

scarcer issues would trade at a premium. Indeed, some are now trading on e-Bay at very considerable prices—or at least were, before the government bullied e-Bay in November 2012 into stopping trades of Libertys on the made-up grounds that they were counterfeit currency.

9. Personal correspondence.

10. The Liberty Dollar company went to great lengths to distinguish itself from official U.S. coinage. As we have seen (see note 5), they not only scrupulously avoided using the term "coin," but they also avoided the term "legal tender": to quote one of their statements, "The Liberty Dollar has *never* claimed to be, does *not* claim to be, is *not*, and does *not* purport to be, legal tender." Instead, it saw the Liberty Dollar as a form of barter—their preferred wording was "private voluntary barter currency"—which people could use for exchange if they wished to. They would also stress that barter and legal tender are mutually exclusive concepts.

11. The word "counterfeit" seems never to have been used, but the meaning is clear. To quote the U.S. Attorney's press release of March 18, 2011, the charge was that the company had been "making coins resembling and similar to United States coins" in violation of 18 USC § 485.

12. A very interesting historical parallel exists of the type of mind-shift required to be able to understand the basic issues. Before Ronald Coase, it was taken as self-evident that radio-broadcasting wavelengths should be allocated by government bureaucrats. Coase then came up with the idea that they could be allocated by auction, only to be met with incredulity and resistance. When he presented his views in testimony to a Federal Communications Commission hearing on the future of broadcasting, a commissioner rebuked him for making a joke at the expense of the hearing! Invited to prepare a report on the subject for the Rand Corporation, Coase and his colleagues met with the most severe criticism, and Rand refused to publish the report: in the unshakable conviction that the broadcasting spectrum was by definition a public good, Rand concluded that publishing the report would be a waste of its resources. Even Milton Friedman and George Stigler at the University of Chicago were initially skeptical, but they soon changed their minds.

13. See http://www.newlibertydollar.com. In particular, the New Liberty Dollar omits any appearance of "USA"; "TRUST IN GOD" is replaced by "RIGHT TO CONTRACT"; and buyers are asked to affirm that they understand that they are not getting government coin that relies on legal tender for its value but are instead getting a product that derives its value from its precious metal content, its numismatic appeal, and so on. It will be interesting to see how the Department of Justice handles this one.

14. A second trial is also in process, in which holders of the silver and gold seized by the government in the Idaho raid sought to have their property returned. In a memorable judgment, Judge Martin Reidinger, who happens to be in the same federal district where von NotHaus was convicted, denounced the government in no uncertain terms. He said: (1) "The Government has completely lost sight of the purpose of this proceeding and the purpose of the forfeiture statute"; (2) "The Government seeks to deprive them [the petitioners] of their hard-earned retirement funds and assets based on absurd contortions of the forfeiture statute"; and (3) "This is the sort of behavior that diminishes the public trust in government, as well as the justice system in general." (The ruling is available on the Web at http://www.libertydollarnews .org/2013june/2013_02_25_reidinger_dismisal_order.pdf.) The Department of Justice walked off with its tail between its legs: they not only lost the case but did not appeal it.

15. The motion for acquittal is available on the Web at http://www.gata.org/files/VonNotHausRetrialMotion-03-25-2013.pdf. This Introductory Statement is on page 2.

16. Ven grew out of a Facebook application launched in July 2007 and was launched on the general Web in January 2011 as what its authors enthusiastically describe as "an open payment digital ecosystem." Ven is a digital currency traded among members of the Hub Culture network system and is targeted at people who want to have their own currency system and save the rainforests at the same time. As their website explains:

> The value of Ven is determined by the financial markets in a weighted basket of currencies, commodities and carbon futures trading against other major currencies at floating exchange rates. Ven is the first digital currency to float, and the first to include carbon in its pricing, making it the only environmentally linked currency in existence. Since Ven is 100% backed by reserve assets equivalent to Ven in circulation, the inclusion of these assets in the reserve basket provide [sic] a demand source for Carbon, with material benefits to the environment at large. Over 25,000 acres of Amazon rainforest and other environmental investments have been made as a result of Ven trading.

Woolly stuff this may be, hard verifiable facts about the size of the Ven monetary system and how it actually operates are difficult to come by, but one gets the impression that Ven is still a fairly small-scale digital currency. One wonders how it has fared since the market for carbon futures collapsed.

17. Liberty Reserve was a Costa Rica–based digital currency company that was shut down by U.S. federal prosecutors in May 2013. Prosecutors alleged that criminal activity went largely undetected because the company made no effort to verify the identities of its users, which made it attractive for scam artists and money launderers. The founder, Arthur Budovsky, and six others were themselves charged with money laundering as well as with operating an unlicensed money-transfer company. Liberty Reserve was said to have been used to launder more than $6 billion in criminal proceeds and to have had 1 million clients when it was closed down.

18. Some background on e-gold can be found in Grow et al. (2006) and Zetter (2009).

19. It was widely said that transactions of e-gold were anonymous, but in private correspondence Jackson is emphatic that e-gold never promoted itself as anonymous and explicitly dispelled any such impression. He also informs me that it was U.S. law enforcement itself that started to disseminate this view around 2001: this would suggest that even then law enforcement was already planning to use e-gold to lure criminals into their grasp.

20. Far from turning a blind eye, as he was later accused of doing, Jackson did investigate suspicious clients and turned over the results of his investigations to law enforcement. As he wrote to me:

> [P]ractically speaking, e-gold was the opposite of anonymous. We could and did connect the dots that enable identification of the most disciplined of chameleons. Even Russian virtuosos, with impeccable anonymizing techniques were at the mercy of transactional counterparties who might be dumb wannabe punks living in Omaha in

248

their grandma's basement. A Spend to or from an idiot would create a permanent link flagging them in our database.

E-gold investigators were instrumental in identifying and locating the crème de la crème of international hard case cyber criminals, a cohort whose career-ending mistake was to believe the misinformation about e-gold being anonymous.

Over time, the pressure from law enforcement increased—it was no longer enough to comply with legal subpoenas, but e-gold was increasingly expected to proactively spy on its clients and report its results. The company complied, too—not that this was to stop it also becoming a target for law enforcement. See also Zetter (2009).

21. The reason for law enforcement's turning on e-gold is not clear but appears to boil down to some Justice Department or Secret Service agenda—perhaps something as petty as individual officials with ambitions for self-promotion, e-gold being a high-profile "catch." However, from the perspective of U.S. law enforcement as a whole, given the quality catches that e-gold itself had been bringing in, taking the firm down can only be regarded as a spectacular score for the opposing team.

22. Jackson was right to be worried. As Chetson (2011) explains, the concept of relevant conduct "allows the judge to punish the defendant for uncharged crimes, or crimes for which a jury acquitted (found not guilty!) the defendant, when sentencing the defendant following the conviction on even tenuously related charges."

23. For more information about Bitcoin, in addition to the other sources cited in this chapter, a good source is Jon Matonis's blog, The Monetary Future (http://the-monetaryfuture.blogspot.co.uk/). Lew Rockwell also has some good commentary on Bitcoin on his site, LewRockwell.com.

24. The first cryptocurrency was B-money. This was invented by Wei Dai in 1998 and was a direct precursor to Bitcoin but did not catch on because of its impracticality; in particular, it required that all transactions be broadcast to all participants, each of whom was to keep a record of them; it also stipulated a rather cumbersome dispute resolution procedure.

25. The notion of cryptoanarchy was first put forward by Tim May in his "Crypto-Anarchist Manifesto," announced to like-minded techno-anarchists at Crypto 88. The most distinctive feature of cryptoanarchism is the use of cryptography to protect the privacy of consensual economic arrangements from state interference and so evade both censorship and prohibition.

26. http://www.weidai.com/bmoney.txt.

27. The identity of Satoshi Nakamoto has spawned a media mystery hunt. Despite many claims to the contrary, his/her/their true identity remains unknown.

28. Bitcoin is often compared to gold, and it is true that both have highly inelastic supply schedules in the short run. However, they differ in that Bitcoin has a very inelastic supply schedule in the long run as well, whereas the long-run supply of gold is more elastic. They also differ in that the long-run supply of Bitcoin is perfectly predictable (if one ignores attrition), but the future stock of gold is less predictable because of the possibility of unexpected gold discoveries or improvements to extraction technology.

29. Thus, regardless of monetary economists' theoretical arguments over whether it should exist or not, the demand for Bitcoin already exists—and the fact that monetary economists might not understand it is another matter.

30. An analogy here is with the early adoption of Esperanto as a new language: the exact same argument (that is, that no one would move first) would similarly "prove" that Esperanto couldn't take off either. Yet it did, up to a point.

31. This explanation fits with what is known about the genesis of the Bitcoin market. The earliest Bitcoiners shared a communitarian spirit. Shortly after Bitcoin started, Gavin Andresen bought 10,000 BTC for $50 and then gave them away to encourage their use. The first "real" trade then took place when Lazslo Hanyecx paid 10,000 BTC for a pizza delivery (an expensive pizza even then; this involved paying a volunteer to order a transatlantic credit card delivery from England). In one of his last public statements in December 2010, in response to a suggestion that Bitcoin be accepted by WikiLeaks, Nakamoto weighed in strongly against on the grounds that the Bitcoin project was not ready and was still vulnerable: "No, don't bring it on," he wrote. "The project needs to grow gradually so the software can be strengthened along the way. To WikiLeaks I make this appeal not to try to use bitcoin. Bitcoin is a small beta community in its infancy. You would not stand to get more than pocket change, and the heat you would bring would likely destroy us at this stage" (Wallace 2011).

32. A very informative history of the early days of Bitcoin can be found in Wallace (2011).

33. These data refer to prices and quantities traded on the Mt. Gox exchange based in Tokyo, which is the first and still the biggest of the Bitcoin exchanges. The first reported day of trading on this exchange was July 17, 2010.

34. The rise in price from 3 cents to US$121.90 represents a rate of increase of 406,300 percent (!) since the reported first day of trading, equivalent to an annual rate of increase of 126,760 percent. Given such a return, it is presumably safe to speculate that the demand for Bitcoin might include a considerable speculative component too.

35. Nor should we forget that Bitcoin is still mainly used for online trading. It is accepted and traded on or by a large number of exchanges and financial institutions and is widely accepted on sites specializing in gambling, gaming, entertainment, music, marketing, and Web services; a large but partial list of sites accepting Bitcoin can be found at https://en.bitcoin.it/wiki/Trade. Well-known organizations accepting Bitcoin include Reddit, the Internet Archive, WordPress, Mega, and WikiLeaks.

36. One also sees the emergence of Bitcoin financial derivatives: these currently consist of futures and contracts for difference, but considerable speculation anticipates that options should soon follow. New accounts are also being offered by brokers and exchanges to allow short selling and margin trading in Bitcoin, and Bitcoin hedge funds and Exchange-Traded Funds are starting to appear. These should facilitate both risk management and speculation in Bitcoin markets and deepen and liquefy those markets.

37. This parameter controls the overall rate of Bitcoin production. It is calculated approximately every 14 days from the global mining speed experience over the previous 14 days and then reset to keep the overall mining rate of the whole network at an approximately constant rate, now set to one block every 20 minutes.

38. Another threat is from Internet theft, but this problem is in no way unique to Bitcoin, and the lesson—as always—is not to cut corners on security.

39. Mt. Gox has come under considerable criticism because of weaknesses in its own security, but as new exchanges enter the market we can expect to see security standards improve and market prices become harder to manipulate or attack.

40. The Web has various Bitcoin mining calculators, and these allow one to infer the profitability of both legitimate and botnet mining. Paganini (2013) offers some illustrative numbers for April 24, 2013, that suggest a botnet with 1,000 bots would generate a monthly profit of US$210. This profit rate is also directly scalable, so, for example, a botnet with 100,000 bots would generate a monthly profit of US$21,000.

41. However, the price of Bitcoin could take a long time to stop growing, and until that happens the price would be rising by over 1.5 percent a year, and a Bitcoin price level would fall at a correspondingly faster rate—and it would fall even faster if the economic growth or attrition rates were higher than assumed.

Interestingly, this projected rate of increase in the Bitcoin price is not that far from a plausible real interest rate, and under some asset price models we would expect the price to rise with the real interest rate. Thus, two alternative approaches to the long-term behavior of the price of Bitcoin give answers of much the same order of magnitude.

42. An informal overview of some of these alt-currencies is provided by Bradbury (2013), but hard details are difficult to find. In terms of market share, however, these new cryptocurrencies are totally dwarfed by Bitcoin, which has at least 99.9 percent of the market. The next biggest is Litecoin (market cap $57.9 million) with a market share of 0.05 percent, and the others are much smaller still.

43. It was closed to U.S. residents in May 2013—presumably in response to U.S. government pressure—but other sites are still available, and doubtless new ones will continue to emerge to meet the demand.

44. Donations may be sent to http://shop.wikileaks.org/donate.

45. The standard reaction is that al Qaeda and the like pose a threat of terrorism. They do, indeed. However, we should put this threat into perspective: leaving aside issues of whether such terrorism is a response to western governments' meddling in their countries—which it surely is, without excusing it—a recent article in *The Atlantic* examined this issue and concluded that Americans were as likely to be killed by their own furniture (TV sets falling onto them, etc.) as by terrorists. But I digress.

46. https://github.com/FellowTraveler/Open-Transactions.

47. In the European Union, the last country holding out to protect bank secrecy is Austria, which passed bank secrecy legislation in 1978 as part of a belated effort to get some of Switzerland's business. To quote Hutchinson (2013) again: "It was said to be tighter than Swiss legislation, because you never needed to give your real name, merely show the nationality of your passport. If you said your name was Mickey Mouse, the bank staff would accept this, and when you visited the bank cheerfully greet you with 'Gruss Gott, Doktor Maus!'"

48. Indeed, the government has already made several attempts to harass Bitcoin organizations. In May 2013, the Department of Homeland Security seized Mt. Gox's Dwolla electronic payments account because of alleged paperwork violations, and in June the California Department of Financial Institutions issued cease-and-desist orders against the Bitcoin Foundation on the spurious grounds that it was involved in transferring money, which it was not. This latter operation, in particular, was the subject of considerable ridicule on the blogosphere.

49. We wouldn't even know about much of this activity if it weren't for whistle-blowers like WikiLeaks and Ed Snowden, who are now being persecuted for their efforts to keep the public informed about what the government is really up to.

50. Not to be outdone, the U.K. government recently proposed a law that would allow it to monitor all Internet traffic through the United Kingdom, and it is already a criminal offense to refuse to hand over passwords when government officials demand them.

51. See Tim May's prophetic Crypto-Anarchist Manifesto (1988).

References

Ball, James. 2013. "Bitcoin Will Continue to Function beyond the Reach of Government and Law." *The Guardian*, May 30.

Barnard, B. W. 1917. "The Use of Private Tokens for Money in the United States." *Quarterly Journal of Economics* 31 (4): 617–26.

Baxendale, Toby. 2011. "Reforming Fractional Reserve Banking." Posting on the Cobden Centre website, March 8, 2013. http://www.cobdencentre.org/author /tbaxendale/#. (This is the author's expert testimony to Ron Paul's *Monetary Policy Anthology*.)

Bradbury, Danny. 2013. "Bitcoin's Successors: From Litecoin to Freicoin and Onwards." *The Guardian*, June 25.

Brough, William. 1898. *Open Mints and Free Banking*. New York: Putnam.

Chetson, Damon. 2011. "Relevant Conduct and Federal Sentencing." Blog: Wake County Criminal Lawyer, December 3. http://www.raleighcriminallawyer .org/2011/12/relevant-conduct-and-federal-sentencing/.

Connolly, Kate, and Guy Grandjean. 2013. "Bitcoin: The Berlin Streets Where You Can Shop with Virtual Money." *The Guardian*, April 26.

Christin, Nicolas. 2012. "Traveling the Silk Road: A Measurement Analysis of a Large Anonymous Online Marketplace." Working Paper, August 1 version Carnegie Mellon University CyLab, Pittsburgh, PA.

Dowd, Kevin. 1990. "Did Central Banks Evolve Naturally? A Review Essay of Charles Goodhart's *The Evolution of Central Banks*." *Scottish Journal of Political Economy* 37 (1): 96–104.

Foxton, Willard. 2013. "The Online Drug Marketplace Silk Road Is Collapsing: Did Hackers, Government or Bitcoin Kill It?" *Daily Telegraph* blogs, May 1.

Franklin, Oliver. 2013. "Unravelling the Dark Web." *GQ British*, February 7. http:// www.gq-magazine.co.uk/comment/articles/2013-02/07/silk-road-online-drugs -guns-black-market.

Goodhart, Charles. 1988. *The Evolution of Central Banks*. Cambridge, MA: MIT Press.

Grinberg, Reuben. 2012. "Bitcoin: An Innovative Alternative Digital Currency." *Hastings Science and Technology Law Journal* 4 (1): 159–207.

Grow, Brian, with John Cady, Susann Rutledge, and David Polek. 2006. "Gold Rush." *Businessweek.com*, January 8. http://www.businessweek.com/stories/2006-01-08 /gold-rush.

Güring, Philipp, and Ian Grigg. 2011. "Bitcoin and Gresham's Law: The Economic Inevitability of Collapse." October–December. http://iang.org/papers/Bitcoin -BreachesGreshamsLaw.pdf.

Hutchinson, Martin. 2013. "The Bear's Lair: Banking Secrecy Is a Key Civil Liberty." The Prudent Bear (blog), April 29.

Lee, Timothy B. 2011. "Bitcoin's Collusion Problem." Bottom-up (blog), April 19. http://timothyblee.com/2011/04/19/bitcoins-collusion-problem/.

Matonis, Jon. 2012. "WikiLeaks Bypasses Financial Blockade with Bitcoin." *Forbes*, August 20.

May, Tim. 1988. "The Crypto-Anarchist Manifesto." http://invisiblemolotov.files
.wordpress.com/2008/06/cryptoanarchist-manifesto.pdf.

Nakamoto, Satoshi. 2009a. "Bitcoin: A Peer-to-Peer Electronic Cash System." http://
bitcoin.org/bitcoin.pdf.

———. 2009b. "Bitcoin Open Source Implementation of P2P Currency." Posted on
P2P Foundation website, February 11. http://p2pfoundation.ning.com/forum
/topics/bitcoin-open-source.

NotHaus, Bernard von, ed. 2003. *The Liberty Dollar Solution to the Federal Reserve*. Evan-
sville, IN: American Financial Press.

Paganini, Pierluigi. 2013. "How to Profit Illegally from Bitcoin … Cybercrime and
Much More." Infosec Institute Resources, May 3. http://resources.infosecinstitute
.com/how-to-profit-illegally-from-bitcoin-cybercrime-and-much-more/.

Pratt, Jason. 2011. "A Free Market Standard: Transitioning from a Government Fiat
Currency to a Private, Value-Based, Free-Market Money System Based 100% on
Gold and Silver." Unpublished manuscript, November 16.

Rounds, Bill. 2011. "Liberty Dollar II: Did Prosecutor Anne Tompkins Violate Ethics Rules?" How to Vanish.com, April 11. http://www.howtovanish.com/2011/04
/liberty-dollar-ii-prosecutor-anne-tompkins-made-false-statement-of-law/.

Schlichter, Detlev. 2011. "Bitcoin, Gold and the Demise of Fiat Money." Navigating
the Monetary Meltdown (blog), June 30. http://detlevschlichter.com/2011/06
/bitcoin-gold-and-the-demise-of-fiat-money/.

Selgin, George A. 2008. *Good Money: Birmingham Button Makers, the Royal Mint, and the
Beginnings of Modern Coinage, 1775–1821*. Ann Arbor: University of Michigan Press.

Timberlake, Richard H. 1984. "The Central Banking Role of Clearinghouse Associations." *Journal of Money, Credit and Banking* 16 (1): 1–15.

———. 1987. "Private Production of Scrip Money in the Isolated Community." *Journal
of Money, Credit and Banking* 19 (4): 437–47.

U.S. Attorney's Office, Western District of North Carolina. 2011. "Defendant Convicted of
Minting His Own Currency." Press Release, FBI Charlotte Division, March 18. http://
www.fbi.gov/charlotte/press-releases/2011/defendant-convicted-of-minting
-his-own-currency.

U.S. Mint. 2006. "Liberty Dollars Not Legal Tender, United States Mint Warns
Consumers." Press release, September 14. http://www.usmint.gov/pressroom
/?action=press_release&id=710.

Wallace, Benjamin. 2011. "The Rise and Fall of Bitcoin." *Wired*. December. http://
www.wired.com/magazine/2011/11/mf_bitcoin/.

Zetter, Kim. 2009. "Bullion and Bandits: The Improbable Rise and Fall of E-Gold."
Wired, June 9. http://www.wired.com/threatlevel/2009/06/e-gold/all/1.

11. Central Banks: Reform or Abolish?

Gerald P. O'Driscoll, Jr.

Advocates of central-bank reform must examine why central banks emerged and what forces sustain them. They did not arise in an institutional vacuum and will not be reformed in an institutional vacuum. The historical origins of central banks explain how they came into existence. The forces sustaining and feeding their growth may differ from those explaining their origin.

Plans to abolish central banks constitute an extreme reform. It is doubtful that such plans can succeed without broader institutional change, occurring either first or simultaneously. That is likely true regardless of the strength of evidence on central-bank performance. I examine these issues in what follows.

Why Central Banks?

> The superiority of central banking over the alternative became a dogma which never again came up for discussion and was accepted without question or comment in all the later foundations of central banks.
>
> —V. Smith (1936) 1990, 167–68

Vera Smith wrote her dissertation on central banking under Friedrich Hayek in the 1930s at the University of London.[1] In book

The comments of the participants in the Liberty Fund seminar "In Search of a Monetary Constitution—Revisited" are gratefully acknowledged. The paper was also presented at St. John's University in New York City; Trinity College in Hartford, CT; and the Summer Institute for the History of Economic Thought at the Jepson School of Leadership Studies at the University of Richmond; the comments received there are gratefully acknowledged. I also gratefully acknowledge the comments of Steve Horwitz, Leonard Liggio, Maralene Martin, and Lew Randall. A version of the paper appeared in the Cato Working Paper series.

form, she titled it *The Rationale of Central Banking*. The reader soon discovers that the case for central banking was less a reasoned exposition of principles and more a set of myths. In Smith's words, it had become dogma. In this chapter, I reexamine the dogma and see if a rationale can be teased out of central-banking myths.

I begin by making a basic point. Central banking is suspect because it violates the general economic principle that presumptively favors competitive markets for producing goods and services. In general economic theory, monopoly is bad and an affirmative case must be made for it. When it comes to central banking, most economists no longer make the case for it. If they did, their reasoning would not pass muster in other areas. Dogma rules more so than even in Smith's time.

To his credit, Milton Friedman argued that the case for monopoly in banking could not go unexamined. Friedman (1960, 4) noted that "control over monetary and banking arrangements is a particularly dangerous power to entrust to government because of its far reaching effects on economic activity at large—as numerous episodes from ancient times to the present and over the whole of the globe tragically demonstrate." He acknowledged that a pure commodity-money system is viable. He argued that bankers and their customers would have incentives to find substitutes for the commodity. These have historically been currency and later bank deposits: "fiduciary elements" in Friedman's terminology (Friedman 1960, 5–6).

Friedman (1960, 6–7) further argued that fiduciary elements would dominate because they are cheaper to produce than the commodity money. Banks would overissue currency and be unable to honor their obligations to pay out units of the commodity money on demand in exchange for their currency and deposits. Friedman made the case for the inherent instability of a competitive monetary system.

Because the enforcement of contracts is a basic function of government in a classical liberal order, Friedman (1960, 6–7) noted that one liberal principle (enforcement of contracts) comes into conflict with another (freedom to compete). Competition would not provide an effective limit to the issuance of money and, hence, its value could not be preserved. Friedman (1960, 7) concluded that the production of "fiduciary currency" is "a technical monopoly" and "there is no such presumption in favor of the private market as there is when competition is feasible." In short, we need a central bank to provide a nominal anchor.[2]

Friedman's argument is the classic case against free banking. I reference it because, in his telling of it, the argument is particularly clear. And he attended to liberal presumptions favoring liberty over coercion in all matters. I also invoke Friedman on this point because he linked the question of banking reform to that of monetary reform. That linkage is a theme of this chapter.

As Friedman was well aware, his argument did not ipso facto make the case for central banking. In one version of his plan for a monetary rule, a functionary in the Treasury Department could make the daily calculation of how much base money to create. Friedman's 1960 argument was long accepted, however, as a rationale for central banking. Call it the classical liberal rationale for the Fed.

The problem is that Friedman's argument against competitive banking is fallacious. As one of his students, Benjamin Klein, later pointed out, Friedman had a model of competition without competitors (Klein 1974). More precisely, the money in Friedman's model is not branded. When firms produce superior products, they enhance the value of the firm (brand-name capital). Markets provide incentives to improve products, not produce shoddy output. In a competitive monetary system, banks would compete to produce superior money that held its value.[3] A virtuous cycle toward high-quality money would take place, not the race to the bottom that Friedman predicted.[4]

Benjamin Klein (1974) modeled a competitive system of money under a fiat standard. That aspect was unpersuasive to Friedman and many others. But Klein was surely correct that competition results in better products and services. Friedman offered a lemons model for competitive money (and, not as he suggested, a natural monopoly).

Now I pause to point out a conundrum. Friedman would not have made his argument as he did had he known of *The Rationale of Central Banking*. He would certainly have had to take note of the argument and historical evidence in that book and perhaps even rethought his position. And he certainly knew Vera (Smith) Lutz. She and her husband were longtime members of the Mont Pelerin Society, of which Friedman was also a member. Friedrich Lutz was president of the society from 1964 to 1967 (Yeager 1990, xv). Additionally, Hayek and Friedman regularly attended meetings, and Vera Lutz's work had influenced Hayek. Anyone attending those meetings knows that monetary topics frequently came up. So I am puzzled by Friedman's apparent ignorance of her contribution. I am only more so because he was later to write a blurb for the jacket of the Liberty Fund edition of her book.[5]

I will not repeat the arguments of more recent contributions to the free-banking literature, likely well known to the readers of this chapter. Building on the earlier work of others, Lawrence White (1984b) marked the renaissance of free-banking theory. The earlier work included Hugh Rockoff (1974) and Arthur Rolnick and Warren Weber (1982). White was followed by numerous other works. George Selgin (1988), Kevin Dowd (1989), White (1989), Steven Horwitz (1990), and Dowd and Richard Timberlake (1998) are just a sampling. The kind of argument made by Friedman (1960) can no longer be taken seriously by students of monetary history. Indeed, Friedman recanted in the face of the work of White and others (Friedman and Schwartz 1986).[6]

Ralph Hawtrey and others have viewed the lender-of-last-resort role of central banks as their primary function (V. Smith [1936] 1990, 141). Walter Bagehot coined the phrase and first explicated how a central bank should act in a liquidity crisis. Economists who justify central banks by their ability to act as lender of last resort get Bagehot's argument exactly backward. Bagehot thought that it was unfortunate that the banking system had evolved as it had. Bagehot ([1873] 2011, 130) described "the natural system" as the one "which would have sprung up if Government had let banking alone." There would be "many banks of equal or not altogether unequal size." In a decentralized banking system, each bank would hold its own reserves and provide for its own liquidity. Reserves would not be concentrated in one place, a practice he thought unwise. Bagehot ([1873] 2011, 134) described it as "the many reserve system." In times of illiquidity, the scramble by all banks for the common pool of reserves leads to the multiple contraction of the money supply (White 1998, 389).

Serving as lender of last resort is *not* then an argument in favor of central banking. Rather, the lender-of-last-resort role is a necessity, given that a country has a central bank. When a central bank exists, reserves concentrate on its balance sheet. In time of crisis, it alone has the wherewithal to lend. Hence the contradiction Bagehot noted. In his view, better the system of central banking with its concentration of reserves had never arisen. Given that Britain had a central bank, however, it was critical that it follow the policies presented in *Lombard Street*. It is a second-best policy.

In fact, central banks today do not follow Bagehot's strictures for a lender of last resort (Humphrey 2010). In times of liquidity crisis, the central bank should lend freely on good collateral at penalty rates. Instead, they now typically lend freely at subsidized rates for periods well beyond any liquidity crisis.

In the United States, this practice has been in place since the 1984 failure of Continental Illinois National Bank (Gelinas 2009, 5, 43–51, 156–57).[7] It has very much been the practice during the current financial crisis, already evident by 2008 and continuing today. "Central banks … did not sufficiently heed Bagehot's admonition to provide liquidity only at a penalty rate. Not designing the financial incentives faced by their counterparties in these new facilities to minimize moral hazard has turned out to be the central banks' Achilles heel in the current crisis. It will come back to haunt us in the next crisis" (Buiter 2008, 27).

Bagehot wanted to ensure that central banks lent only to solvent institutions experiencing liquidity problems. If institutions have good, unpledged collateral, it indicates they are solvent. The penalty rate motivates banks to pay off emergency borrowings as soon as financial markets return to normal.

If central banks relax collateral requirements and lend at subsidized interest rates, they risk lending to insolvent institutions. Keeping insolvent institutions open and operating by lending directly to them at subsidized rates misallocates resources. Resources are taken from solvent banks, which could lend productively, and instead provided to insolvent banks, which are not in a position to lend. Credit is constrained, and normal economic activity stifled.

Current central-bank practice creates "zombie" banks. Think of the savings and loan crisis in the United States in the 1980s, the Japanese banking crisis of the 1990s, or the European banking crisis of today.[8]

As this is being written, the Fed has renewed currency swap lines with the European Central Bank and four others (Canada, the United Kingdom, Switzerland, and Japan). It lends at 50 basis points above the overnight index swap rate. The European Central Bank (and others drawing on the lines) then lends dollars to its banks.

European banks engage in dollar lending in global markets. Funding dollar assets with dollar liabilities is least costly. As Buiter (2008, 34) observed, however, "expensive is not illiquid." European banks could issue debt instruments denominated in euros and purchase dollars in the foreign-exchange markets. If the banks are unable to raise euro funds, it suggests they are not perceived to be solvent. The swaps arrangement has put the Fed in a position of funding a cross-border bailout of foreign banks. It is an escalation of bad central-bank practice.

Notably, in the recent round of swaps, the Fed cut its interest rate from 100 basis points to 50 basis points. Even in an earlier round of swaps, Buiter (2008, 34) concluded the swap arrangement provided "unwarranted subsidies to euro area- and Switzerland-based banks needing US dollar liquidity." That is even truer today.

What I have been describing is credit allocation. Subsidized lending to favored financial institutions is inherently so. The Fed did this also by targeting certain securities, such as mortgage-backed securities, for open-market purchases. In the process, the Fed accepted dubious assets, likely at inflated valuations. The European Central Bank is reportedly doing the same. Richmond Fed president Jeffrey Lacker (2011) criticized the practice, "Credit allocation can redirect revenues from taxpayers to financial market investors, and over time can expand moral hazard and distort the allocation of credit." It transfers resources from solvent banks, which would fund profitable investment, to unsound or even insolvent banks. The latter are constrained in lending. It is a recipe for creating a Japan-style "lost decade" of economic stagnation.

Central banks are not following Bagehot's rule for the lender of last resort. But they do continue to conduct monetary policy in part by using the discount window ("rediscounting" in the older terminology). As long ago noted by Friedman (1960, 38), "rediscounting is a technically defective tool" for conducting monetary policy. Better just to use open-market operations, which were infeasible in Bagehot's time. Using the discount window makes the central bank a passive agent dependent on banks coming to it. By engaging in open-market operations, the central bank can take an active approach in a financial panic and provide liquidity to the entire banking and financial system. To conclude, central banks are no longer adhering to Bagehot's sound rule, but they are wedded to an archaic policy procedure.

I now focus on the origins of the first major central bank.[9]

The Bank of England

We need to understand the fiscal history of Europe, England, and the Continent. In *The Wealth of Nations*, Adam Smith ([1776] 1981, 907, 908) distinguished between two eras: that "rude state of society which precedes the extension of commerce and the improvement of manufactures, when those expensive luxuries which commerce and manufactures can alone introduce, are altogether unknown" and "a commercial country with every sort of expensive luxury." In the modern commercial society, "the sovereign, in the same manner as almost all the great proprietors in his dominions, naturally spends a great part of his revenue in purchasing those luxuries." The lure of luxuries leads to overindulgence in them: "His [the sovereign's] ordinary expenses become equal to his ordinary revenue, and it is well if it does not frequently exceed it" (A. Smith [1776] 1981, 909).

This dynamic leads the sovereign into a chronic statement of impecuniousness. It is aggravated by the proclivity of kings to go to war. "The want of parsimony in time of peace, imposes the necessity of contracting debt in time of war" (A. Smith [1776] 1981, 909). Much of the remainder of the chapter "Of publick Debts" details the sad fiscal record in England, France, and Italy. It is an early public choice accounting of the costs of war, empire, and royal luxuries.

Kings used a variety of expedients to raise revenues, especially to fund wars. They sold monopolies, made arrangements with guilds, seized church lands and revenues, seized the property of Jews and expelled them, and clipped coins. These were often temporary expedients. In England, the king eventually created Parliament to collect taxes (Liggio 1999). The rise of the Estates-General in France was a product of the same fiscal dynamic (Aftalion 1990).

The Bank of England was created as another fiscal expedient and with no thought to anything we would call monetary policy. Charles II spent and borrowed heavily and eventually defaulted on his loans to bankers. The king's credit was left in ruin. As Vera Smith ([1936] 1990, 12) phrased it, William III "fell in with a scheme" to raise 1,200,000 pounds. The government did so in a clause of the Tunnage Act of 1694 by creating the Governor and Company of the Bank of England. That sum was raised as capital and immediately lent to the government. In turn, the bank was permitted to issue notes in that amount. As Smith ([1936] 1990, 12) summarizes it, "the early history of the Bank was a series of exchanges of favours between a needy Government and an accommodating corporation."

Kings had heretofore entered into many arrangements in which money was lent to the government in return for favors. It was their stock in trade, and there was nothing notable in that accommodation. In 1697, however, the government renewed and extended the privileges of the bank. The bank was allowed to increase its capital to lend more to the government and issue more notes. That model would be followed a total of seven times between 1694 and the beginning of the 19th century: a renewal of charter, more loans to the government, and more notes outstanding (V. Smith [1936] 1990, 13).

What was momentous in 1697 was the inclusion of the privilege of limited liability for the members of the corporation. "This was a favour which was to be denied to all other banking associations for another one and a half centuries" (V. Smith [1936] 1990,12). Even when laws of general incorporation emerged in England and America, they were not automatically extended to banks. Banking was viewed as privilege. Extending limited liability to the Bank of England compounded one privilege with another.

The Bank of England was born in fiscal iniquity, a corporation endowed with privileges—like so many before it—for the sole purpose of financing the king's extravagances. It served no other function, no grand public purpose, and certainly no monetary role. It acquired a monetary role over time only though the accumulation of more privileges, such as the exclusive right to note issuance in greater London. The granting of legal-tender status to Bank of England notes in 1812 was extremely important in cementing the bank's monopoly status (V. Smith [1936] 1990, 15–16).

The extension of the bank's privileges proceeded more rapidly as the government's funding needs grew during the Napoleonic Wars. It was more of the exchange of favors between the bank and the government. Early in the Napoleonic Wars, the government's demands on the bank became so severe that it threatened the bank's survival. Parliament passed an act suspending cash payments. Vera Smith ([1936] 1990, 15) observed that this amounted to legalizing the bank's bankruptcy "and it created a precedent which led the public in the future always to expect the Government to come to the aid of the Bank in difficult circumstances."

As practice evolved, the bank underwrote the government's finances, and the government provided the privileges needed to render that a profitable business model. Ultimately, it amounted to the bank's guaranteeing the government and the government's guaranteeing the bank. The eventual monopoly of the production of paper money assured that no default in nominal terms would occur for either partner in the scheme.

The experience of suspension motivated Henry Thornton to write his treatise on *Paper Credit* in 1802. It was a brilliant exposition of central-bank practice incorporated within monetary theory. It was a much deeper and more comprehensive analysis than Bagehot provided later in the century. Thornton analyzed such matters as the divergence of money rates of interest from their equilibrium level, the inflationary process that resulted, and price expectations effects on nominal interest rates. It was a prime example of a phenomenon noted by Hayek: the best monetary theory often arises out of the worst monetary practice. That is why Italy has produced so many notable monetary economists.[10]

After the Napoleonic Wars, Britain implemented a series of mutually reinforcing, benign policies. With the Coinage Act of 1816 and the Resumption Act of 1819, it adopted the gold standard (Steil and Hinds 2009, 80–81, 156). With the repeal of the Corn Laws in 1846, it began the process of adopting free trade. It also adopted fiscal rectitude.

After the 1840s, the growth of incomes took off in Britain. Even with an empire weighing it down and the costs of protecting the seas, Britain experienced enough economic growth to generate the tax revenues needed to fund its government. And, of course, Britain had established a firm rule of law protecting private property rights.

The Bank of England was not called upon to finance the government. Instead, it managed the gold standard through its adjustments to the Bank Rate. It was born of fiscal necessity but flourished when released from the demands of the Crown for funds. That was true so long as the mix of other good policies remained intact. It ended with World War I.

Other countries emulated Britain's sound policies in trade, finance, and money. Central banking spread but was not adopted uniformly.

The rule of law, free trade, and sound money was the policy formula for sustained economic growth (Steil and Hinds 2009). History suggests that central banking was adventitious.

Other Central Banks

In the aftermath of the collapse of John Law's scheme, France saw revulsion against note issues. Eventually private note issuance was allowed to resume. By the 1790s, limited banking freedom existed. "The freedom prevailing at this time in banking in France seems to have proved very satisfactory, and no disasters occurred, but the march of political events destined this state of affairs for a short existence" (V. Smith [1936] 1990, 29).

The march of events was the rise of Napoleon Bonaparte and his incessant war making. With that came the need for finance. It led to the creation of the Bank of France, preference in note issuing, and then effective monopoly of note issuance. Added to the familiar dynamic was "Napoleon's mania for centralization" (V. Smith [1936] 1990, 29). Attempts were made later in the century to introduce competition in banking, but to no avail.

The story of Germany is more complex because of the many separate states. Vera Smith ([1936] 1990, 58) reported that princes and nobles started banks "motivated by fiscal needs." In Prussia, Frederick the Great founded the Royal Bank of Berlin as a privileged bank. During the Napoleonic Wars, it lent heavily to the state and suffered losses. The Royal Bank was reconstituted as the Prussian Bank in 1846 (V. Smith [1936] 1990, 61). Finally, in 1875 the Reichsbank was constituted out of the Prussian Bank, and Germany had a central bank (V. Smith [1936] 1990, 68–69). The origins of banking and central banking stemmed from the need of the Prussian state to finance itself. Banks and the state were intertwined.

The United States is a still more complex story because of its many states. Before the Civil War, banking was mostly governed by state law and regulation. Texas, to cite one extreme, forbade the business of banking in its state constitution. Another issue was the complexity of the First (1791–1811) and Second Banks (1816–36) of the United States, each a federally chartered institution and neither of which saw renewal of its charter. Generally, the chartering of banks evolved from at first being institutions specially chartered by legislatures with grants of limited liability. Beginning with a New York law in 1838, bank charters were given under a general law of incorporation specifying in advance general rules and regulations of such matters as coverage for note issues and capitalization. The era of free banking, American style, began. It was aptly described by Vera Smith as decentralization without freedom.[11]

The system had a number of weaknesses. State-chartered banks were restricted to branching within the boundaries of the states, if at all. This produced a system of small, often financially undiversified institutions. Further, banks might be required to hold state bonds as backing for currency issues. In that sense, we see the linkage of banking and government in the U.S. story, albeit with state governments. The federal government was relatively unimportant in the antebellum era. In some instances, banks could value state bonds at par even if they traded at a discount. That produced an incentive for overissuance of currency. Nonetheless, Vera Smith ([1936] 1990, 53) judged that the banking system in the 20 years leading up to the Civil War was "far steadier" than before.

The Civil War required financing. The strains of managing the government's finances led to the National Banking Acts of 1863 and 1864. They created nationally chartered banks of issue, whose notes were backed by U.S. Treasury bonds. The acts attempted to reform the U.S. banking system, but financing the war deficit was the strong motivating factor (Salsman 1993, 89).

Until the creation of the Federal Reserve System, the United States operated with a national banking system. It had a number of flaws and has been much maligned. It has been portrayed as prone to bank panics and crises in 1873, 1884, 1890, 1893, and 1907. Yet the national-bank era was one of the strongest periods of economic growth in the country's history. Salsman (1993, 86) argues that the 19th-century crises "were briefer, milder, and involved acute illiquidity, whereas this [20th] century crises have involved prolonged periods of recession and depression, widespread bank failure, and chronic insolvency." The 21st century appears to be following suit.

The system proved inflexible in panics when currency demand rose during bank runs. This inflexibility was a product of the law rather than an inherent flaw of competitive note issuance. By imposing legal minimum-reserve requirements, the law made reserves unusable when needed. Far from guaranteeing bank liquidity, the requirements rendered banks illiquid (Salsman 1993, 88). The reserve requirement was rendered more stringent by the fact that the Treasury was paying down debt, which constituted the reserves behind national-bank notes (V. Smith [1936] 1990, 149).[12] Friedman and Schwartz (1963, 117–18n44) noted that, in his 1894 *Annual Report*, Comptroller of the Currency Eckels called for repeal of all laws requiring U.S. bonds as security for national bank notes and adoption of an asset-backed currency. There were also reserve requirements on deposits: "At that time and for at least the next half-century, the U.S. was the only major country in the world that had legal reserve requirements for commercial bank deposits."

After the Panic of 1907, calls for an alternative increased. Reform was all that was needed, but major banks and Progressives came together in support of some type of central bank. Kolko (1963) cites the creation of the Federal Reserve as an important factor in the triumph of "conservatism," but I would say it would be more conventional to term it the triumph of corporatism. It was part of the Progressive vision of government management of the economy. It was less about monetary policy and more about control of big finance. As Kolko argued, however, it became a way for big finance to influence government policies. But the Fed did not originally fit the model of banking in the service of government finances, although it would quickly become so with the outbreak of World War I. Yet after the war and depression of 1920–21, tax reform and strong economic growth would again produce budget surpluses. The Fed as financer of large, peacetime budget deficits awaited the New Deal.

I tentatively suggest that the history tells us that chronic government budget deficits are a sufficient, but not a necessary, condition for the rise of a central bank in a country. Canada got through the Great Depression without a central bank and experienced no major bank failures. The Bank of Canada was created in 1935 mainly to conform to international practice (Selgin, Lastrapes, and White 2012, 583).

By that logic, ending chronic deficits is a necessary condition for the elimination of a country's central bank. It is scarcely possible to imagine a permanent end to deficits without a downsizing of the modern welfare/warfare state. Notably, the fiscal surpluses of the Clinton administration were, at least in part, a product of the peace dividend following on the end of the Cold War and welfare reform.

266

The British experience provides an alternative model for monetary reform. The Bank of England was retained in the era of classical liberalism. But it was reduced to managing the operation of the gold standard. The gold standard functioned as a binding monetary rule on the bank. The gold standard was the effective rule for which monetary economists have been searching. That case clarifies that it is possible to have free trade, free movement of capital, a gold standard, and a central bank.

O'Driscoll (2012) argues that the gold standard worked with a number of banking arrangements. There was the English case with a central bank. For a time, in neighboring Scotland, free banking flourished. The flawed free-banking system in the United States worked, as did the national-bank system. Canada offered yet another model: a small number of banks emerged with national branching and note issuance under the gold standard.[13]

A return to a gold standard would be a return to the monetary system that historically accompanied the classical liberal system. Global fiat money is a discordant element in a system of free trade and free capital movements. Steil and Hinds (2009, 8) observe that "national monies and global markets simply do not mix; together they make a deadly brew of currency crises and geopolitical tensions and create ready pretexts for damaging protectionism." The current conflict over "currency manipulation" between the United States, on the one hand, and China and now Japan, on the other hand, illustrates their point.

Steil and Hinds treat the evolution of sound money on a par with the rule of law in making globalization possible. They note that the evolution of contract merchant law, *lex mercatoria*, was critical for the global extension of commerce. Merchants came together from great distances and different countries to trade.[14] They needed to be governed by common rules of contract and behavior. Those rules became merchant law, which only later became absorbed into national law (Steil and Hinds 2009, 23–26). Just as merchants required a common law, they also required a common money. Commodity money, mainly silver and gold, was the common money.

Mises also portrayed "sound money," for him a gold standard, as part of a wider liberal program.[15] Mises ([1952] 1971, 413–14) characterized the chief political problem as "how to prevent the rulers from becoming despots and enslaving the citizenry." Mises ([1952] 1971, 414) further stated that "the idea of sound money ... was devised as an instrument for the preservation of civil liberties against despotic inroads on the part of governments." For Mises, sound money is as much a political institution as an economic one. "Ideologically it belongs in the same class with political institutions and bills of rights. The demand for constitutional guarantees and for bills of rights was a reaction against arbitrary rule and non-observance of old customs by kings" (Mises [1952] 1971, 414). Steil and Hinds, and Mises, provide complementary arguments for why a gold standard is an essential part of a liberal order.

Returning to a gold (or other commodity) standard would be necessary to implement a system of competitive banking with note-issuing private banks. O'Driscoll (2012) argues that a restoration of the gold standard is a necessary condition for reform of the monetary *and* banking systems. White (2012) provides a practical path for restoration.

My point can be restated as follows. Commodity money is liberalism's money. By imposing a rule on central banks, a true gold standard (not a gold-exchange standard) accomplished much of what free-bank advocates desire. It would constitute a major reform and end most of the discretion that central banks have acquired under global fiat money. Additionally, a gold standard provides fiscal discipline. "A gold standard does help to ensure budget balance in the desirable present-value or long-run, by constraining a government that wants to sell its bonds in the international market to a fiscal path consistent with full repayment in gold" (White 2012, 11).

Adopting a gold standard is a way station for a return to free banking. Many people have lived under at least the vestige of the gold standard. No one alive today has lived in a free-banking system. It will be a more difficult case to make.

Having made this point, however, I turn to recent arguments in favor of free banking. The case is today stronger than it has been for many years.

Why Free Banking?

Hayek ([1937] 1989, 13) identified the "fundamental dilemma" of central banking:

> The only effective means by which a central bank can control an expansion of the generally used media of circulation is by making it clear in advance that it will not provide the cash (in the narrower sense) which will be required in consequence of such expansion, but at the same time it is recognised the paramount duty of a central bank to provide the cash once the expansion of bank deposits has actually occurred and the public begins to demand that they should be converted into notes or gold.

Hayek has told us that central banks face an inherent time-inconsistency problem (Kydland and Prescott 1977). It must promise today to limit the creation of base money, but the public knows that in the future it will be forced to do so. Hence, its promise is not credible. White (1998, 390) characterized it as "the classic conflict between fighting external and internal drains placed in a dynamic context." So the goals of a central bank are placed in conflict with the gold standard.

The lender-of-last-resort function may also conflict with a gold standard. The practical resolution under a classical gold standard was that liquidity crises were of short duration. And the lending at penalty rates meant that short-term capital inflows would be attracted. The ultimate resolution of the conflict was that one goal was paramount under the classical gold standard: protecting against external drain, that is, staying on the gold standard.[16] Exception was made for times of war, which came under force majeure. Still, the conflict was always present.

For a fiat-money system, the conflict is unresolvable. For the gold-exchange standard of the interwar years and the Bretton Woods system, we know from history that Hayek's "fundamental dilemma" could not be resolved. Each system was abandoned when imperatives led countries to make domestic considerations paramount.

The best free-banking argument is not that central banking and the gold standard are incompatible. They were not so historically. The best argument is that central banks are superfluous under a gold standard. Or as White (2012, 8) put it, "because the nation's money stock becomes endogenous, no monetary policy is needed under a gold standard." Before moving into powerful government positions, Alan Greenspan (1966) used to make much the same point. "Under the gold standard, a free-banking system stands as the protector of an economy's stability and balanced growth."[17]

The free-banking argument is not far from Bagehot's argument of more than a century ago. Free banking is the natural system. Central banking was an accident of history. The best outcome is to devise policies for a central bank to mimic how a free-banking system would work. In essence, White (2012, 8) accepted the first part of Bagehot's thesis but doubted the second can be implemented. He presented a three-part argument:

1. A central bank undermines the automatic operation of the gold standard and "does more harm than good."
2. A central bank inevitably faces political pressures to pursue policies that undermine the gold standard.
3. When conflicts arise between central-bank policies and the dictates of the gold standard, "typically the gold standard gives."

White (2012, 9) proceeded to remind the reader that both Canada and, to a lesser extent, the United States did well under the classical gold standard, 1879–1914. So, too, did Britain with a central bank. We must view White's three points as contingent facts. They may or may not come into play. The best way to address such contingent facts is to look at history. Fortuitously, we now have more history.

Heretofore, the case for free banking has relied on (a) theoretical arguments and (b) history from the 18th and 19th centuries. The theoretical arguments are persuasive but come up against institutional inertia. We have central banking. Even if we thought it would have been better had there never been such an institution, the cost/benefit calculation for abolishing the institution has not been convincingly made.[18]

The historical argument has likely not persuaded many because financial services have changed so much. Banking is an ever-declining part of the financial services industry. And the emphasis on note issuance perhaps seems quaint as the payments system moves away from notes.[19] Deposits have long since eclipsed notes for payments, and now electronic payments are eclipsing deposits. The need for Citi or Wells currency does not seem compelling for many in the modern world of the payments system.

In addition, the Greenspan era and the Great Moderation gained the Fed new respect. Central banks around the world seemed finally to have gotten it right. One thinks of Milton Friedman's 2006 encomium in the *Wall Street Journal* to the departing Alan Greenspan, "He Has Set a Standard." Well, it turns out that Friedman and much of the rest of the profession may have gotten it all wrong.

Selgin, Lastrapes, and White (2012) provide an important revisionist history of the Fed's performance. It does not compare the Fed's performance to an ideal free-banking system but to the far-from-ideal national-banking system. It surveys the modern historical work on both the Fed and the pre-Fed system. Its criteria are the performance of prices and of output. It examines both averages and standard deviations of variables.

The paper's first observation is perhaps the most telling point. The Fed's performance on long-run price stability has been abysmal. A basket of goods that cost $100 in 1790 cost only $108 in 1913. By 2008, a basket cost $2,422 (Selgin, Lastrapes, and White 2012, 570). What they don't say explicitly, but which is obvious, is that long-run price stability has simply not been a consistent goal of the Fed. Only in times of unusually high inflation, such as the 1980s, when public opinion turns strongly against its policies, will the Fed tighten at the expense of substantially higher unemployment. That was the conclusion of Allan Meltzer after completing his three-volume history of the Fed.

Most of the decline in the value of the dollar has occurred since 1970. Under Richard Nixon, the United States abandoned the last vestige of the gold standard (exited the Bretton Woods system). That removed the only constraint, admittedly a weak one by then, on the Fed's proclivity to engage in stabilization policies whose byproduct is price-level uncertainty. Selgin, Lastrapes, and White (2012, 572) note that the price level has become less rather than more predictable under the Fed. "As the Fed gained greater control over long-run price level movements, those movements became increasingly difficult to forecast."

The Fed has expanded money pro-cyclically in response to positive spending shocks, but "was *less* effective than the classical gold standard had been in expanding the money supply in response to unpredictable reduction in money's velocity" (Selgin, Lastrapes, and White 2012, 578–79, emphasis in original).

The Fed's performance in the interwar years was so poor and universally criticized that Selgin, Lastrapes, and White make many of their comparisons between the post–World War II era and the pre-Fed era. Even then, comparisons are often not favorable to the central bank.

Selgin, Lastrapes, and White (2012, 584) cite Thomas Humphrey (2010) on the Fed's role as lender of last resort. During the subprime crisis, the Fed, in Humphrey's (2010, 333) words, "deviated from the classical model in so many ways as to make a mockery of the notion that it is a LLR." (Humphrey is one of the most knowledgeable historians of lender of last resort.) It accepted toxic assets without giving them a haircut (discounting their price as collateral), lending to firms known to be insolvent, and sterilized lending through the discount window prior to the fall of 2008. The last procedure transferred resources "from solvent firms to potentially insolvent ones—a strategy precisely opposite Bagehot's" (Selgin, Lastrapes, and White 2012, 585).

In summary, Selgin, Lastrapes, and White found that the performance of the national banking system was better than has been conventionally portrayed. And the performance of the Fed has been worse than has been portrayed.

My quick tour through the pages of this important paper does not do it justice. Selgin, Lastrapes, and White have provided a systematic analysis of actual, historical monetary and banking institutions. It is just the kind of comparative institutional analysis needed to challenge the dogma of central banking and to move the debate forward.

Conclusion

The theory and history of banking and central banking has many moving parts. Banking developed at different periods and evolved differently across countries.[20] That makes generalizations difficult. Particularly in modern times, money and finance have never evolved wholly spontaneously and have occurred within a heavily regulated environment. It is out of the process of banking evolution that a monetary system develops. Reform of money and banking are inextricably intertwined.

Many issues have necessarily been touched upon only lightly or not at all. The development of central banking in countries other than the United States and the United Kingdom has been only briefly discussed. The development of shadow banking has been entirely ignored, as it has been largely ignored in policy discussions generally.[21] That development complicates most analysis of money, credit, and commercial banking.[22]

I have suggested that the rise of the central bank coincides with the rise of nation-states, whose spending commitments exceed their capacity to finance those commitments. Historically, wars were the chief source of fiscal embarrassment to monarchs. Early central banks, like the Bank of England, were not conceived as monetary institutions but as banks to the king. Even the Federal Reserve was not conceived as a monetary authority. "The responsibilities originally assigned to the Fed did not need to include, and in fact did not include that of managing the stock of money or the price level" (Selgin, Lastrapes, and White 2012, 588). It did not arise for fiscal reasons but became indispensable to a growing federal government both in wartime and peacetime. Standard economic justifications for central banking do not take adequate account of historical reality. Consequently, they are theoretically naïve.

Wars are still expensive, but most governments no longer fight major wars. The United States is a conspicuous exception. The modern welfare state with its vast array of entitlements drives government finances into deficit (Buchanan and Wagner 1977). Currently, the European Union is suffering an acute financial crisis. Its economies grow too slowly to generate the tax revenues to finance the benefits promised to the citizens of those countries. The governments borrow chronically to help pay for ordinary, current expenses. Unforeseen events, such as recessions or housing bubbles bursting, throw governments deeper into deficit. The modern European sovereign finds himself in much the same situation as his 18th-century predecessor.

The European Union is an interesting case because its own central bank is limited in its ability to finance government deficits. So the commercial banking system has become a huge holder of sovereign debt. Partly that reflects the favorable treatment given to government securities under the Basel rules (Basel II). Banks do not need to hold capital against the sovereign debt of members of the Organisation for Economic Co-operation and Development. Because all such debt was preferred by regulators, bankers choose to hold the highest-yielding and riskiest sovereign debt, for example, that of Greece instead of Germany.[23] Governments also pressured their own banks to hold sovereign debt to keep funding costs down. That pressure is being very much felt today. So the European Union banking system is in crisis along with its governments.

We Americans should not cultivate schadenfreude at the plight of Europe. The United States is not far behind Europe on its fiscal trajectory to default, or what amounts to the same thing, high inflation. We benefit temporarily because, relatively speaking, U.S. assets offer a safe haven for investors. If that changes, and global capital repositions elsewhere, borrowing costs for everyone, including the federal government, will rise. That by itself could produce a fiscal crisis here. A U.S. fiscal crisis is being postponed but not avoided.

Ending central banking in this environment is institutionally impossible. I certainly do not mean that it should not be discussed. But, as they have always been in the history of central banking, monetary and fiscal institutions are linked. Monetary reform will need to go hand in hand with fiscal reform.

I end with an assessment of modern ("independent") central banks offered by Milton Friedman (1962, 50) almost 50 years ago. It is appropriate today and addresses the question asked in the title of my paper.

> It may be that these mistakes were excusable on the basis of the knowledge available to men at the time—though I happen to think not. But that is really beside the point. Any system which gives so much power and so much discretion to a few men that mistakes—excusable or not—can have such far-reaching effects is a bad system. It is a bad system to believers in freedom just because it gives a few men such power without an effective check by the body politic—this is the key political argument against an "independent" central bank. But it is a bad system even to those who set security higher than freedom. Mistakes, excusable or not, cannot be avoided in a system which disperses responsibility yet gives a few men great power, and which thereby makes important policy actions highly dependent on accidents of personality. This is the key technical argument against an "independent" bank. To paraphrase Clemenceau, money is much too serious a matter to be left to the Central Bankers.[24]

We have two bad systems: the fiscal and the monetary. They are intertwined now as they were in the 18th and 19th centuries. They

274

must be reformed, or together they will destroy the economic system that sustains them. They have become parasitical. The unsettled question is whether anything less than radical reform of both will work. Can central banks be constrained to a Bagehot-like role, or must they be abolished? Can a "bad system" be made better, or do we need wholesale replacement? That is the question that monetary economists should be discussing.

Notes

1. In his preface to *The Rationale of Central Banking*, Leland Yeager (1990) provides some useful biographical details. I will add one provided me by Professor Hayek. Though a distinguished economist in her own right, Vera Lutz (her married name) could never attend the seminars at Princeton because she was a woman.

2. In much of the rest of his monetary work, Friedman documented the proclivity of central banks to overissue, including in Friedman (1960).

3. Kevin Dowd (1990, 101) argued in similar fashion in his review essay of Charles Goodhart's *The Evolution of Central Banks*.

4. Daniel Klein (1997) generalized the argument to all manner of social interaction. Individuals value their reputation and so do not cheat.

5. Larry White reminded me that Gary Becker ([1956] 1993) had provided an argument for limited free banking, to which Friedman (1960, 108n10) alluded. Still, Friedman held to his instability thesis.

6. A separate literature exists on laissez faire banking based on equity payments systems. It is sometime called the BFH (Black/Fama/Hall) system and was presented by Greenfield and Yeager (1983). White (1984a) and O'Driscoll (1985, 1986) criticized it. Woolsey (1992) updated BFH, and Cronin (2012) has recently revived what is now called Monetary Separation on empirical grounds. I do not deal with that literature in this chapter.

7. The failure of Franklin National Bank in 1974 was a precursor. The Fed kept it open while uninsured deposits ran off.

8. Kane (1987) originated the concept of "zombie" financial institutions.

9. The Swedish Riksbank was founded in 1668 and was the first central bank (Riksbank 2013).

10. See Hayek's Introduction to the *Paper Credit* for both a brief bibliography and assessment of Thornton's contributions (Hayek [1939] 1978). See also Meltzer (2003, 19–64).

11. The discussion generally follows Smith's account.

12. Horwitz (1990) delved into the constraints on expeditiously increasing the supply of notes in response to higher demand for them. And he detailed market responses in the form of currency substitutes.

13. Dowd and Timberlake (1998, 7) point out that "the development of legal tender money and central banking had only a limited impact so long as most countries remained on the gold standard."

14. Pirenne (1937) provides a classic account of medieval fairs and merchant trading.

15. O'Driscoll (2010) elucidates the idea of sound money in economics.

16. As Bagehot ([1873] 2011, 113) put it, "unless you can stop the foreign export [of bullion], you cannot allay the domestic alarm." Preserving the gold standard was paramount even when a domestic panic was also in progress. The maxim to lend freely at a penalty rate derived from that realization.

17. Since departing the Fed, Greenspan has returned to the same position. White (2012, 8n9) cites a 2007 interview in which the former Fed chairman reiterates that "you didn't need a central bank" under the 19th-century gold standard.

18. Bagehot thought the cost/benefit calculation argued overwhelmingly against abolishing the Bank of England.

19. Cronin (2012) documents that central-bank reserves are also of declining importance in developed countries. The advent of private, real-time net settlement systems enables financial institutions to increasingly economize on these reserves.

20. Cipolla (1976, 182–89) provides a brief and informative overview of aspects of the development in the medieval world.

21. Gorton (2010) is a notable exception and good starting point.

22. Within the last year, I asked a senior official at a reserve bank whether anyone in the Federal Reserve had been studying the rise of shadow banking. He responded "no."

23. In the face of the threat of sovereign debt default (economically, a reality in the case of Greece), banks have now shut down crossborder lending. German bunds are the only exception.

24. Bagehot (1873, 66) said much the same thing. He described allowing the directors of the Bank of England so much power as "very anomalous [and] very dangerous."

References

Aftalion, Florin. 1990. *The French Revolution: An Economic Interpretation.* Cambridge: Cambridge University Press.

Bagehot, Walter. (1873) 2011. Lombard Street. N. L.: *A Description of the Money Market.* New York: Scribner.

Becker, Gary S. (1956) 1993. "A Proposal for Free Banking." In *Free Banking*, edited by Lawrence H. White, vol. 3, pp. 20–25. Aldershot, UK: Edward Elgar.

Buchanan, James M., and Richard E. Wagner. 1977. *Democracy in Deficit: The Political Legacy of Lord Keynes.* New York: Academic Press.

Buiter, Willem H. 2008. "Central Banks and Financial Crises." Paper presented at the Federal Reserve Bank of Kansas City 2008 Economic Symposium, Jackson Hole, WY, August 21–23.

Cipolla, Carlo M. 1976. *Before the Industrial Revolution: European Society and Economy, 1000–1700.* New York: W.W. Norton.

Cronin, David. 2012. "The New Monetary Economics Revisited." *Cato Journal* 32 (3): 581–94.

Dowd, Kevin. 1989. *The State and the Monetary System.* New York: St. Martin's Press.

———. 1990. "Did Central Banks Evolve Naturally? A Review Essay of Charles Goodhart's *The Evolution of Central Banks.*" *Scottish Journal of Political Economy* 37 (1): 96–104.

Dowd, Kevin, and Richard H. Timberlake, Jr., eds. 1998. *Money and the Nation State.* Oakland, CA: Independent Institute.

Friedman, Milton. 1960. *A Program for Monetary Stability.* New York: Fordham University Press.

———. 1962. *Capitalism and Freedom.* Chicago: University of Chicago Press.

Friedman, Milton, and Anna J. Schwartz. 1963. *A Monetary History of the United States, 1867–1963.* Princeton: Princeton University Press.

———. 1986. "Has Government Any Role in Money?" *Journal of Monetary Economics* 17 (1): 37–62.

Gelinas, Nicole. 2009. *After the Fall: Saving Capitalism from Wall Street—and Washington.* New York and London: Encounter Books.

Gorton, Gary B. 2010. *Slapped by the Invisible Hand: The Panic of 2007.* Oxford: Oxford University Press.

Greenfield, Robert L., and Leland B. Yeager. 1983. "A Laissez-Faire Approach to Monetary Stability." *Journal of Money, Credit and Banking* 15 (3): 302–15.

Greenspan, Alan. 1966. "Gold and Economic Freedom." *The Objectivist.* http://www.321gold.com/fed/greenspan/1966.html.

Hayek, Friedrich A. (1937) 1989. *Monetary Nationalism and International Stability.* Fairfield, NJ: Augustus M. Kelley.

———, ed. (1939) 1978. *An Inquiry into the Nature and Effects of the Paper Credit of Great Britain.* Fairfield, NJ: Augustus M. Kelley.

Horwitz, Steven. 1990. "Competitive Currencies, Legal Restrictions, and the Origin of the Fed: Some Evidence from the Panic of 1907." *Southern Economic Journal* 56 (3): 639–49.

Humphrey, Thomas. 2010. "Lender of Last Resort: What It Is, Whence It Came, and Why the Fed Isn't It." *Cato Journal* 30 (2): 333–64.

Kane, Edward J. 1987. "Dangers of Capital Forbearance: The Case of the FSLIC and 'Zombie' S&Ls." *Contemporary Economic Policy* 5 (1): 77–83.

Klein, Benjamin. 1974. "The Competitive Supply of Money." *Journal of Money, Credit and Banking* 6 (4): 423–53.

Klein, Daniel B., ed. 1997. *Reputation: Studies in the Voluntary Elicitation of Good Conduct.* Ann Arbor: University of Michigan Press.

Kolko, Gabriel. 1963. *The Triumph of Conservatism.* New York: Free Press of Glencoe.

Kydland, Finn E., and Edward C. Prescott. 1977. "Rules Rather Than Discretion: The Inconsistency of Optimal Plans." *Journal of Political Economy* 85 (3): 473–91.

Lacker, Jeffrey M. 2011. "Understanding the Interventionist Impulse of the Modern Central Bank." Paper presented at the Cato Institute Annual Monetary Conference, Washington, DC, November 16. http://www.richmondfed.org/press_room/speeches/president_jeff_lacker/2011/lacker_speech_20111116.cfm.

Liggio, Leonard. 1999. "The Medieval Law Merchant: Economic Growth Challenged by the Public Choice State." *Journal des économistes et des études humaines* 9 (1): 63–82.

Meltzer, Allan H. 2003. *A History of the Federal Reserve, Volume 1: 1913–1951.* Chicago and London: University of Chicago Press.

Mises, Ludwig von. (1952) 1971. *The Theory of Money and Credit.* Irvington-on-Hudson, NY: Foundation for Economic Education.

O'Driscoll, Gerald P., Jr. 1985. "Money in a Deregulated Financial System." *Federal Reserve Bank of Dallas Economic Review* (May): 1–12.

———. 1986. "Deregulation and Monetary Reform." *Federal Reserve Bank of Dallas Economic Review* (July): 19–31

———. 2010. "What Is Sound Money?" Paper presented at the 2010 Association of Private Enterprise Education Conference, Las Vegas, NV, April 11–13.

———. 2012. "Toward a Global Monetary Order." *Cato Journal* 32 (2): 439–48.

Pirenne, Henri. 1937. *Economic and Social History of Medieval Europe.* New York: Harcourt, Brace & World.

Riksbank. 2013. Riksbank History. http: www.riksbank.se/en/The-Riksbank /History.

Rockoff, Hugh. 1974. "The Free Banking Era: A Re-examination." *Journal of Money, Credit and Banking* 6 (2): 141–67.

Rolnick, Arthur J., and Warren E. Weber. 1982. "Free Banking, Wildcat Banking, and Shinplasters." *Federal Reserve Bank of Minneapolis Quarterly Review* 6 (3): 10–19.

Salsman, Richard M. 1993. "Bankers as Scapegoats for Government-Created Banking Crises in U.S. History." In *The Crisis in American Banking*, edited by Lawrence H. White, pp. 81–118. New York and London: New York University Press.

Selgin, George A. 1988. *The Theory of Free Banking: Money Supply under Competitive Note Issue.* Totowa, NJ: Rowman and Littlefield.

Selgin, George, William D. Lastrapes, and Lawrence H. White. 2012. "Has the Fed Been a Failure?" *Journal of Macroeconomics* 34 (3): 569–96.

Smith, Adam. (1776) 1981. *An Inquiry into the Nature and Causes of the Wealth of Nations.* Two volumes. Indianapolis: Liberty Press (a reprint of the 1776 Oxford University Press edition).

Smith, Vera C. (1936) 1990. *The Rationale of Central Banking and the Free Banking Alternative.* Indianapolis: Liberty Press.

Steil, Benn, and Manuel Hinds. 2009. *Money, Markets and Sovereignty.* New Haven and London: Yale University Press.

White, Lawrence H. 1984a. "Competitive Payments Systems and the Unit of Account." *American Economic Review* 74 (4): 699–712.

———. 1984b. *Free Banking in Britain: Theory, Evidence and Debate, 1800–1845.* Cambridge and New York: Cambridge University Press.

———. 1989. *Competition and Currency: Essays on Free Banking and Money.* New York and London: New York University Press.

———. 1998. "Monetary Nationalism Reconsidered." In *Money and the Nation State*, edited by Kevin Dowd and Richard H. Timberlake, pp. 377–401. New Brunswick, NJ, and London: Transaction Publishers.

———. 2012. "Making the Transition to a New Gold Standard." *Cato Journal* 32 (2): 411–21.

Woolsey, W. William. 1992. "A Model of the BFH Payments System." *Southern Economic Journal* 59 (2): 260–72

Yeager, Leland. 1990. "Preface." In Vera C. Smith, *The Rationale of Central Banking and the Free Banking Alternative*, pp. xiii–xxvi. Indianapolis: Liberty Press.

Index

Note to index: Page references followed by t or f indicate tables and figures, respectively; n designates a numbered note.

About the Editors

Lawrence H. White is Professor of Economics at George Mason University and a Senior Fellow of the Cato Institute. Best known for his work on free banking, White is the author of *The Clash of Economic Ideas* (2012), *The Theory of Monetary Institutions* (1999), *Free Banking in Britain* (2nd ed., 1995), and *Competition and Currency* (1989). His research has appeared in the *American Economic Review* and other leading economics journals. His popular writings have appeared in the *Wall Street Journal* and elsewhere.

Dr. Viktor Vanberg is Senior Research Fellow, Chairman of the Board, and former Director of the Walter Eucken Institut in Freiburg-im-Breisgau, Germany. He was for many years Professor of Economic Policy at the University of Freiburg and previously Professor of Economics at George Mason University.

Ekkehard Köhler is Research Fellow at the Walter Eucken Institut. His main research interests are Comparative Institutional Analyses, Monetary Institutional Economics, Monetary Policy, New Institutional Economics, and Constitutional Economics. His work has been supported by the Friedrich Naumann Foundation for Freedom and the German Academic Exchange Service. He holds an economics degree from Albert-Ludwigs-University, Freiburg.

Cato Institute

Founded in 1977, the Cato Institute is a public policy research foundation dedicated to broadening the parameters of policy debate to allow consideration of more options that are consistent with the traditional American principles of limited government, individual liberty, and peace. To that end, the Institute strives to achieve greater involvement of the intelligent, concerned lay public in questions of policy and the proper role of government.

The Institute is named for *Cato's Letters*, libertarian pamphlets that were widely read in the American Colonies in the early 18th century and played a major role in laying the philosophical foundation for the American Revolution.

Despite the achievement of the nation's Founders, today virtually no aspect of life is free from government encroachment. A pervasive intolerance for individual rights is shown by government's arbitrary intrusions into private economic transactions and its disregard for civil liberties.

To counter that trend, the Cato Institute undertakes an extensive publications program that addresses the complete spectrum of policy issues. Books, monographs, and shorter studies are commissioned to examine the federal budget, Social Security, regulation, military spending, international trade, and myriad other issues. Major policy conferences are held throughout the year, from which papers are published thrice yearly in the *Cato Journal*. The Institute also publishes the quarterly magazine *Regulation*.

To maintain its independence, the Cato Institute accepts no government funding. Contributions are received from foundations, corporations, and individuals, and other revenue is generated from the sale of publications. The Institute is a nonprofit, tax-exempt, educational foundation under Section 501(c)3 of the Internal Revenue Code.

CATO INSTITUTE
1000 Massachusetts Ave., N.W.
Washington, DC 20001
www.cato.org